James BOND
A CELEBRATION

007 Mark I:
Sean Connery

007 Mark II:
George Lazenby

Created by
Ian Fleming

007 Mark III:
Roger Moore

007 Mark IV:
Timothy Dalton

James BOND
A CELEBRATION

Peter Haining

PLANET

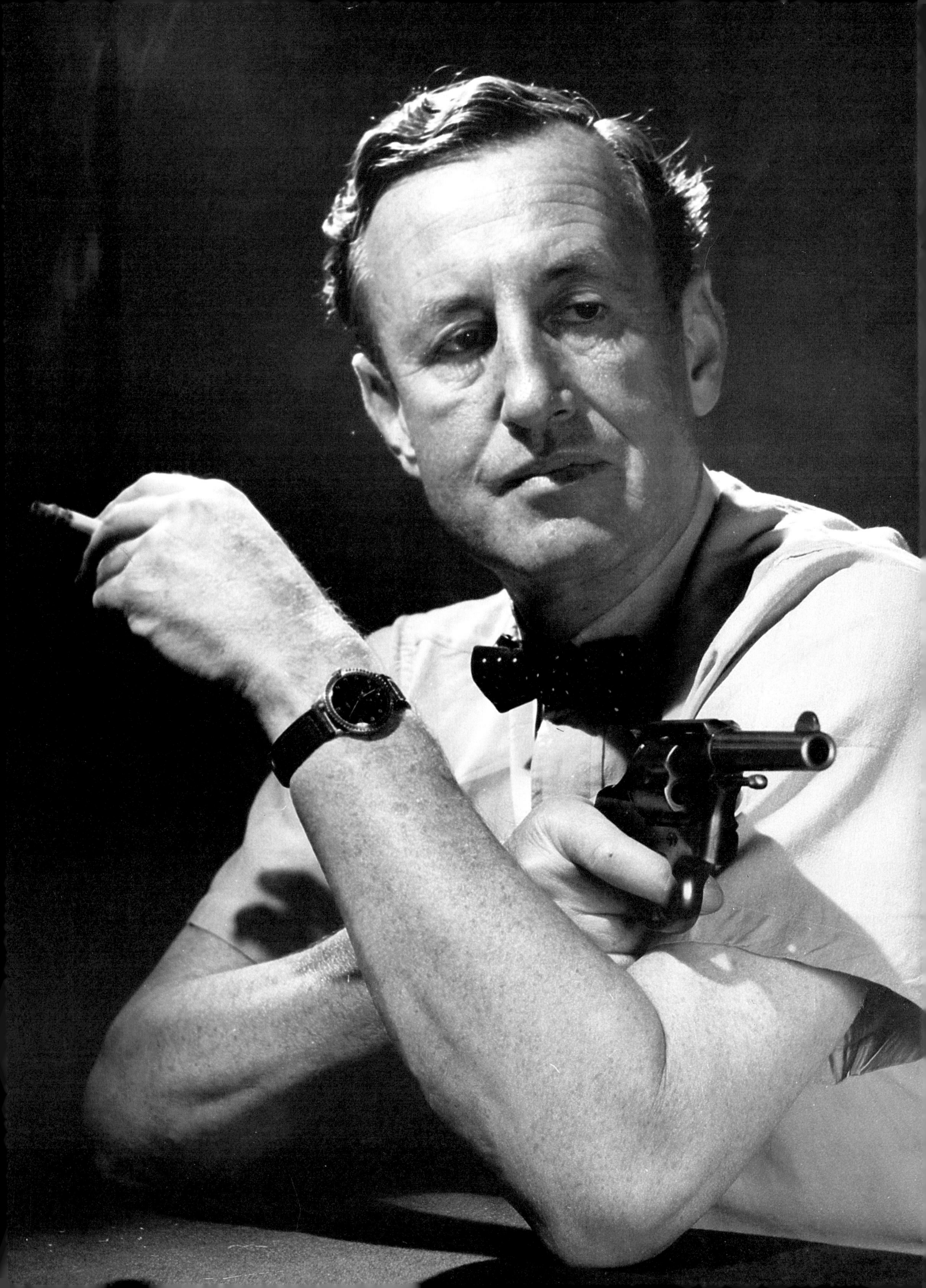

'I wrote Bond as an antidote to my hysterical alarm at facing up to marriage for the first time at 43. I write for warm-blooded heterosexuals in railway trains, aeroplanes – and beds.'
IAN FLEMING

'James Bond is the invincible figure every man would like to be, every woman is excited by, and is everyone's survival symbol.'
SEAN CONNERY

James BOND
A CELEBRATION

First published in 1987 by Planet Books,
a division of W.H. Allen & Co Plc

Typeset in Bembo
by Phoenix Photosetting, Chatham, Kent
Printed and bound in Singapore
for the publishers W.H. Allen & Co Plc,
44 Hill Street, London W1X 8LB

ISBN 1–85227–020–9

Design by Cecil Smith

ACKNOWLEDGEMENTS

The author would like to thank the following for their kind permission to reproduce the black and white illustrations in this book:

Popperfoto, Keystone Press Agency, The Photo Source, Express Newspapers, Punch Magazine, Playboy Inc, Times Newspapers, Associated Newspapers, British Film Institute, Sygma, & William Collins & Sons & Co.

Contents

Introduction – A Double-O Celebration

The year 1987 marks a double celebration for 007. It is just thirty-five years since James Bond sprang to life from the fertile imagination of his creator, Ian Fleming, and just twenty-five years since the first of the continuing series of films about the secret agent burst upon the world's cinema screens. In the intervening period, as a result of the huge sales of Fleming's books (not to mention their sequels) and the record-breaking box office appeal of the movies, Bond has become a world-wide cult figure crossing all race and language barriers and can now be numbered among the half-dozen most famous characters in literature.

It is a truly remarkable achievement for a character created, initially, as a money-spinner and means of escape from routine for his author. In return, James Bond, British secret agent 007, has provided escape and enjoyment for 100 million readers and one and a half billion cinemagoers, and has earned a permanent place in the world's consciousness.

The start of the two legends which have brought such astonishing fame to James Bond can be dated precisely. It was on the morning of Tuesday, 15 January 1952, that Ian Fleming sat down in front of his battered Imperial portable typewriter in the living-room of his holiday home, Goldeneye, on the island of Jamaica and, without preparatory notes or planning, began to write Bond's first adventure, *Casino Royale*. It was to take just two months of solid work each morning, before, on Tuesday, 18 March, he typed the last page of the manuscript and a character destined for immortality was ready for the world.

Almost ten years later, at 8.30 am on the morning of Monday, 26 February 1962, the film cameras rolled at Pinewood Studios in England to begin making *Dr No*, the first of what has proved a hugely popular series of movies which, it is estimated, have now been seen by one in four of the world's population – excluding Russia and China where this 'capitalist hyena' is neither politically nor morally welcome.

The men behind the James Bond legend. (Above) Ian Fleming at a Foyle's Literary Luncheon in 1963 to mark the astonishing success of his 007 novels. (Below) Cubby Broccoli, as dapper as Bond himself, at the première of *From Russia With Love* in 1963.

The Bond of literature – from the cover of the 1955 Pan edition of *Casino Royale.*

In both instances, the omens for success were not immediately very promising: 'At first I was so ashamed of what I had written that I used to worry about what my friends would say if they read it,' Ian Fleming was to say later of *Casino Royale*. 'I went into writing like a blind man. After I had finished a page I used to hide it away under the others, never daring to look at it, in case I despaired for ever when I realised that this utter rubbish, this piffle, was my handiwork. It was just a case of keeping my head down and typing like mad. In the end, I think this resulted in a fast narrative speed, which was what I was aiming at in the books. I just let it zip on – in the same way as Bond went about life. Very fast.'

A decade later, after the first screening of *Dr No* for the executives of United Artists of America who had put up the money for the making of the picture, one voice was heard to say, 'Well, we're not going to make any money out of *this*. How can we show a picture which has a limey truck driver playing the lead?'

Both estimations were, of course, hopelessly wrong. Ian Fleming's books were to earn a huge international readership, and the admiration of literary critics as well as fans as diverse as US Presidents Kennedy and Reagan, film stars like Bob Hope and Joan

The first screen Bond – Sean Connery with Shirley Eaton while shooting the famous 'golden girl' scene for *Goldfinger* in 1964.

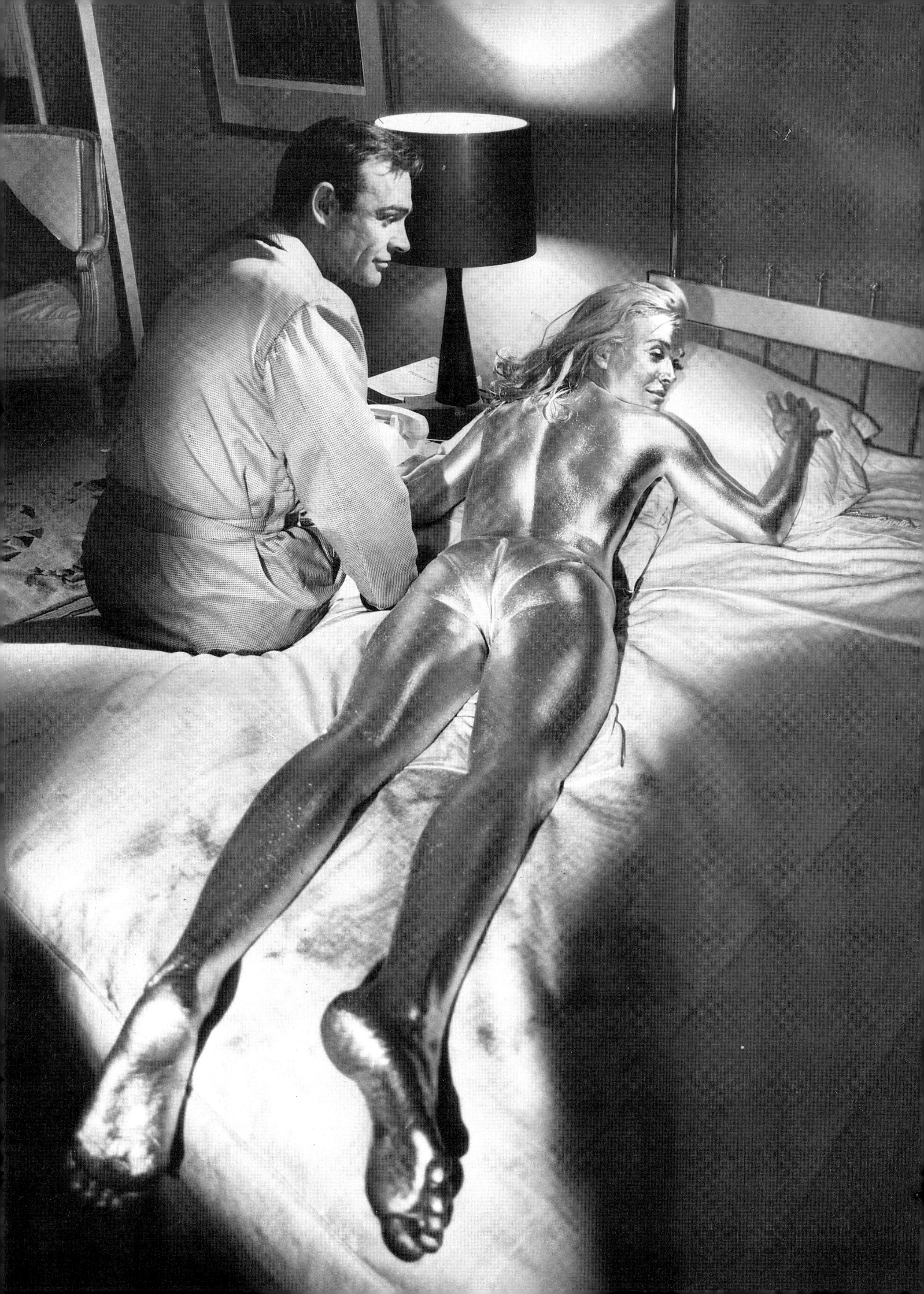

Collins, sportsmen such as Mohammed Ali and Bjorn Borg, and singing stars as widely different as Liberace and Paul McCartney.

Equally, the film so disparagingly dismissed was to be the first of many box office sensations, and the 'limey truck driver' (actually Sean Connery was neither: he was a Scot and the son of a lorry driver) was to create a legendary super-hero. This man, and his successors in the role, initiated an era of Bondomania which shows no signs of diminishing.

With the benefit of hindsight, it is possible to put into clear perspective what actually happened in both cases:

Looking at the phenomenon from a literary point of view, fellow spy writer Len Deighton has said, 'Ian Fleming introduced the element of the adventure story into the spy story. He took all those big 1930s Bentleys on the highways and put them into his work. Nobody had done anything like that before.'

The *New York Times* agreed with this view, calling Fleming an innovator with an original vision. 'His central device, the wildly improbable story set against a meticulously detailed and somehow believable background, is vastly entertaining; and his redoubtable, implacable, indestructible protagonist, though some think him a strangely flat character, may well be not so much the child of this century as of the next.'

The impact of the films was equally impressive. 'The popularity of the Bond films changed the course of film history,' the *Sunday Express* said in February 1986. 'They helped to make the cinema more permissive and proved that the British could make films better than the Americans – and have a far greater impact world-wide.'

The prestigious cinema magazine, *Films and Filming*, in reviewing the Bond story went still further: 'James Bond is not just a screen hero,' it said, 'he is an institution, and as such has influenced world affairs, art, music, motion pictures and fashion. In his heyday, probably 1965, stores around the world were selling 007 shirts, suits, ties, cuff-links, vodka, cologne, shaving cream. The Hilton chain of hotels even had a 007 suite for the more adventurous types. And that was just for grown-ups! The children had 007 guns, rifles, identification cards, fan clubs, miniature toy Aston Martins, and even Bond attaché cases!'

James Bond has become a unique success story – perhaps *the* success story of our times. Yet somehow the explanation for this remains elusive – in itself perhaps a major part of the success? In the pages that follow, however, I hope to offer some clues from the experiences and recollections of those who have been involved in the making of the legend – both in print and on the screen.

It has to be said that Bond's status as an anti-hero is vitally important. He is an opponent of the system; shuns the nine-to-five workaday world; makes his own rules and retains his own individuality. Most of his enemies have epitomised the corporate world gone haywire, and by destroying them he has struck a blow for the civilised world and proved that no matter how corrupt the system, it can be cleaned up.

James Bond became, initially, the cultural hero of the Sixties, but has proved himself a man of the Seventies and Eighties too. He has also evolved into an art form of his own, and fully deserves the title of a legend.

A Legend in the Making

A selection of reviews of the Bond books and films covering thirty-five years of the development of the 007 legend, with contributions by a number of famous writers, including Ian Fleming's great friend, the American 'hard-boiled' writer Raymond Chandler; critic Paul Johnson who called the novels a mixture of 'Sex, Snobbery and Sadism'; a similarly stinging attack from the Russian journalist, Yuri Zhukov, the chief polemicist of *Pravda*; novelist Kingsley Amis, a great admirer of 007 and author of *The James Bond Dossier*; and the modern master of the tale of espionage, John Le Carré.

AN EXTREMELY ENGAGING AFFAIR

Anonymous

From *Times Literary Supplement*, 17 April 1953

Mr Ian Fleming's first novel, *Casino Royale*, is an extremely engaging affair, dealing with espionage in the 'Sapper' manner, but with a hero who, although taking a great many cold showers and never letting sex interfere with work, is somewhat more sophisticated. At any rate, he takes very great care over his food and drink, and sees women's clothes with an expertness of which Bulldog Drummond would have been ashamed.

The main plot of the book deals with the attempt of a British secret agent to out-gamble a Communist agent whose sexual predilections have cost him a lot of money and who must play for high stakes to make up the Party funds and carry out his programme.

The game concerned is baccarat and the especial charm of Mr Fleming's book is the

Enter James Bond – strip cartoon hero in the *Sunday Express* drawn by John McLusky.

high poetry with which he invests the green baize lagoons of the casino tables. The setting in a French resort somewhere near Le Touquet is given great local atmosphere and while the plot itself has a shade too many improbabilities, the secret service details are convincing.

Altogether, Mr Fleming has produced a book that is both exciting and extremely civilised.

BONDED GOODS
by Raymond Chandler

From the *Sunday Times*, 25 March 1956

Some three years ago Mr Ian Fleming produced a thriller which was about as tough an item as ever came out of England in the way of thriller writing, on any respectable level. *Casino Royale* contained a superb gambling scene, a torture scene which still haunts me, and, of course, a beautiful girl.

His second book, *Live and Let Die*, was memorable in that he entered the American scene with perfect poise, did a brutal sketch of Harlem, and another of St Petersburg, Florida. His third, *Moonraker*, was, by comparison with the first two explosions, merely a spasm.

We now have his fourth book, *Diamonds Are Forever*, which has the preliminary distinction of a sweet title, and of being about the nicest piece of book-making in this type of literature which I have seen for a long time.

Diamonds Are Forever concerns, nominally, the smashing of an international diamond smuggling ring. But actually apart from the charms and faults I am going to mention, it is just another American gangster story, and not a very original one at that.

Raymond Chandler – Ian Fleming's great friend, and admirer of James Bond.

In Chapter One, Mr Fleming very nearly becomes atmospheric, and with Mr James Bond as your protagonist, a character about as atmospheric as a dinosaur, it just doesn't pay off.

In Chapter Two we learn quite a few facts about diamonds, and we then get a fairly detailed description of Saratoga and its sins, and a gang execution which is as nasty as any I have read.

Later, there is a more detailed, more fantastic, more appalling description of Las Vegas and its daily life. To a Californian, Las Vegas is a cliché. You don't make it fantastic, because it was designed that way and it is funny rather than terrifying.

From then on there is some very fast and dangerous action, and of course Mr Bond finally has his way with the beautiful girl. Sadly enough his beautiful girls have no future, because it is the curse of the 'series character' that he always has to go back to where he began.

Mr Fleming writes a journalistic style, neat, clean, spare and never pretentious. He writes of brutal things, and as though he liked them.

The trouble with brutality in writing is that it has to grow out of something. The best hard-boiled writers never try to be tough, they allow toughness to happen when it seems inevitable for its time, place and conditions.

I don't think *Diamonds are Forever* measures up to either *Casino Royale* or *Live and Let Die*. Frankly, I think there is a certain amount of padding in it and there are pages in which James Bond thinks.

I don't like James Bond thinking. His thoughts are superfluous. I like him when he is in a dangerous card game; I like him when he is exposing himself unarmed to half a dozen thin-lipped professional killers, and neatly dumping them into a heap of fractured bones; I like him when he finally takes the beautiful girl in his arms, and teaches her about one-tenth of the facts of life she knew already.

I have left the remarkable thing about this book to the last. And that is that it is written by an Englishman. The scene is almost entirely American, and it rings true to an American. I am unaware of any other writer who has accomplished this.

But let me plead with Mr Fleming not to allow himself to become a stunt writer, or he will end up no better than the rest of us.

SEX, SNOBBERY AND SADISM
by Paul Johnson

From *New Statesman*, 5 April 1958

I have just finished what is, without doubt, the nastiest book I have ever read. It is a new novel entitled *Doctor No* and the author is Mr Ian Fleming. Echoes of Mr Fleming's fame had reached me before, and I had been repeatedly urged to read his books by literary friends whose judgment I normally respect. When his new novel appeared, therefore, I obtained a copy and started to read. By the time I was a third of the way through, I had to suppress a strong impulse to throw the thing away, and only continued reading because I realised that here was a social phenomenon of some importance.

There are three basic ingredients in *Doctor No*, all unhealthy, all thoroughly English: the sadism of a schoolboy bully, the mechanical, two-dimensional sex-longings of a frustrated adolescent, and the crude, snob-cravings of a suburban adult. Mr Fleming has no literary skill, the construction of the book is chaotic, and entire incidents and situations are inserted, and then forgotten, in a haphazard manner. But the three ingredients are manufactured and blended with deliberate, professional precision; Mr Fleming dishes up his recipe with all the calculated accountancy of a Lyons Corner House . . .

Fleming deliberately and systematically excites and then satisfies the very worst instincts of his readers. This seems to me far more dangerous than straight pornography. In 1944, George Orwell took issue with a book which in some ways resembles Fleming's novels – *No Orchids for Miss Blandish*. He saw the success of *No Orchids*, published in 1940, as part of a discernible psychological climate, whose other products were Fascism, the Gestapo, mass-bombing and war. But in condemning *No Orchids*, Orwell made two reservations. First, he conceded that it was brilliantly written, and that the acts of cruelty it described sprang from the subtle and inte-

The designation 007 became the title of the Bond strip cartoon when it transferred to the *Daily Star* in 1981.

grated, though perverse, view of human nature. Secondly, in contrasting *No Orchids* with *Raffles* – which he judged a healthy and harmless book – he pointed out that *No Orchids* was evil precisely because it lacked the restraint of conventional upper-class values; and this led him to the astonishing but intelligible conclusion that perhaps, after all, snobbery, like hypocrisy, was occasionally useful to society.

What, I wonder, would he have said of *Doctor No*? For this novel is badly written to the point of incoherence and none of the 500,000 people who, I am told are expected to buy it, could conceivably be giving the publishers, Cape, 13s 6d to savour its literary merits. Moreover, both its hero and its author are unquestionably members of the Establishment. Bond is an ex-Royal Navy Commander and belongs to Blades, a sort of super-Whites. Mr Fleming was educated at Eton and Sandhurst, and is married to a prominent society hostess, the ex-wife of Lord Rothermere. He is the foreign manager of that austere and respectable newspaper, the *Sunday Times*, owned by an elderly fuddy-duddy called Lord Kemsley, who once tried to sell a popular tabloid with the slogan (or rather his wife's slogan) of 'clean and clever'. Fleming belongs to the Turf and Boodle's and lists among his hobbies the collecting of first editions. He is also the owner of Goldeneye, a house made famous by Sir Anthony Eden's retreat from Suez. Eden's uneasy slumbers, it will be remembered, were disturbed by giant rats which, after they had been disposed of by his detectives, turned out to be specially trained ones kept by Mr Fleming.

Orwell, in fact, was wrong. Snobbery is no protection: on the contrary, the social appeal of the dual Bond-Fleming personality has added an additional flavour to his brew of sex and sadism. Fleming's novels are not only successful, like *No Orchids*; they are also smart. The *Daily Express*, pursuing its task of bringing glamour and sophistication to the masses, has serialised the last three. Our curious post-war society, with its obsessive interest in debutantes, its cult of U and non-U, its working-class graduates educated into snobbery by the welfare state, is a soft market for Mr Fleming's poison. Bond's warmest admirers are among the Top People. Of his last adventure, *From Russia With Love*, his publishers claim, with reason, that it 'won approval from the sternest critics in the world of letters'. The *Times Literary Supplement* found it 'most brilliant', the *Sunday Times* 'highly polished', the *Observer* 'stupendous', the *Spectator* 'rather pleasant'. And this journal, most susceptible of all, described it as 'irresistible'.

It has become easier than it was in Orwell's day to make cruelty attractive. We have gone just that much farther down the slope. Recently I read Henri Alleg's horrifying account of his tortures in an Algiers prison; and I have on my desk a documented study of how we treat our prisoners in Cyprus. I am no longer astonished that these things can happen. Indeed, after reflecting on the Fleming phenomenon, they seem to me almost inevitable.

◆

A PLEASANT FILM
by Angela Milne
From *Punch*, 17 October 1962

'Pleasant' is the last word I expected to choose for the first film of one of Ian Fleming's James Bond novels. But *Dr No* (Director: Terence Young) has managed to cut out the nastiness, the sadism which in this novel at any rate (it happens to be the first and last Bond I ever read) so carefully unbalances plot and human interest. Here the story's the thing: a ridiculous thing of Secret Agent versus Master Mind, but the rewriting and direction ensure that you don't take anything very seriously – not even the nuclear reactor to-do which has taken the place of those very explicit tortures.

Sean Connery is a delightful Bond,

The first of several Bond cartoons which Ffolkes has drawn for *Punch*. This accompanied the review of *Dr No* in October 1962.

stunningly handsome and nicely light-hearted as he pursues the forces of evil from his glossy London world to an even glossier Jamaica. But his metamorphosis (even his well-known sexual prowess is turned into a joke, a 'you know *him*' between film and audience) produces one jarring note and an important one; the callous killings now seem the more callous. That problem will have to be worked out before the Bond image is all set for a series.

BONDOMANIA

From *Time*, 11 June 1965

There seems to be no geographical limit to the appeal of sex, violence and snobbery with which Ian Fleming endowed his British secret agent, James Bond.

In Tokyo, for instance, the queue for *Goldfinger*, the third Bond film, stretches half a mile. In Brazil, where the second, *From Russia With Love*, broke all Rio and Sao Paulo records, one unemployed TV actor had only to change his name to Jaime Bonde to be swamped with offers. In Beirut, where *Goldfinger* outdrew *My Fair Lady*, even Goldfinger's hat-hurling bodyguard, Oddjob, has become a minor hero.

And in New York, the ads and marquees scream: 'JAMES BOND IS BACK . . . TO BACK!' The first movies, *Dr No* and *From Russia With Love*, both less than three years old, are being double-billed here and all across the US. In the New York area, they jammed twenty-six theatres and grossed $650,000 for the week. The same crowds, the same large grosses in Boston, Buffalo, Chicago, Los Angeles and Washington; at the drive-ins, traffic rivalled the commuting hour.

What makes the box-office figures that more astonishing is that both films are

Bondomania – Sean Connery surrounded by pretty girls as 007 fever spread around the world in 1965.

grossing nearly as much the second time around as the first. Sparking the revival is the success of *Goldfinger*, still finishing its first run and heading for a gross that now seems likely to reach $30 million.

Nor is Bondomania restricted to the US. In England, all three films broke box-office records, and Ian Fleming's last book, the posthumous *Man with the Golden Gun*, has already climbed to the top of the best seller list.

To date, in hard cover and paperbacks, Bond books have been read by some 30 million people, and United Artists estimate that 25 million have seen Bond in reel life. By the time all three current Bond films have been milked dry, the take may top $100 million.

The fact that James Bond has developed into the biggest mass-cult hero of the decade has given serious pause to such as Britain's novelist Kingsley Amis who ranks Fleming 'with those demi-giants of an earlier day, Jules Verne, Rider Haggard and Conan Doyle'; and to Columbia University's Jacques Barzun, who deplores 'the studies by academic critics who have argued over Fleming's morals and philosophies.'

British columnist Malcolm Muggeridge is also appalled. While admitting that Bond's 'instant appeal to attractive women, his dash and daring and smartness combined with toughness, make him every inch a hero of our time,' he also notes that 'insofar as one can focus on so shadowy and unreal a character, he is utterly despicable: obsequious to his superiors, pretentious in his tastes, callous and brutal in his ways, with strong undertones of sadism, and an unspeakable cad in his relations with women, toward whom sexual appetite represents the only approach.'

What Fleming's literary critics overlook is that in transferring Bond from fiction to film, and endowing him with all the attributes of Scottish-born actor, Sean Connery, a new twist has been added. Says chief scriptwriter Richard Maibaum, 'The common denominator is deadpan spoofing. We know it, the audience knows it, yet they are perfectly willing to alternately believe and disbelieve what is happening on the screen.'

To help illusion along, there are not only gadgets galore – Bond's tricked-up Aston Martin is now a major attraction at the New York World's Fair – but there is also Pussy Galore, to say nothing of Tilly Masterson and her gilded sister, Jill, Tatiana Romanova and Honeychile Rider.

Currently, the producers are completing the next Bond film, *Thunderball*, in Nassau and London. Nassau has been in an uproar for weeks.

The company staged an out-of-season Junkanoo carnival parade for background shots that laid up half the island with hangovers, invited over the whole jet set from Palm Beach for other background shots, and built the 'Kiss Kiss Club' on Huntington Hartford's Paradise Island with such style that one old Nassauvian remarked, 'Best damned nightclub on the island. They should have left it there.'

But it all left Sean Connery himself on the blah side. 'There's an awful lot of this stuff,' he groused. 'Next they'll be making *Son of*. . . It's got so one needs the constitution of a rugby player.'

Nor is Connery backward about claiming that he has helped the James Bond image along no end.

'You must realise,' he says, 'that Ian Fleming's books began coming out after the war and rationing and all that, and they had all this selectivity of detail about eating and drinking. It was marvellous journalism. But Ian told me it was nothing but padding. You know, vodka must be shaken and not stirred, that kind of razzmatazz. But he did write with a bit of size.'

The only thing the Fleming books lacked, in Connery's view, was a sense of humour. 'I discussed it with Ian, and he thought there was humour in them. But the director Terence Young and I did not. So we injected some.'

Terence Young agrees. 'In a Bond film you aren't involved in *cinéma verite* or *avant-garde*. One is involved in colossal *fun*.'

PREACHING A LICENCE TO KILL
by Yuri Zhukov

From *Pravda*, 30 September 1965

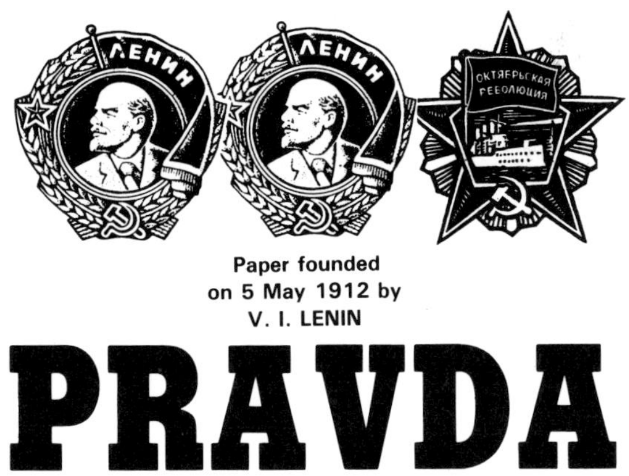

James Bond lives in a nightmarish world where laws are written at the point of a gun, where coercion and rape is considered valour and murder is a funny trick. All this is invested to teach people to accept the antics of American marines somewhere in the Mekong Delta in Vietnam and Her Majesty's Intelligence agents in Hong Kong and Aden.

Bond's job is to guard the interests of the

property class, and he is no better than the youths Hitler boasted he would bring up like wild beasts to be able to kill without thinking.

His creator is Ian Fleming, who posed as *The Times* correspondent in Russia in 1939 but was in truth a spy for the capitalist nations. Although he is now dead, James Bond cannot be allowed to die because he teaches those sent to kill in Vietnam, the Congo, the Dominican Republic and many other places.

It is no accident that sham agents of the Soviet counter-intelligence, represented in caricature form, invariably figure in the role of Bond's opponents, because Bond kills right and left the men Fleming wanted to kill – Russians, Reds and Yellows. Bond is portrayed as a sort of white archangel, destroying the impure races.

The Bond cult started in 1963 when the American leader, President Kennedy, unsuspecting that some American hero [a reference to Lee Harvey Oswald] with the right to kill would shoot him, too, declared that Fleming's books were his bedside reading.

As if by a magic wand, everything changed. The mighty forces of reaction immediately gave the green light to Fleming. And in James Bond he has created a symbol of the civilisation which has used bombs to drown the voice of conscience.

The men and women who allow their talents to be used in the making of films about the exploits of this man are also guilty of furthering the shameful aims of the Western capitalists.

THE STORY FLEMING DARED NOT TELL!

by Kingsley Amis

From *New Statesman*, 2 April 1965

In most of the Bond books it was the central villain on whom interest in character was fixed. *Moonraker*, for instance, is filled with the physical presence of Hugo Drax with his red hair and scarred face, bustling about, puffing cigars, playing the genial host when he isn't working on his scheme to obliterate London. Scaramanga, in the last of them, *The Man With The Golden Gun*, is just a dandy with a special (and ineffective) gun, a stock of outdated American slang, and a third nipple on his left breast. We hear a lot about him early on in the ten-page dossier 'M' consults, including mentions of homosexuality and pistol-fetishism, but these aren't followed up anywhere. Why not?

It may be relevant to consider an outstandingly clumsy turn in the narrative. Bond has always been good at ingratiating himself with his enemies, notably with Goldfinger, who took him on as his personal assistant for the Fort Knox project. Goldfinger, however, had fairly good reason to believe Bond to be a clever and experienced operator on the wrong side of the law. Scaramanga hires him after a few minutes' conversation in the bar of a brothel. (At this stage he has no idea that there's a British agent within a hundred miles, so he can't be hiring him to keep him under his eye.) Bond wonders what Scaramanga wants with him: 'it was odd, to say the least of it . . . the strong smell of a trap.' This hefty hint of a concealed motive on Scaramanga's part is never taken up. Why not?

I strongly suspect – on deduction alone, let it be said – that these unanswered questions represent traces of an earlier draft, perhaps never committed to paper, wherein Scaramanga hires Bond because he's sexually interested in him. A supposition of this kind would also take care of other difficulties or deficiencies in the book as it stands, the insubstantiality of the character of Scaramanga, just referred to, and the feeling of suppressed emotion, at any rate the build-up to and the space for some kind of climax of emotion, in the final confrontation of the two men. But of course Ian Fleming wouldn't have dared to complete the story along those lines. Imagine what the critics would have said!

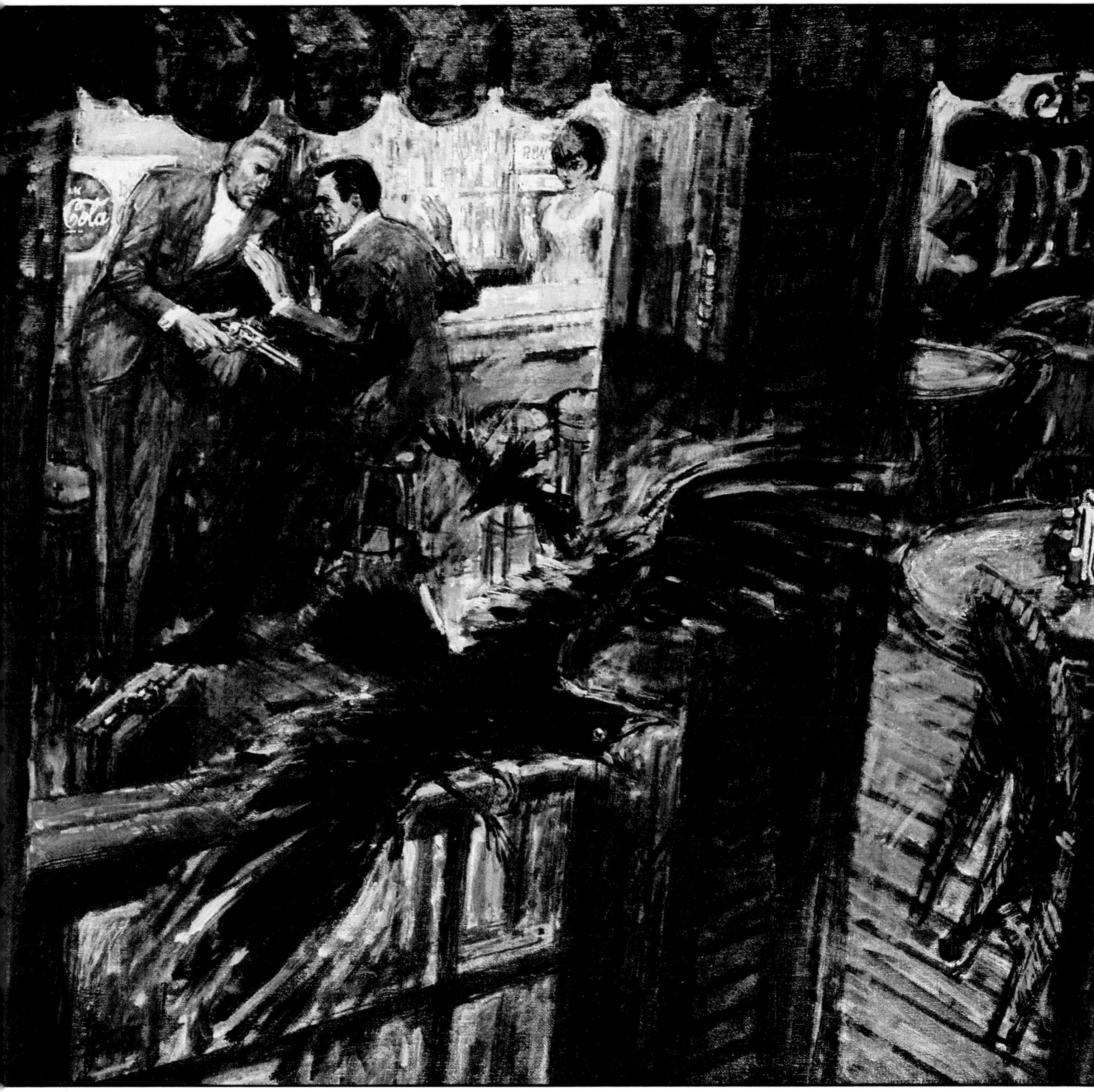

Playboy illustration for the serialisation of the controversial story, *The Man With The Golden Gun*, in 1965.

To read some of their extant efforts, one would think that Bond's creator was a sort of psychological Ernst Stavro Blofeld, bent on poisoning British morality. An article in this journal in 1958 helped to initiate a whole series of attacks on the supposed 'sex, snobbery and sadism' of the books, as if sex were bad *per se*, and as if snobbery resided in a few glossy-magazine references to Aston-Martin cars and Pinaud shampoos and what-not, and as if sadism could be attributed to a character who never wantonly inflicts pain. (Contrast Bulldog Drummond and Spillane's Mike Hammer.)

These are matters that can't be argued through in this review. But it seems clear that Ian Fleming took such charges seriously. Violent and bloody action, the infliction of pain in general, was very much scaled down in what he wrote after 1958. Many will regard this as a negative gain, though others may feel that a secret-agent story without violence would be like, say, a naval story without battles. As regards 'sex' and 'snobbery' and the memorable meals and the high-level gambling, these, however unedifying, were part of the unique Fleming world, and the denaturing of that world in *The Man With The Golden Gun* and parts of its immediate forerunners is a loss. Nobody can write at his best with part of his attention on puritanical readers over his shoulder.

Ian Fleming was a good writer, occasionally a brilliant one, as the gypsy-encampment scene in *From Russia With Love* (however sadistic) and the bridge-game in *Moonraker* (however snobbish) will suggest. His gifts for sustaining and varying action, and for holding down the wildest fantasies with cleverly synthesised pseudo-facts, give him a place beside long-defunct entertainer-virtuosos like Jules Verne and Conan Doyle, though he was more fully master of his material than either of these. When shall we see another?

THE CONSUMER-GOODS HERO
by John Le Carré
From the *Listener*, 14 April 1966

I don't believe in the notion of the anti-hero. George Orwell once said that we either write for the hero or the victim. You could translate that in modern terms into the difference between the literature of escapism and the literature of involvement. In the literature of escapism we have really run to two different kinds of hero. If one could sub-divide that particular paragraph, we have had in the past the Sandy Arbuthnots, the Buchan figures, the Geoffrey Household figures, who act within the realms of a discernible ethic, who are defending a society which we know and understand – the upper-middle-class society of England and the whole tradition of power which we have had. Since then something else has emerged, something very interesting. That is the James Bond kind of hero. I call this the consumer-goods hero.

This is the man who surrounds himself with all the things which are technique – with the charms of super cars, super and expendable girls, with cigarette lighters that go off with a bang, with everything which in artistic terms replaces love or emotion. You could take James Bond on that magic carpet and, given the prerequisities of the affluent society, given above all an indefinable villain of whatever kind – and weak people need enemies – you could dump him in the middle of Moscow and you would get a ready-made Soviet agent. I find him in this sense extremely cosmopolitan. He is an Etonian and so on, but in fact he seems to me to correspond more to the kind of international manager type – the rich young fellow of thirty-eight or thirty-nine who has discovered that promiscuity is one of the privileges of wealth; who has developed a pretty hard-nosed cynicism

Not a martini in sight! Sean Connery advertising American Bourbon Whiskey in 1967.

SEE SEAN CONNERY STARRING IN "YOU ONLY LIVE TWICE."

GIFT-WRAPPED WITH OUR COMPLIMENTS.
JIM BEAM 86 PROOF KENTUCKY STRAIGHT BOURBON WHISKEY DISTILLED AND BOTTLED BY THE JAMES B. BEAM DISTILLING CO., CLERMONT, BEAM, KENTUCKY

The gift is distinctive.
The season is merry.
The man is Sean Connery.
The Bourbon is JIM BEAM.

towards any sense of moral obligation.

This is, I think, an unconscious but pretty accurate reflection of some of the worst things in Western society. And it will soon reflect on the worst things in Eastern society. What I tried to do in my books, *The Spy Who Came In From The Cold* and *The Looking-Glass War*, was to remake a figure who was involved in the dilemma of our time: that we cannot continue with the war epic. In the past we have shown that war was a legitimate means of self-defence or even, when we were empire building, a legitimate means of aggression. Now we have got the Bomb instead. We have not got an identifiable enemy; we have an ideology instead with which we must come to terms, and it seemed to me that the Western dilemma of the small man is that the institutions we create to combat the ideology to fight the cold war are getting so big that the individual himself is losing his identity in our society, just as he is in Eastern society.

We have always argued that in the West we may be amorphous, we may be vague, we may contain a great variety of beliefs, but the one thing we have in common in a non-communist world is supposed to be the belief that the individual is worth more than the idea; that whatever we believe in, we will defend to the death the individual's right to dissent; and yet in the cold war, we are doing something *in fact* which I believe we are already doing *in principle* elsewhere – that is to say, we are sacrificing the individual in our battle against the collective. This is the supreme paradox. I want people when they open my books and begin reading to feel, 'God, this *could* be me!' When they are reading this other type of heroic book like James Bond, I think they are saying, 'Oh, gosh, I *wish* this were me,' and that is a sharp difference. Both may be, in long-haired terms, pop art, but I believe that mine at the moment have more application to our dilemma than the other.

INHUMAN BONDAGE
by Dilys Powell
From *Punch*, 4 July 1979

Too bad that, as *Moonraker* appears, Ian Fleming is no longer with us. Too bad at any time, but particularly now when the narrative invention of his tales, extravagant from the start, has been allowed to get completely out of hand. He enjoyed his creation of the indestructible James Bond; but at his best he always related the extravagance to some sort of reality; and the adventure was terrestrial, not planetary. Bond survived partly, it is true, by the use of gadgets, but basically by courage and wit; and the films followed the same line. Little by little the gadgets have been winning. With *Moonraker* (director, Lewis Gilbert) they have taken over; *Moonraker* is the adventure not of Agent 007 but of rear-activated speedboat torpedos and a handy little wrist-attached exterminator.

The film doesn't lack jokes in the Bond style. Some of them are reference-jokes: the hero (Roger Moore, insouciant as ever) emulates Superman, excusing himself when asked why he is late by saying, 'I fell out of a plane.' I doubt whether the surrender of Jaws (himself, of course, a reference-joke) to the diminutive blonde would have seemed as funny if one didn't remember Frankenstein's Monster encountering the innocent child. The fights, though, with the oriental type employed by world-villain Drax (Michael Lonsdale) pass almost unregarded; the martial arts are old arts to us by now. But now and then a brief visual jest comes off; smart when Bond loses a gondolier – but lives to wear his hat. And there are the verbal sex-jokes. One knows what Miss Moneypenny means when, asked whether 007 has finished his African assignment, she says she thinks he is on his last leg.

Most of the action depends on the impossible. The audience doesn't believe that James Bond can float to earth without a parachute, and laughs because it doesn't have to believe. And the impossible comes every ten minutes. *Moonraker* takes in two continents, moving from Californian nuclear-plant to Venetian glass-factory and back across the Atlantic to Carnival in Rio de Janeiro; it moves disjointedly. Its two hours could be divided into independent episodes: Bond at the pigeon-shoot, Bond in the velocity-test, Bond attacked from a canal-hearse, or acrobatic in a cable-car, or resourceful with a tropical reptile. (Species? With a crowd of Bond beauties watching one really hasn't time to identify.) In fact *Moonraker* is a serial; it would gratify the desire, common in the silent days, to see all the episodes in one go. It was startling therefore to find myself, towards the end, reflecting that something was a bit tedious.

I know why. The last part of *Moonraker* is space-adventure. The insecure assembly of wire and what-not assumed by sci-fi to be capable of whizzing through space, the long bare corridors which make up the architecture of a sci-fi metropolis – it is all here, and once too often. Sci-fi repeats itself, feeds on itself. If I too may make a reference, the sameness of these eternal space-ships is driving me nuts. Return Bond to earth!

THE LAST OF THE BYRONIC HEROES?

by Philip Larkin

From the *Times Literary Supplement*, 5 June 1981

The first pseudo-Bond novel, *Colonel Sun*, written by Robert Markham (aka, Kingsley Amis a first class writer and a Bond fan), appeared in 1968, four years after Ian Fleming's death: here, thirteen years later, is the second, *Licence Renewed* by John Gardner, an experienced thriller writer. At first this suggests, hearteningly, that James Bond has joined that small but select club of characters who have been brought back to life after the death of their creators simply because their readers want more of them. But thirteen years is a long time, and

Another of Ffolkes' cartoons for *Punch*, 4 July 1979.

during it there has been ample reason to fear that Bond had floated (literally at times) out of the world of fiction into that of cinematic fantasy, which is not quite the same thing. As everyone knows, the Bond novels were an adroit blend of realism and extravagance, and both were necessary: the one helped us swallow the other. Because Sir Hugo Drax had red hair, one ear larger than the other through plastic surgery, and wore a plain gold Patek Phillipe watch with a black leather strap, we accepted that his *Moonraker* rocket could blow London to bits. The Bond films, on the other hand, dispensed with the realism and concentrated on the extravagance, becoming exercises in camped-up absurdity. In this way there became two Bonds, book-Bond and film-Bond, each with his separate public. And a certain hostility arose between them: for the readers, the films were ludicrous and childish travesties; the viewers, if they had ever heard of the books, saw them simply as material to be guyed, perhaps deservedly. Since Gresham's Law operates in the world of entertainment as well as anywhere else, it looked as if the films were winning. But here is another novel. Is book-Bond making a come-back?

The trouble is that to resurrect Bond you have to be Fleming, for he was his creator in a way that Tarzan or Sherlock Holmes or Billy Bunter clearly weren't theirs. It was Fleming who smoked seventy cigarettes a day, who wore dark blue Sea Island cotton shirts and loved scramble eggs and double portions of orange juice for breakfast; Bond was a kind of *döppelgänger* sent out to enact what Fleming himself had never achieved. The ease with which Bond appeared suggests the tapping of deep imaginative springs. And the novels that succeeded them drew on the same dark source: 'the next volume of my autobiography,' he would call the book currently in progress, masking his personal involvement by mocking it. Of course the springs were not inexhaustible; by *Thunderball* (1961), Fleming admitted he had 'run out of puff', and his last five books are not as good as his first seven. But since they were instinct with a personality much more complex, much more intelligent, much more imaginative than Bond's – the personality, in short, of Fleming himself – they remain alive in a way that *Colonel Sun* and now *Licence Renewed* cannot hope to do.

Why then persist in trying to raise the book-Bond from the dead, if such efforts can never succeed? The prospect, no doubt, of making money for somebody; perhaps – the ultimate grisly irony – the necessity of providing new vehicles for film-Bond. But one would like to think that there is also an element of homage, and a faint hoping-beyond-hope that one day the sorcery will really work, and we shall be rewarded with another unmistakable instalment of the latest – perhaps the last – of the Byronic heroes.

Bond in the Eighties – the Byronic hero of a role-playing game from Victory Games Inc.

James BOND A CELEBRATION

PART ONE

Bond In Literature

Ian Fleming – The Man With The Golden Pen

Ian Lancaster Fleming was born on 28 May 1908, the second of four sons of Major Valentine Fleming, a Conservative MP and winner of a DSO during the First World War, in which he also lost his life. Ian's mother was Evelyn Fleming, considered one of the most beautiful women in England, and it was from his parents that he inherited his distinguished looks and sophisticated manners.

He was educated at Eton and then went to the Royal Military College at Sandhurst, passed out, but had second thoughts about an Army career and instead decided to study for the Diplomatic Service and spent some time at the Universities of Munich and Geneva. However, he again changed his mind and in 1929 opted for a career in journalism, joining Reuters at a time when all the international wire serviçes were struggling for supremacy.

'Reuters was great fun in those days,' he was to recall later, 'a very good mill. The training there gives you a good, straightforward style. Above all, I have to thank Reuters for getting the facts in my books right.'

Ian Fleming was sent to Russia to work in the Moscow bureau and came face to face with several of the elements which were to directly inspire the Bond novels. It was a tough assignment for the young man, and he found himself in direct competition with the veteran American correspondents. A friend from Fleming's journalist days, Geoffrey Bocca, now a writer living in the South of France, told me about this crucial period in his life.

'Ian may have been young and a bit green, but already one could see the older, ever-curious Fleming peeping out,' he said. 'Many correspondents hated Moscow, but he loved it and quickly added Russian to his fluent German and French. He was also fascinated by the Russian secret police who were everywhere.'

In the Spring of 1933 he actually came face to face with some of them when he covered the trial of six British engineers working in Russia for the Metropolitan-Vickers

Company who were charged with spying, plotting against the Soviet State by sabotaging machinery at power stations, and bribing Russians for secret information. This introduction to the world of OGPU, the Russian secret police, and their use of violence and torture to extract confessions, made a deep impression on him as he sat taking notes in the court room. Like all independent observers, however, he was sure the trial was a sham.

Alongside the six accused engineers was a darkly-beautiful Russian girl, Anna Kutusova, a secretary at the company, who was said to have been the mistress of one of the men, Leslie Thornton, and also involved in the spying. Fleming never forgot her, and she later became Tatiana in arguably the best of all the Bond novels, *From Russia With Love*.

His reports sent back to London – carried verbatim by *The Times* amongst other newspapers (see a typical report of 13 April 1933 reproduced here) – were models of brevity and information. In them can be seen the first flowering of the style that was to be so perfectly executed when he came to write his novels, as well as the origin of the harsh worlds of SMERSH, SPECTRE and their employees.

After three years with Reuters, Fleming was offered the job of their assistant general manager in the Far East, but decided against this and instead sought to make his fortune in the City – an attempt which continued without much success first as a banker and then as a stockbroker. In 1939 he made a brief return to Moscow for *The Times* to cover the activities of a British Trade Mission. When he returned to London with war clouds beginning to gather on the horizon, his life underwent a dramatic change.

'When I got back in April 1939 I suddenly began to hear that funny questions were being asked about me,' he was to recall in later years. 'Friends of mine told me that people had been asking about me and where I had been and who I knew. It turned out I was being investigated for a job in Naval Intelligence. Someone in the city had been asked to find a chap about my age with good knowledge of both finance and languages to do some hush-hush work at the Admiralty.'

And so at the age of thirty-one, Ian Fleming entered the world of James Bond. Like his hero-to-be he was made a Lieutenant Commander, and posted to the Special Branch of the Royal Naval Volunteer Reserve, where, for the duration of the war, he served as Personal Assistant to the Director of Naval Intelligence, Admiral John Godfrey. He worked in the famous Room 19, and many of his activities – which included preparing assault groups to go in with invading forces to seize enemy codes and secret equipment – have remained on the secret list to this day.

His friend Geoffrey Bocca recalls that the stories he told of those days 'tended to be farcical rather than dare-devil'.

'There was one occasion, though, in 1941 which he talked about because it gave him the idea for his first James Bond story,' Geoffrey recalls. 'He was on his way to Washington for secret talks with the American Office of Naval Intelligence. En route he stopped at Estoril and there at the casino saw some German secret agents playing chemin de fer.

'He knew who they were, but they did not know who he was, and he had a brilliant idea. He would play them and take them for all the secret funds they had got. But it didn't quite work out that way!

'Instead of cleaning out the Nazis, Fleming was cleaned out himself!' says Geoffrey. 'But it wasn't altogether a waste of time – for as you know, he let James avenge him in that dramatic game with Le Chiffre in *Casino Royale*.'

Although Fleming himself said his war was 'intensely exciting', Bocca believes it was also very gruelling.

'We don't really know what he did,' he says. 'Much of his work is still classified under the Official Secrets Act – but it was grim, you can be sure. Readers of the Bond novels are often horrified by the gruesome tortures which Fleming describes. But he knew from experience what happened to secret agents in Occupied Europe, and he once told me that what he described in his books was mild compared to some of the tortures the agents actually suffered.'

At the end of the war in 1945, Fleming was lured back into journalism again when Lord Kemsley offered him the job of foreign manager of his newspapers – *The Times* and the *Sunday Times*. With his insider's knowledge of reporting abroad, Ian Fleming set about creating an efficient news gathering team based all over the world.

Another employee at Kemsley Newspapers at that time was Godfrey Smith, now a columnist on the *Sunday Times*. He was then Personal Assistant to Lord Kemsley and worked on the third floor of the *Sunday Times* building. He has vivid memories of his colleague, Ian Fleming.

'His handsome, battered face would appear round my door most days,' Godfrey Smith says. 'His greeting was always the same: "Hello, old boy. Could I possibly have the key to the loo?" Only certain privileged figures were allowed into the third floor loo. Ian Fleming was one of them.'

Godfrey Smith was then twenty-five, and Ian Fleming forty-two, earning a salary of £5,000 per year to which you could add another nought for a comparable figure today. The veteran newsman recalls how Fleming joined Kemsley Newspapers.

'He had met Lord and Lady Kemsley at wartime bridge parties at the Dorchester. They were both smitten by the debonair commander in naval intelligence who smoked seventy Morland cigarettes a day, drank a good many very dry Martinis, and collected first editions.

'At any rate, Lord Kemsley gave Ian a job after the war, very much on Ian's terms. He insisted on having eight weeks' paid leave each year to go to Goldeneye, his seaside house on the north coast of Jamaica which he had bought at the end of the war. Even in London he would get away to play golf on Friday afternoons, much to the envy of us lesser mortals. Still, he was a healthy influence on the old *Sunday Times*,' Godfrey adds.

The columnist also remembers going to lunch with Fleming in his Ford Thunderbird which he would leave parked outside his office all day.

'He was the first man I had ever met who drank pink gins,' Godfrey Smith continues. 'I remember him saying that no newsman should ever use subordinate clauses. And I remember thinking how odd it was that such an elegant man should have no cuffs; he always wore short-sleeved shirts under his suits.'

Godfrey Smith was also an eye-witness to Ian Fleming's romance with Ann Rothermere which led to his marriage at the age of forty-four. She was the former wife of another newspaper proprietor, Lord Northcliffe, and one of the most brilliant hostesses in London.

'The romance was common knowledge – Ian was known in the office as Lady Rothermere's fan – and he married her in 1952,' he says. 'In fact she wrote a playful letter to him claiming that in her travels round the world she seldom visited a capital city where she did not meet some woman with whom he had had carnal relations! Yet the marriage was a good one; and Ann Rothermere was probably the only woman he ever loved.'

This love for beautiful women was as much a part of Fleming as of Bond, and again Godfrey Smith can fill in the background to the first book.

'It was to get used to the shock of marriage that he went to Goldeneye and wrote his first thriller, *Casino Royale*, in just seven weeks, pounding his old fashioned type-writer

THE MOSCOW CHARGES

FIRST DAY OF "TRIAL"

THE SOVIET CASE

TWO PRISONERS QUESTIONED

The " trial " opened in Moscow yesterday of the six British employees of the Metropolitan-Vickers Company on an indictment charging them with belonging to counter-revolutionary organizations and of engaging in espionage, sabotage, and of bribery. The names of the British accused are :—

Mr. A. Monkhouse	Mr. W. H. Macdonald
Mr. L. C. Thornton	Mr. C. de Nordwall
Mr. J. Cushny	Mr. A. W. Gregory

With the British accused are charged 11 Russians, including Mme. Kutuzova, the company's secretary in Moscow. An engineer, Vitvitsky, who is also charged, is ill, and was absent when the trial opened yesterday. He will be tried separately.

The indictment, together with the charges, is summarized on page 9. Five of the accused British employees pleaded " Not Guilty." Mr. Macdonald pleaded " Guilty," as did the whole of the Russian prisoners. Our Riga Correspondent describes the opening proceedings as showing that the case is uniform with earlier Soviet prosecutions.

PRISONERS SEPARATED

A summary of the opening proceedings of the trial, which is being held in the Hall of the Trades Unions, was issued by the Foreign Office last night. It was noticeable, the summary says, that the slogans emblazoned on cotton streamers which usually adorn Soviet Courts were absent. The Englishmen and the Russians accused with them all sat together, the two Englishmen on whom the prosecution sets the greatest store, Messrs. Macdonald and Thornton, being marshalled as far as possible from their four companions, Messrs. Monkhouse, Cushny, Gregory, and Nordwall, who occupied the back rows.

After the usual formalities, the indictment was read to the Court. The evidence which the prosecution advanced in this document in support of the charges consisted almost exclusively of the depositions of the Russian accused, and of the deposition of one of the English accused, Macdonald, who had not been allowed out on bail and has during the last four weeks been in the Ogpu prison without being allowed to receive advice or to discuss his case with anyone except the Prosecutor or his State-paid Soviet counsel.

" EVIDENCE " IN PRISON

The evidence containing direct insinuation of the guilt of the accused apart from that which has been secured from the accused themselves consists of some extracts from the findings of a Soviet State Commission and of the testimony of two Russians.

One of the latter gave part of his evidence in the Ogpu prison, while the other's evidence consists of a statement to the effect that he had immediately handed to the Ogpu money he had received from Thornton.

After the reading of the indictment the accused were interrogated as to whether or not they pleaded guilty. Macdonald, who was interrogated first of the Englishmen—*i.e.*, out of his order in the list of the accused—pleaded " Guilty." The five other Englishmen interrogated after him pleaded " Not Guilty."

The Court at yesterday's sitting examined Gusev, one of the accused Russians, and Mr. Macdonald and Mr. Thornton were also questioned. The proceedings did not end until 10 p.m. and were then adjourned until this morning.

Ian Fleming's report from Moscow in *The Times* of 13 April 1933, on the spy trial which inspired *From Russia With Love*.

MOSCOW TRIAL.—A photograph taken during the holding of the trial of the British employees of the Metropolitan-Vickers Company in Moscow. On the judges' bench are (left to right) M. Martens, M. Ulrich (the presiding Judge), M. Dmitrieff, and M. Zelikoff.

COURT
BUCKINGHAM PALACE
WINDSOR CASTLE
SHAKESPEARES
FLEMING
LOVE LET ME NOT HUNGER
An Illustrated History of ENGLAND
André Maurois
LAROUSSE GASTRONOMIQUE
PAUL HAMLYN
MY NAME IS MORGAN
Arthur Bryant
THE AGE OF CHIVALRY
The Story of England
THE GROVE OF EAGLES
SIMENON

for three hours each morning between his swim and his zizz,' he recalls. 'He disclaimed any similarities between himself and 007, however, but there were plenty. Both were naval officers, both were *aficionados* of food, drink, cards and cars; both knew the seamier sides of the world's great cities. Yet I think Ian was a much nicer man than Bond. I still miss him today.'

It was at the little house in Jamaica which he had bought for £5,000 that Fleming wrote most of the Bond books – initially during his breaks from duty on the *Sunday Times*, and then when fame and fortune came and he resigned from the newspaper group in 1959. Another journalist who knew him and visited him in the West Indies was Rene MacColl, a famous reporter on the *Daily Express*, whose proprietor, Lord Beaverbrook, once called Fleming 'The Chocolate Soldier' because he thought there was something sugar-coated about his worldly facade. (He was, though, keen enough on the Bond novels to serialise them in the *Express* and buy the rights to use 007 as the subject of a daily strip cartoon which has continued to the present day!)

MacColl last visited Fleming at Goldeneye in February 1964, just six months before the author's death on 12 August 1964.

'It was difficult not to envy him,' MacColl said later. 'The superb tropical garden . . . the private beach from which he swam . . the retinue of faithful coloured servants. But that day, under the sparkling sunshine, with all the trappings of wealth and success about him, Fleming possibly did betray an inkling of some apprehension.

'He asked me my age and told me his own. He made some jests about virility. And it was noticeable that he was pacing himself very carefully indeed. Back in 1961 he suffered a heart attack, and he told me rather wistfully that he wasn't turning out his wordage at the old rate, that the production per day was off by several hundred words.'

He was though, said MacColl, taking great pleasure from the continuing success of his novels and the films based on the books. He thought Sean Connery was an inspired choice as Bond.

'But in my mind,' MacColl added, 'there was no doubt that he identified himself with Bond, heart attack or no. Just as the American thriller master, the late Raymond Chandler whom Fleming and I both knew and liked, identified himself with the tough private eye he created, Philip Marlowe. But whereas Chandler bore no resemblance whatever to Marlowe, Fleming would not have done badly as Bond – as I told him, to his evident pleasure!'

Rene MacColl's verdict of Fleming was that he was 'a great, big glorious snob' – but from his glorious snobbery and sense of just what made the postwar world of affluence and precariousness tick, he made a fortune.

'James Bond,' said MacColl in an affectionate obituary tribute to Fleming in the *Express* of 13 August 1964, 'his inspired secret agent, was an amalgam of all the daydreams of not only Fleming himself, but of several million other men all over the world. He hit it just right.

'Bond became absolutely compulsive reading. And as Britain jumped into prosperity, into an understanding of winemanship, motorcarmanship – remember those throwaway bits in the Bond books about his cars? – hotelmanship, travelmanship, and, above all, expertise about women, Fleming became a sort of high priest of the secret life of all the Walter Mittys all over the world.'

On the subject of Bond's women, MacColl also recounted a story about the eminent

Ian Fleming photographed at London Airport in 1963 before leaving for Jamaica to write another Bond novel.

novelist, Evelyn Waugh, who stayed with the Flemings at Goldeneye on several occasions.

Apparently, Fleming told Waugh that he knew he was writing well if he became excited by what he had put down.

'Oh,' Waugh is said to have replied, 'and what were you writing about this morning?'

'I was describing Bond's latest girl,' Fleming replied.

'Well,' the novelist grunted, 'and did she excite you?'

'Actually, no,' a rather shamefaced Fleming admitted.

'Then get back to your typewriter and *start* all over again!' thundered Evelyn Waugh.

Though the enormous success of the Bond books delighted Ian Fleming, he was hurt by some of the swingeing criticisms directed at his character – and particularly that he as a writer traded in sex, snobbery and sadism. He once replied to the attacks in these words:

'I wanted to show a hero without any characteristics, who was simply the blunt instrument in the hands of the government. Then he started eating a number of meals and dressing in a certain way so that he became encrusted with characteristics much against my will . . . Apart from the fact that he wears the same clothes that I wear, he and I really have very little in common. I do rather envy him his blondes and his efficiency, but I can't say I much like the chap.'

He also didn't much like the theories and debates which began to proliferate among scholars and critics about the alleged motives and philosophies of his work. He saw the books as entertainment, pure and simple: 'They're reading too much into the man,' he once said, 'He's not all *that* important.'

I also wonder what he might have thought of the theory advanced by Dr Joshua Bierer, a retired Harley Street consultant psychiatrist, who said in February 1983 that Fleming actually invented Bond to live out his own tortured fantasies in the pages of books rather than in real life!

Dr Bierer claimed that in 1927 he had been asked to treat Fleming by British Consular Officials in Austria where the young man was studying for the Diplomatic service. They had called him in because Fleming's drunken affairs and aggressive behaviour had stretched even the tolerance of pre-war diplomatic circles.

Posing as a tutor in the art of diplomacy, said Dr Bierer, he got Ian Fleming to reveal his self-doubts and compulsive urges. 'He was the classic psychopath. I suggested he should begin writing because the thoughts of a mind as brilliant as his should be shared. That, very simply, is how James Bond was born. He was the fantasy figure which kept his creator sane.'

Whatever validity there might be in this claim, it was to be a quarter of a century before Fleming began 'exorcising his demons' by writing *Casino Royale*. And if there is to be an analysis of the creation of Bond, then I think David Holloway in the *Daily Telegraph* was as close as anyone when he wrote in August 1964:

'James Bond was an intensely personal creation, like all the great thriller heroes from Sexton Blake to Philip Marlowe. Already there have been imitations, but James Bond will stand alone as the creation of a well-stocked mind and an uninhibited imagination.'

Where psychology undoubtedly *did* come in is that Fleming realised just what sort of book the public was ready for after the dark years of war and the new threat of the nuclear bomb: fictionalised violence by recognisable crooks along with improbable sex. He hit the market right on the button.

His insight also told him that it would be films rather than just books that would make his character a superstar. And though the process of invention grew more difficult for him towards the end of his life, the snowball of success gained still further momentum in

James Bond was created in the tradition of all the great thriller heroes from Sexton Blake to Philip Marlowe – two typical illustrations of the super sleuths by Arthur Meadows (above) and LR Summers.

the hands of the film makers. What they did was to give Bond a sense of humour and thrust him into ever-more outlandish adventures, thereby propelling the legend of 007 into its second and even more amazing stage, which I will discuss in Part Two.

I was lucky enough to have an interview with Ian Fleming less than a year before his death, when he let me into some secrets both about himself and his creation, James Bond. That meeting has remained vividly in my mind ever since. We met in London's Fleet Street, the famous heart of the newspaper industry. I was working for a weekly magazine at the time, and was in the process of writing a series of articles about popular modern writers. I got the chance to interview Fleming shortly before he was due to leave the country, as was his custom, to begin work on his thirteenth book.

I have to confess that I was a little apprehensive about meeting the man who was undisputably the doyen of spy novelists, already enjoying sales in excess of 30 million copies. Part of my apprehension about the meeting in the little office he kept in Mitre Court, just off the top of Fleet Street, was that I knew he had not long finished with two legal entanglements. One with a newspaper which had infringed his copyright, and the other a claim of infringement against him.

In the previous month, November, he had taken legal action against the *Daily Sketch* for revealing that in the next Bond book, *You Only Live Twice*, not actually scheduled for publication until March 1964, the enviable hero was seemingly to die at the hands of his villainous enemies Blofeld and Irma Bunt!

The *Sketch* had apparently obtained an early proof copy of the book, and on Friday, 15 November ran an article entitled, 'In Memoriam James Bond'. Although as a former

IN MEMORIAM

JAMES BOND

IT HAD TO HAPPEN SOMETIME...AND HERE IS WHAT 'M' WROTE ON THE DAY HE KNEW 007 WAS DEAD

By ARTHUR POTTERSMAN

M, HIS shoulders hunched inside the square-cut blue suit, stood by the big window looking out across the park.

The loaded pipe lay cold in a big copper ashtray. The empty desk, the empty chair opposite his own, were the final accusation. But there was no more holding back on this news.

The mission, which Bond had christened "You only live twice," was ended. And so was Bond.

He turned and walked across to his desk. Nothing was reflected in the lined, sailor's face as he reached for the Cabinet telephone.

"M speaking," he said into the green receiver. "I want the Prime Minister personally."

In the line of duty . . .

He waited, remembering Bond, who in the line of duty had been tortured to the edge of death, till his eyes were like blackcurrants poached in blood, and his body an inert and quivering lump.

He had shot and knifed his way out of hell a dozen times. Blood-lusting barracuda had chased him. He had fought a giant squid, for all its forest of tentacles and the suckers that tore flesh and drew blood with the merest touch. And won with a puny table knife.

Well, all that was over now. No more of James' messy bird nests of plans. No more arguments about guns. The Beretta and the Smith and Wesson—who cared for such trivia now.

It sounded as if M cared very much when the Prime Minister came on the line. Softly M spoke: "I've had news from Tokyo, sir. Bad news. 007 is dead."

And that is what caused the obituary (right) to be published in The Times, according to Ian Fleming's next thriller, which will be published in the spring.

The Daily Sketch article of 15 November 1963 which Ian Fleming claimed gave away the secrets of *You Only Live Twice.*

newspaperman himself Fleming knew all about scoops and was only too well aware of the public interest in Bond, he felt the story gave away an important twist to the plot of the forthcoming book.

Therefore he had obtained an injunction against the newspaper, but his post had been deluged with letters from fans demanding to know whether he had taken the same course of action as Sir Arthur Conan Doyle when he wearied of Sherlock Holmes and tried to kill him off. Fleming had been able to assure everyone that the book did *not* mark the end of Bond's career, and had added with a wry smile and a touch of the humour that I found typical of the man, 'I would have thought the title might have given *some* discerning people a clue as to my intentions . . .'

Hard on the heels of this business had come a High Court action brought by film producer Kevin McClory in which he claimed, along with Hollywood screenwriter Jack

Obituary

CDR. JAMES BOND C.M.G., R.N.V.R.

M. writes:—

As your readers will have learned from earlier issues, a senior officer of the Ministry of Defence, Commander James Bond, CMG, RNVR, is missing, believed killed while on an official mission to Japan. It grieves me to have to report that hopes of his survival must now be abandoned. It therefore falls to my lot as the Head of the Department he served so well, to give some account of this officer and of his outstanding services to his country.

James Bond was born of a Scottish father, Andrew Bond of Glencoe, and a Swiss mother, Monique Delacroix, from the Canton de Vaud. His father being a foreign representative of the Vickers armaments firm, his early education, from which he inherited a first-class command of French and German, was entirely abroad.

At the age of twelve or thereabouts, he passed satisfactorily into Eton, for which College he had been entered at birth.

It must be admitted that his career at Eton was brief and undistinguished, and, after only two halves, as a result, it pains me to record of some alleged trouble with one of the boys' maids he was removed and transferred to Fettes, his father's old school. Here the atmosphere was somewhat Calvinistic, and both academic and athletic standards were rigorous. By the time he left, at the early age of seventeen, he had twice fought for the school as a lightweight and had, in addition, founded the first serious judo class at an English public school. By now it was 1941, and, by claiming an age of nineteen and with the help of an old Vickers colleague of his father, he entered what was to become the Ministry of Defence.

To serve the confidential nature of his duties, he was accorded the rank of lieutenant in the Special Branch of the RNVR, and it is a measure of the satisfaction his services gave to his superiors that he ended the war with the rank of Commander. It was about this time that the writer became associated with certain aspects of the Ministry's work, and it was with much gratification that I accepted Commander Bond's post-war application to continue working for the Ministry.

The nature of Commander Bond's duties with the Ministry, which were, incidentally, recognised by the appointment of CMG in 1954, must remain confidential, nay secret, but his colleagues at the Ministry will allow that he performed them with outstanding bravery and distinction, although occasionally, through an impetuous strain in his nature, with a streak of the foolhardy that brought him in conflict with higher authority. But he possessed what almost amounted to "The Nelson Touch" in emergencies.

The publicity, particularly in the foreign Press, accorded some of his adventures, made him, much against his will, something of a public figure, with the inevitable result that a series of popular books came to be written around him by a personal friend and former colleague of James Bond. If the quality of these books, or their degree of veracity, had been any higher, the author would certainly have been prosecuted under the Official Secrets Act. It is a measure of the disdain in which these fictions are held at the Ministry, that action has not yet—I emphasise the qualification—been taken.

It only remains to assure his friends that Commander Bond's last mission was one of supreme importance to the State. Although it now appears that, alas, he will not return from it, I have the authority of the highest quarters in the land to confirm that the mission proved one hundred per cent. successful. It is no exaggeration to pronounce unequivocally that, through the recent valorous efforts of this one man, the safety of the Realm had received mighty reassurance.

James Bond was briefly married in 1962 to Teresa, only daughter of Marc-Ange Draco, of Marseilles. The marriage ended in tragic circumstances. There was no issue.

Ian Fleming with his wife, Ann, outside the Law Courts in London in December 1963 during the *Thunderball* trial.

Whittingham, to have created the basis of the Bond adventure later novelised by Ian Fleming as *Thunderball.* Although McClory acknowledged that Fleming had acted in good faith believing it to be in the best interests of everyone concerned in the project that he wrote and published the novel, it had still not been a pleasant experience for the author to sit through ten days in the High Court. At the conclusion, he was left with the book rights while agreeing to assign to McClory all film rights to the story.

After the hearing, Fleming had told reporters, 'I am glad the whole expensive misunderstanding has now been disposed of. It's a pity it ever had to come to Court.' And when asked if he might use the experience in a future Bond book he had added with a smile, 'I don't think James Bond would feel at home in the Chancery Division.'

When I arrived at Ian Fleming's office, I was surprised at how tall, lean and handsome my host was. Fifty-five years old, he had high Scottish cheekbones betraying his ancestry and close-set, slightly-hooded pale blue eyes. His hair was dark and wavy, greying around the ears. There was definitely something rather sardonic-looking about his features, and although he had a slightly superior look about him, it belied his gentle nature which was expressed in his well-modulated and straightforward manner of speaking. He moved a little slowly, a result, no doubt, of the heart attack he had suffered two years earlier.

I was momentarily startled by the revolver that lay just to the right hand side of his desk – and then realised it was made of china.

He offered me a chair, proferred a box of cigarettes, and put one in his own tortoiseshell cigarette holder.

Ian Fleming talking to the author in his Mitre Court office in London in December 1963.

'I am trying to cut down,' he confessed. 'I would like to smoke less, which is why I've got this box which only holds ten at a time. Trouble is, I find I refill it more often.' He smiled and applied the lighter to the end of the cigarette.

Ian Fleming's years in journalism had taught him all about the needs of reporters and I was conscious throughout our conversation that many of his answers were well-rehearsed and, indeed, when I came to look up the cuttings on other interviews he had given, there were many phrases in common. Yet, this said, he showed no sense of boredom in talking about his remarkable super agent.

'Do you know,' Fleming said after he had drawn heavily on his cigarette, 'I've been writing the Bond books for twelve years now and I can't help wondering if I'm not getting too old for blondes and guns. The trouble with my kind of writing is that the action must be constant. And that requires a great deal of invention.

'Talking of invention,' he said and a smile crossed his face as the memory of what he was about to tell me slipped into his mind, 'an accountant I know came up with a good idea for tax exemption recently. He said that as so many of my books were about gambling why didn't I take my gambling losses as a business deduction from my income tax?'

Fleming paused. 'The trouble was,' he said, 'that I usually win when I gamble and the Government could therefore tax me on my winnings!'

He laughed gently, and the slightly formal atmosphere of the interview was broken. I used the opportunity to ask him how the 'gamble' of creating James Bond had all come about.

'He came out of thin air really,' he said, drawing again on his cigarette holder and letting a stream of smoke pour through his nostrils. 'He was a compound of all the secret agents and commando types that I met during the Second World War when I was Personal Assistant to the Director of Naval Intelligence.

'The thing was my job got me right into the heart of things, even the most secret affairs. No one could have wished for a more exciting or interesting war. And it was all the things that I heard and learned about secret operations that finally led me to write about them in a disguised way and with James Bond as the central character.'

Fleming lent back in his chair and then almost contradicted himself in the next breath. 'The odd thing about Bond is that I didn't think of him as a "character" at all. I didn't intend that he would have any characteristics at all – except to be a blunt instrument in the hands of the British Government. He's a cipher, in fact. What's happened over the years is that he has become a "character" largely exaggerated in the public mind.

'The paradox is that I quite deliberately made him rather anonymous. This was to enable the reader to identify with him. People have only to put their own clothes on Bond and build him into whatever sort of person they admire. If you read my books you'll find that I don't actually describe him at all.'

I said that I was aware of this, but what sort of *person* was he?

'He's got his vices obviously,' Fleming said, 'and some virtues like patriotism and courage – though I'm not sure just how much of a virtue they are. He's got a little bit of culture. He's a man of action primarily, and he's not a person of much social attractiveness. But then I never intended him to be a particularly likeable person which makes me wonder a bit about the real motives of people who treat him like a cult.'

Fleming ground the remains of his cigarette out into the ashtray, and fitted a fresh one into the tortoiseshell holder.

'I suppose you could best describe Bond as a highly romanticised amalgam of the tough guy, dressed up in twentieth century clothes and using twentieth century language. I do think he's more true to the modern kind of hero – the secret service men and commandos who inspired him – than the cardboard heroes of the old fashioned thrillers.

'You probably know there are all sorts of popular theories about him. They say he's a gourmet. In fact he just happens to have a good meal now and then like most of us enjoy from time to time. He's not a wine snob either, as some people would have it. He very seldom drinks wine, just an occasional glass of champagne. Basically he is a hard liquor man.

'There is also this business about Bond being fastidious over clothes. His shoes, for example. In fact, I've never mentioned them except to say he doesn't like laces. Any more than he likes buttons, studs or long-sleeved shirts. The reason for that is that *I* hate the things and wear short-sleeved shirts because I cannot stand dirty shirt cuffs!'

'Bond is fond of black silk knitted ties, I agree,' he went on. 'But there really is no snobbery about his clothes.'

What, then, about his cigarettes specially made by Morlands of Grosvenor Street?

Fleming blew what seemed like a slightly exasperated puff of smoke between his teeth.

'But that's not snobbery,' he replied evenly. 'Of course, no real secret agent would be so ostentatious – if he smoked he'd stick to Players or one of the commoner American brands. The reason for the Morlands is that the readers enjoy such little idiosyncrasies. And I put them in because little things like that interest *me*. I'm always collecting facts about people and places, and I note them down to use in the stories. Such things all make the character that much more interesting.

'I don't think I could argue with anyone who said that there wasn't much secrecy about my secret agent. He is certainly pretty obvious wherever he goes. But the pace of the story gets over such objections. The reader gets so caught up in the sheer speed of the narrative that he isn't worried by such incongruities.

'And I *do* take a lot of my plots from life,' Fleming continued. 'They are certainly bizarre, but they are also made up of real things. Espionage is like an iceberg. So much more is hidden beneath the waves. The trouble is, espionage always goes one better than a plot I can think up myself.'

My host paused for a moment, and then from his memory dug out another story which illustrated his theme.

'A while back I met this old friend from my Intelligence days who told me how he had carried out an experiment to survive in the Arctic wastes. He had lived on grass, weeds and the snails which are found on the screes there. I was fascinated by this, and asked if someone desperate from hunger could survive on grass alone.

'My friend said no – and cited the example of cows. They have to eat all day long just to stay alive and still have no energy. Then another thought came into my mind.

"Suppose," I said to my friend, "a nice, clean Russian stood between you and starvation and so you killed him. Which would be the best part to eat?"

' "How should I know?" he replied. "But I've been told that the palm of the hand is the tastiest part," I said. He shook his head. "What about the buttocks?" I persisted. Still he shook his head.

' "So, *what* then?" I nagged him. And he looked me straight in the eyes and said without so much as a blink, "A cut off the ribs – that's the best part!" '

I swallowed hard at the thought and didn't quite know whether to feel nauseated or to laugh at the idea. It was, though, an ideal moment to raise the ticklish subject of violence in the Bond stories: an issue which had been raised many times in the press and on which Fleming had expressed himself forcibly already.

'The fact of the matter is,' the author said raising his head in a half-glaring, half-defensive look, 'that Bond reflects the times he lives in. We live in violent times, we all have to accept that. It has been said that I invented all the cruelties and brutalities to which Bond is subjected. But let me tell you, some terrible things were done to secret agents in the last war. I *know* that. And anyone who has been involved in the Secret

Service in recent years certainly won't agree such things are made up.

'I wouldn't like anyone to think that Bond enjoys killing people: he doesn't. It is part of his job and he gets on with it. Violence and death are as much a part of his life as women and seduction,' Fleming said.

I put it to him that there were those critics who complained Bond had an appallingly chauvinistic attitude towards women.

'Oh, nonsense,' he pulled hard on his cigarette. 'Everybody complains he leaves the girl behind in some place like Mexico. But he has to get back to headquarters in London, you see. After all he is on the job!'

His lined and knowing face broke into the kind of grin that has crossed the face of uncounted millions of cinemagoers when the various screen Bonds have uttered just such *double entendres*.

'James Bond is a healthy, violent, non-cerebral man in his middle thirties,' he went on. 'He's a creature of his times. I wouldn't say he's particularly typical of our times, but he is certainly a man *of* his times. I think seduction has now replaced courtship – the direct approach to sex has become the norm. I think Bond is a believable man and I try to weave a great web of excitement and fantasy around him.

'You see I can't really imagine Bond drinking half a pint of beer – even in the company

The original of James Bond as described by Ian Fleming – 'the golfer Henry Cotton in his younger days'.

of people who do. He gets himself into the most dangerous places and suffers rather nastily as a result.

'So,' Fleming went on, 'I really think it is up to me to see that he gets the best of everything when he isn't being tortured or shot at. His basic needs are money, beautiful women, good food and clothes, fast cars and general luxury. Plus, of course, a gun.

'I must confess I quite often get terribly excited myself at his adventures. There are times when I can hardly wait to write the next page.'

I smiled at this useful quote, and just as quickly my host slipped in another, which to this day remains as one of the most frequently used in essays about Ian Fleming.

'I have always said that the target of my books lies somewhere between the solar plexus and the upper thigh,' he said blowing the last smoke from his cigarette before crushing the butt out in his ashtray with the end of his cigarette holder. 'I write for warm-blooded heterosexuals in railway trains, aeroplanes and beds. I suppose you could say Bond is my pillow fantasy – the feverish dreams of the author of what he might have been. It is no more than you would expect from an adolescent mind such as the one I happen to possess.

'I am for the total stimulation of the reader,' he added. 'I suppose really I appeal to the Boy Scout in everybody.'

At this moment the chiming bells of St Dunstan-in-the-West in Fleet Street interrupted our conversation. I realised then that my time with Fleming was growing to a close, as I had known from the start that he had a luncheon appointment. I was, though, anxious to ask him just a few more questions – in particular about the origins of Bond. Firstly, his name.

Fleming meticulously straightened the papers before him on the desk, and I asked if he would just confirm that it had been an American professor who lectured on the science of classifying birds who had been the inspiration.

'As I mentioned earlier,' he said, 'I was determined right from the start that my secret agent should be as anonymous a personality as possible. I wanted him to be just an instrument carried along by the action of the book. And so to be anonymous he needed a brief, unromantic name and yet one which was very masculine.

'The answer came so easily it still surprises me. One of my "Bibles" in Jamaica is a famous ornithological work called *Birds of the West Indies* by James Bond, who is a lecturer at the Academy of National Sciences in Philadelphia. The name sounded just right and so I purloined it!'

Fleming smiled at the memory, and then continued.

'Two years ago I got a letter from the real Mr Bond's wife in which she rather pulled my leg. She said that since the success of the book, they had been receiving phone calls from people either after Bond's help or asking questions about one or other of his adventures. What tickled me was her remark about what she said when callers asked to speak to her husband. She would reply with a barely controlled giggle, "I'm sorry – but he's out right now with Pussy Galore!"'

Had he ever had any living person in mind where the actual *features* of James Bond were concerned, I asked.

'I see him as permanently in his thirties,' he answered non-committally. 'If you must put a face on him, then a bit like the golfer Henry Cotton in his younger days.'

Fleming's desire for Bond to remain, as he put it, as anonymous a personality as possible, meant he was obviously not going to prolong a discussion along these lines, but I did just ask him what he thought of Sean Connery who had then played Bond on screen twice in *Dr No* and *From Russia With Love*. Was he anything like the image of the secret agent as he had conceived him?

'Yes, I believe he is. One thing I put my foot down about when they planned the first film was to choose an unknown actor who wasn't yet typed. Yes, Sean is a good choice.'

And what, I asked next, about Bond's famous prefix, 007 – how had that originated?

'I pinched that idea, too,' Fleming replied, leaning back in his chair once more. 'When I was at the Admiralty at the beginning of the war, all top-secret signals had the double O prefix. Although this was later changed for security reasons, it stuck in my mind and I decided to borrow it for Bond to make his job sound more interesting and provide him with a licence to kill. Of course, in real life any spy may need to kill and probably will, quite irrespective of whether he is authorised to do so!'

These explanations for the origins of the name 'James Bond' and the prefix '007' are both open to some speculation, as the reader will discover in the next section, 'The Spies Who Made Me'.

I was anxious to know the origins of SMERSH, the Russian secret organisation against whom Bond pitted his wits in the early books, before the international band of conspirators named SPECTRE claimed his attentions.

'Well, as you know I worked for Reuters in Moscow in the Thirties and I became fascinated by the Russian secret police who were everywhere. It was through my interest that I learned about SMERSH who had been set up by Stalin to do his dirty work. They were OK as the villains for a while until Khrushchev closed them down, but always a bit restricting because being the real thing there was always only so far I could go with them in a fictional sense. So I invented SPECTRE to give me the freedom of invention I needed for the more recent books.

'Mention of Stalin reminds me of the scoop I very nearly got in Moscow,' he added. 'Of course every journalist there in the Thirties wanted to talk to him, but he usually ignored all requests for interviews. So one day with another journalist friend, Stanley Richardson, we sent a joint letter asking for an interview. Much to our surprise we got a personal reply.

'It was badly typed on a mixture of Cyrillic and Roman keys and addressed to "Micter Richardson and Micter Fleming". Still, we both realised it was a document of some financial value and decided to play poker for it. I won.'

But what did it *say*, I wanted to know.

'I still have the paper today,' Fleming went on. 'Sometimes I think I will give it to Sotheby's to auction because I have long since ceased to dine out on it because of the anticlimax. For when I tell people I have a personal letter from Stalin they ask, "What does it say?" and I have to reply, "Sorry, I cannot see you, J. Stalin." '

Fleming laughed at the memory, and immediately recounted another story from his Russian days. Despite his depiction of Russian espionage in his books, he clearly had an affinity for the Russian *people*, if not an actual liking for the ordinary professional men and women he met. He certainly experienced some moments of good humour in their country.

'I remember when I was due to come home to London I decided to bring back some Russian contraceptives. I had seen them in a Moscow chemist's shop and wondered if they were made of the same latex we had in Britain. So I stuck a packet in my case.

'Well, you've never seen anything like the face of the Russian Customs Officer when he came across the packet while going through my things. He took the contraceptives out of the packet one by one and held them up to the light. I'm sure he was convinced they must have contained secret messages!'

With a real belly laugh, Fleming stood up and offered his hand. 'I'm sorry, I must go now. I hope you have enough.'

As we left the office, Fleming spoke briefly to his secretary and then we walked

'Sean Connery was a good choice as James Bond' – Ian Fleming.

downstairs. He was heading for his appointment at the wine bar, El Vino's, almost literally next door to the office. The old habit of a journalist to meet before lunch for a drink in this famous Fleet Street tavern was obviously still strong in him.

I said before we parted with another handshake that he obviously enjoyed the fame and fortune that James Bond had brought him.

'Oh, it's enormous fun, and I really enjoy knowing that people find my books entertaining,' he replied. 'I never look back on the past. I have no regrets.'

And what of Bond? What plans had he for him after the next book which was evidently already in shape in his mind?

'I can't put him into retirement or anything like that. It's just a question of knowing what he does next. Cheerio!'

And with that, Ian Fleming swung through the side door of El Vino's and was immediately swallowed up by the dark and yet convivial atmosphere of the wine bar.

As I walked back down Fleet Street to my office, I felt I would never again see the stories of James Bond in quite the same light. Though undeniably written as entertainments, there was more in their conception and writing than might at first be evident. Fleming might try to depreciate his characters and his storytelling powers, but he had undoubtedly tapped a rich vein that gave readers all over the world pleasure and satisfaction. And that was something all writers strove for – but only a select few ever achieved.

The Spies Who Made Me

There has been a great deal of discussion during the past thirty-five years since the first James Bond adventure appeared, about 007's literary predecessors as well as the writers who influenced Ian Fleming. At first glance the answers seem readily available – the hints provided by Fleming himself – but once the subject is carefully investigated, it proves to be as tortuous and mysterious as a spy story.

The most obvious comparison between James Bond and his literary predecessors has to be Bulldog Drummond; the secret agent whose adventures were as popular in books and films in Britain in the Twenties and Thirties as the Bond novels today. We know Fleming read these tales of high drama when he was young for he was more than once questioned on the fact by interviewers.

The cult which developed around the figure of Captain Hugh 'Bulldog' Drummond was uncannily similar to that which has embraced James Bond. Both men are remarkably similar in certain respects: both are intensely patriotic, willing to risk their lives, break the law if need be, and commit acts of violence against those who endanger the security of Britain. Both are excellent revolver shots too, adept with their fists and see Russia as their main enemy (Drummond also included the Germans). Both face archvillains of terrible depravity and cunning – while Bond has several such adversaries, the redoubtable Bulldog is primarily concerned with outwitting just one: the fiendish Carl Peterson.

In what is widely considered Drummond's most exciting adventure, *The Final Count* (1926), Peterson is plotting the self-same ambition as most of Bond's enemies – to rule the world: in his case by the use of a deadly poison which will bring instantaneous death to millions. *The Female of the Species*, another popular title which followed in 1928, had Peterson's mistress trying to avenge her dead lover against Drummond.

The series of sixteen Bulldog Drummond films which started in 1922 made ideal cinema material, and also made a star of a young man named Ronald Colman who first appeared in the role in 1929. The series was discontinued in 1951, but following the success of the Bond pictures in the early Sixties, an updated version of the gentleman adventurer reappeared with Richard Johnson in the title role in *Deadlier Than The Male*

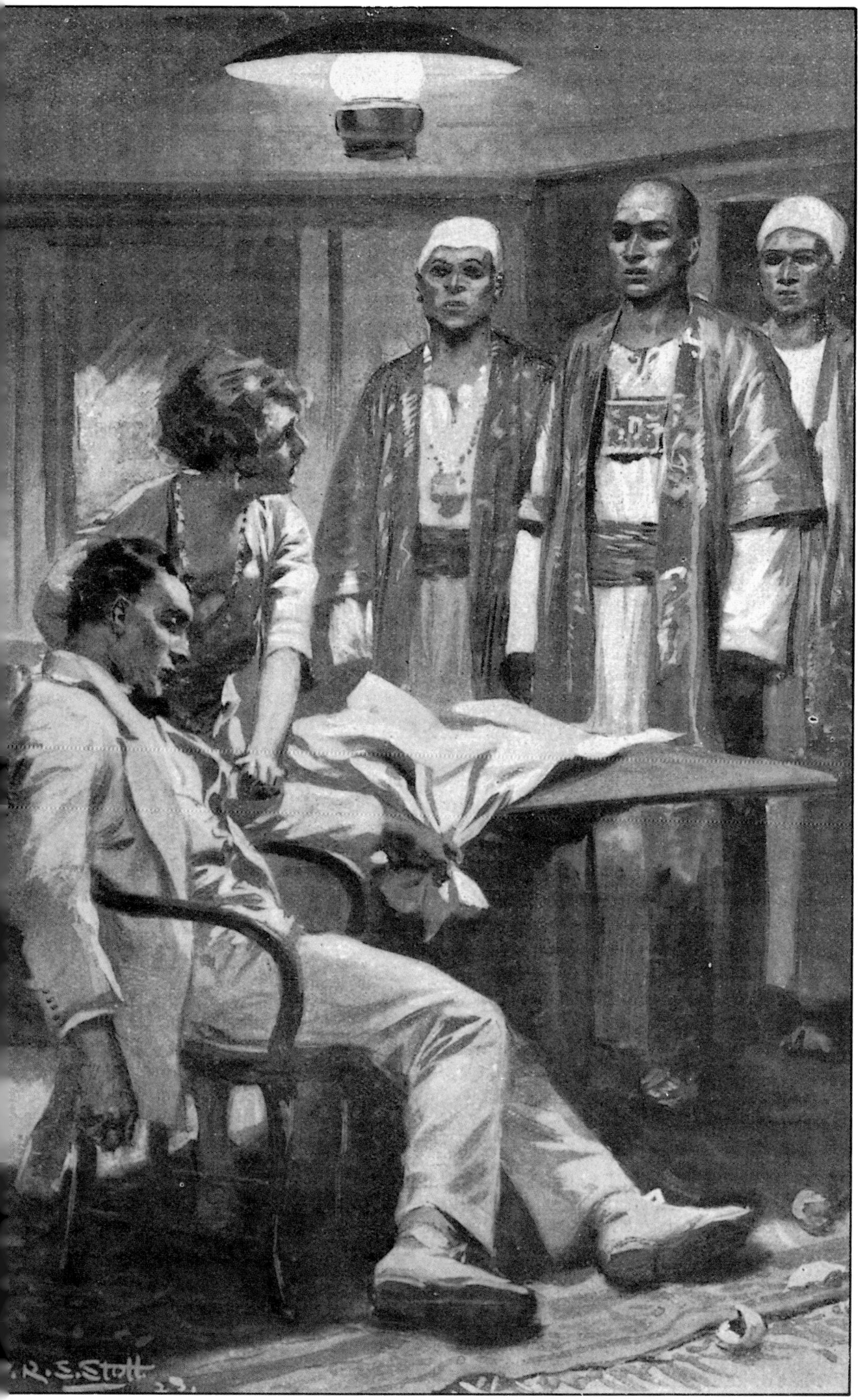

Bond's great forerunner, Bulldog Drummond, was created by Major HC McNeile (above), who wrote under the pen-name 'Sapper'. Drummond is pictured (left) in a tight corner in *The Final Count* (1926), illustrated by WR Stott.

Bulldog Drummond on the screen. Like 007, Bulldog was forever combating arch-villains and rescuing beautiful girls. Ronald Colman played Drummond in this 1929 film with Joan Bennett as his co-star.

(1967) and *Some Girls Do* (1971), during which he battled a team of deadly female robots! (Johnson was also one of the names on the short-list to play 007.)

It is fifty years ago this year that Herman Cyril McNeile (1888–1937), who wrote the Bulldog Drummond stories under the pen-name 'Sapper', died, his name eclipsed by that of his creation. Like Ian Fleming, he saw his character begin what has proved to be a seemingly unending series of films, with his series of books also destined to be continued by another writer, Gerald Fairlie.

Like Fleming, McNeile came from a service background – but although his father was a Navy Captain, it was in the Royal Engineers that he served for twelve years until retiring to write under the pseudonym which he derived from the military slang term for

The modern Bulldog Drummond. Richard Johnson – who was once a favourite for the role of 007 – and Sylva Koscina in *Deadlier Than The Male* (1967).

an engineer. Just as Ian Fleming endowed Bond with some of his likes and dislikes, so McNeile made Drummond a lover of smart restaurants and bars, fine wine and possessing a great thirst for adventure. The books featuring both these heroes are similarly fast-paced, with a skilful use of violence, romance and cliff-hanging suspense. In both, characterisation and realistic storylines take second place to action.

Despite such evident similarities, Ian Fleming denied that Bond owed anything substantial to Drummond when he came to create him. For, as he told an interviewer in the *New Yorker* magazine in April 1962, 'I don't believe in the heroic Bulldog Drummond types. I mean, rather, I don't believe they could exist any longer in literature. I wanted my men to follow the pattern of Raymond Chandler's or Dashiell Hammett's people. They are *believable* heroes.'

What he undeniably *was* doing, however, was continuing a tradition that had begun in the closing years of the previous century. For the spy or 'secret agent' as such did not arrive as a central character in fiction until the year 1890 when a journalist-turned-novelist called William Le Queux wrote a sensational book entitled *Guilty Bonds*!

There is evidence that Ian Fleming knew and read this man's very popular books which were appearing in full flood in Britain during his childhood. The similarities in their interests and the facts of their lives are also something which I feel sure would have intrigued and fascinated the ever-curious Fleming. After setting them down, it is fair to ask, I think, whether the influence on the Bond books by William Le Queux might not be a heretofore unconsidered factor.

William Tufnell Le Queux was born in London on 2 July 1864, the son of a wealthy French father and an English mother. As was customary with such children he was educated privately in London, and then sent to complete his studies in Paris where art was his subject and the Latin Quarter the place were he spent a good deal of his time.

Before the thought of work needed to intrude into the young Le Queux's life, he spent a good many months touring France and Germany on foot, thoroughly acclimatising himself to the countries which were later to feature in his books. Indeed, a career seemed the last thing he had in mind, and his father observed at one point that he was a 'lazy, rackety, good-for-nothing fellow'.

Whether these words influenced Le Queux or not, we have no way of knowing – but not long afterwards he threw himself into the world of journalism and began a hectic love affair with the written word which was to last for the rest of his life.

The similarities between Le Queux's life and that of Fleming become evident when the young writer was made a special correspondent for *The Times*, and in 1890 was sent to Russia.

There is strong circumstantial evidence that by this time Le Queux had been recruited by the British Secret Service, and there seems little doubt that many of his later travels in Europe up the time of the First World War, ostensibly to collect material for his novels, were actually a cover for his espionage activities. In any event, on his return from Russia, Le Queux picked up his pen and wrote *Guilty Bonds*, which dealt with political conspiracy and the work of undercover agents in Russia. The book was an immediate sensation in Britain and Europe – and, like the James Bond novels half a century later, was promptly banned in Russia.

Guilty Bonds was to prove a landmark in popular literature – for despite its obvious shortcomings as a piece of writing, it set the pattern of the straightforward spy story which is still practised today and which reached a kind of apogee in James Bond. The publication of the book was also an important moment for William Le Queux, as his biographer N St Barbe Sladen has recorded in *The Real Le Queux* (1938):

William Le Queux, the master of espionage, who created Duckworth Drew, the unlikely-sounding first spy in literature.

'One of the proudest moments in Le Queux's life was the day of publication, by Messrs George Routledge & Sons, of his first novel: *Guilty Bonds*. This was written on his return from Russia where he had been on a special mission for *The Times*. The novel attracted the attention of the (then) Princess of Wales. Russia, where the scene of the book was laid, was at that time governed by the Emperor Alexander, and people were being exiled to Siberia, without charge made against them. The book sold well and was afterwards dramatised.'

The following year, 1891, Le Queux was made Foreign Editor of the *Globe* (shades of Fleming here again), and travelled throughout Africa, Turkey, Albania and other points in search of the material which he utilised initially in articles for his paper and later in novel form. Then, in 1896, he published a second major novel about spying in Russia which he called *A Secret Service*. In a Preface to the second edition of this he wrote:

'By a special order issued from the Press Bureau at St Petersburg copies of this book are prohibited from entering the Russian Empire, while, not content with the formal interdiction of my novel, *Guilty Bonds*, which deals with a political conspiracy, the Russian Government has also sent one of its emissaries to my house in London to inform me of the fact. This, I believe, is a personal attention received by no other English

The 'father' of James Bond, William Le Queux's Gerry Sant in a situation that could be straight out of a 007 novel. This Michael King illustration (left) was for *Sant of the Secret Service* (1918). (Right) An advertisement for one of Duckworth Drew's adventures, *Number 70 Berlin*, published in 1912.

author. The methods of the agents of the Russian Secret Police in London will probably be a revelation to English readers!'

Indeed they were – and copies of the two books sold in their thousands. Le Queux's continued travels obviously provided him with still more material, and the turn of the century saw him introducing a secret agent by name: Duckworth Drew, the first spy in modern literature and arguably James Bond's 'grandfather'. In his first appearance in *The Man of Mystery* (1903), the curiously-named Drew was described as 'a secret agent in the employ of the Foreign Office, and, next to His Majesty's Secretary of State for Foreign Affairs, one of the most powerful and important pillars of England's supremacy.' From a personal point of view he was also 'one of the most remarkable of men, possessing shrewdness and tact, cunning and daring that are utterly amazing.'

What is also interesting about Drew is the fact that he encounters a number of very 'Bondian' gadgets during his missions. In one he has a narrow escape from an explosive cigar – not the comic variety beloved by comedians, but a 'most deadly and diabolical contrivance' containing a small charge of dynamite and quite capable of blowing a man to bits when lit.

On another mission he discovers the 'Electric Eye', a very fiendish invention which works by remote control to detonate naval mines. Intended to be used by the French in an unsuspected attack on England by warships, the intrepid man from the Foreign Office turns the tables on the enemy and uses the 'Eye' to blow up the leading ship of the strike fleet before it is even in firing range of the White Cliffs of Dover! At this piece of ill-fortune, all the others turn tail and run.

Though Duckworth Drew is important as the first literary spy, he was nowhere near as convincing a figure as Gerry Sant whom Le Queux created in *Sant of the Secret Service*, published in 1918. He is truly the 'father' of James Bond, as this Introduction to the book by Le Queux will make plain:

'To those who, like myself, have moved in the Continental underworld of spies and spying, the name of "Sant of the Secret Service" is synonymous with all that is ingenious, resourceful and daring. In the Intelligence Departments of London, Paris, Rome and New York, the name of "Sant of the Secret Service" is today one to conjure with.

'Cheerful, optimistic, and the most modest of men, Gerry Sant has seldom spoken of his own adventures. The son of a certain nobleman who must here remain nameless, and hence the scion of a noble house, he has graduated through all stages of the dark and devious ways of espionage.

'Our first meeting was ten years ago, in the tribune at the Battle of Flowers at San Remo, where, to be exact, we were fellow-members of the committee, and it is because of our old friendship, and the fact that we have been fellow-spies up and down Europe, that he has permitted me to write down these intensely absorbing memoirs of exciting and unrecorded adventures . . .'

Sant, like Bond, has some of the qualities of his creator. He is a crack shot with a pistol, has an expert knowledge of radio communications and loves motoring and skiing in Switzerland. Le Queux himself was one of the first wireless experimenters in connection with espionage, though he is better known for his broadcasts for children as 'Uncle William' in the Twenties! He was a pioneer motorist too, driving as a companion with his friend, the newspaper proprietor, Lord Northcliffe, one of the first owners of a motor car in Britain. But it was as a spy that he gained the information which made his books so avidly read.

Again I quote from the biography by N St Barbe Sladen: 'I do not recall that anyone who indulged in secret service on a large scale led such an extraordinary life as Le Queux. He delighted in looking the part of a secret agent or counter-spy whilst differing fundamentally from one's preconceived ideas of such an individual's appearance and habits. Such an outstanding figure was Le Queux in his sphere that on one occasion two men came over specially from the United States of America to assassinate him, when he was staying at a London hotel. He discovered the plot in time to escape.'

On his travels in Europe, Le Queux's footsteps were also occasionally dogged by spies, and there is no doubt he was a source of annoyance to both Russia and Germany. Indeed, he later successfully predicted the First World War with Germany in a book entitled *The Invasion of 1910*, published in 1906 and initially greeted with scepticism until grimly vindicated. In all, it was translated into twenty-seven languages and sold about one million copies.

William le Queux was such a larger-than-life figure and his books so widely discussed (one his greatest admirers, A J Balfour, leader of the Conservative Party, for example, said his works were 'worth several thousand votes to the Tories'), that I find it impossible to believe that Ian Fleming did not know about him and was not familiar with at least some of his works. The fact that Le Queux was also a rare book collector of some reknown would surely have brought his name to Fleming's attention as owner of the specialist magazine, *The Book Collector*.

Unfortunately for Le Queux, one difference between the two men was that while Ian Fleming's espionage novels made him a rich man, the reverse was the case with Le Queux, as N St Barbe Sladen has also noted in his biography:

'Some people have asserted that Le Queux made money out of the services he rendered to the British Government. Not a penny was expected or received from public funds; royalties derived from Le Queux's novels were utilised to meet the cost of fifteen years' travel in Europe, Asia Minor and Africa as a spy and counter-spy of Great Britain, and Le Queux defied anyone to prove the contrary. In point of fact, his patriotism was ruinous from a financial aspect and Le Queux was not a wealthy man.'

Several of the authorities who have written about Ian Fleming's life have commented on three specific authors whom we know he read as a child and who must have left a vivid impression on him: Rider Haggard, Jules Verne and Sax Rohmer. Fleming's biographer, John Pearson, who had access to his papers has particularly confirmed these three major influences.

From Sir Henry Rider Haggard (1856–1925) he learned the art of portraying the lonely, heroic figure defying the odds – and the comparisons between Bond and Haggard's great adventurer, Allan Quatermain, who features in a total of eighteen stories, are most evident when both are hurling break-neck through times of crisis and peril. Quatermain was a relentless pursuer of man and beast, and rescued no small number of beautiful girls from evil villains in the series of books about him, ranging from the most famous, *King Solomon's Mines*, first published in 1885, to the curiously futuristic *Allan and the Ice Gods* (1923).

The Quatermain stories have been published over the years in numerous editions, and several have been filmed: *King Solomon's Mines* half a dozen times, with Stewart Granger as Allan in the 1950 British version.

Futuristic gadgets are the highlights of many of the extraordinary fantasies of Jules Verne (1828–1905), who effectively inaugurated the literature of science fiction, and his stories were to be found on young Fleming's book shelves. *Twenty Thousand Leagues Under the Sea* (1870) was one of Ian's favourite books, and introduced him to the wonders of underwater exploration – a fascination which remained with him all his life and which was given its most complete expression whenever he was staying in Jamaica. For as John Pearson wrote in *The Life of Ian Fleming* (1966):

'By the mere act of donning his flippers and mask, he was back in the sort of world Captain Nemo inhabited in the Jules Verne books he read as a child; a world where nobody talks or makes demands or answers back; a world where boredom vanishes, where loneliness no longer matters, where the faintest stroke of a flipper would carry him over canyons, past great rocks, through the forests of tree coral, as he followed the rainbow fish and the blue parrot fish that went flashing between the niggerheads and the great clumps of brain coral in the cold underwater sunlight.'

The books of Jules Verne also opened Fleming's eyes to the wonders of travel, both to exotic corners of the Earth and even into space. *Around The World in Eighty Days* (1873) thrilled him as it has done generations of other readers, with his personal favourite to play Bond on the screen, David Niven, starring in the multi-million dollar version made by Mike Todd in 1956. Verne's space operas captured his fancy too, though by the time he came to write *Moonraker*, for instance, the Frenchman's fantasies about travelling to the Moon were hopelessly outdated. But the seeds had been sown in those imaginative old engravings which decorated the Verne books, *From The Earth To The Moon* (1865) and *Round The Moon* (1870), and showed intrepid voyagers wrestling with the problems of space flight in a small projectile.

We should not overlook the fact that in *Propeller Island* (1895) Verne conceived of a huge artificial secret island of the kind so beloved of Bond adversaries, while in two other books he portrayed unforgettable master villains. In *For The Flag* (1896) there is a power-mad despot called Ker Kerraje who threatens the world with his 'atom bomb' unless all the governments bow to his demands, and in *The Barsac Mission*, a tyrant appropriately named Harry Killer wages a war of attrition on the world from his hideout, Blackland, in the middle of the Sahara Desert.

It was, though, from Sax Rohmer (1886–1959) that he gained inspiration for his villains. Fleming discovered the works of Rohmer while he was at school, and we can find the model for *Doctor No* in the sinister, sardonic oriental villain, Fu Manchu, who features in many of the books. Interestingly, in reviewing *Doctor No* in 1958, *Time* magazine referred to the evil mastermind as 'a sort of rich man's Fu Manchu.'

Rohmer's influence is also strong in *Live and Let Die*, as John Pearson pointed out: 'The whole episode of Mr Big with the table that descends through the floor of the Boneyard Strip Club, the supernatural awfulness of his presence and his reliance on voodoo and black magic to keep his followers in order, is a skilful re-creation of the world of Sax Rohmer and Fu Manchu whose adventures Fleming enjoyed as a boy at Eton.'

Beyond these writers, any other literary influences on Fleming are mere conjecture. It is quite likely he knew of John Buchan's hero Richard Hannay and Dornford Yates' Jonah Mansel, for along with Bulldog Drummond they were popular reading for the masses during Ian's formative years. There are also certainly parallels to be drawn between them and Bond: though the strongest would seem to be that they were household names in their time as 007 is today. What is arguable, I think, is that they will be long forgotten when Bond remains as much a part of literary históry as the immortal Sherlock Holmes.

The other factor of James Bond's creation which remains tantalisingly open to argument is the origin of his name and the number by which he is known in the Secret Service. Fleming told us he purloined the name from the author of a book about birds, and the number from his days working at the Admiralty. But although he repeated this story without variation throughout his life, there are two other very interesting possibilities that deserve consideration: one is that he got the name from another fictional character created in a short story by Agatha Christie; and the second, that the 007 was taken from the title of a short tale by Rudyard Kipling. Let us examine the stories for the clues they offer.

It was some years ago that I first came across an intriguing short story by Agatha Christie in one of her lesser known works called *The Listerdale Mystery*, which had been published in the Collin's 'Crime Club' series. I found the rather worn copy of the collection on the shelves of the London Library while I was researching Miss Christie's work for a book I was writing. As I idly skimmed through the twelve stories making up the compilation, I came to the penultimate tale which was entitled, 'The Rajah's Emerald'. Immediately, a line caught my eye and I wondered if I had picked up the wrong book – or a story had found its way into a collection where it did not belong.

'With a serious effort,' the line of fading type read, 'James Bond bent his attention once more on the little yellow book in his hand.'

What on Earth was Bond doing in a collection by Agatha Christie? As soon as I had convinced myself that my eyes were not playing tricks, I sat down and read the story through very rapidly. Sure enough the hero of this little tale of skulduggery was James Bond – though certainly not the Bond of Ian Fleming's books. As I found when I turned to the reverse of the title page, this book had been published in *1934* – a whole twenty years before 007 made his debut!

The story itself was innocuous enough, but could this be where Ian Fleming had first stumbled across the perfect name for his hero?

The facts of the story are easily told: James Bond is a somewhat impoverished clerk who suddenly and unwittingly finds himself thrust into a case of international jewel-theft. The setting for the tale is Kempton-on-Sea, a fashionable English seaside resort where James is on holiday with his fiancée, Grace, an ambitious young shop assistant whose recent promotion means she now earns more than him. The couple are not, though, staying at the same hotel and apart from the irritation of the wages discrepancy, James, who is booked into a cheap guest house, is not amused by the fact that Grace is staying at the fancy Esplanade Hotel on the seafront.

Agatha Christie's James Bond in 'The Rajah's Emerald' published in *Pearson's Magazine* in July 1934, and later in the collection entitled *The Listerdale Mystery* (1934).

Much of the gossip in Kempton is focused on the town's most wealthy inhabitant, Lord Campion, who is currently entertaining the Rajah of Maraputna, owner of a fabulous egg-sized emerald. Such affairs are of scant concern to James, until he learns that another guest at the Esplanade, a rather poisonous and obviously wealthy man named Claude Sopwith, is pursuing Grace – and that she is not averse to these attentions.

The drama unfolds when James returns from a morning swim and accidently finds himself putting on a pair of shabby grey flannel trousers; in one of the pockets is the Rajah's famous emerald. Although he is naturally startled, James realises this is his chance to impress Grace with his powers of detection, and by some astute detective work he does, indeed, put an end to an attempted robbery and returns the precious stone to its much-relieved owner.

Though Grace is naturally impressed by her fiance's resourcefulness, she remains flattered by the attentions of Claude Sopwith and invites both of them out to the cinema with her. Rather miffed, Bond refused on the grounds that he has a prior engagement! End of story.

By Agatha Christie's standards, 'The Rajah's Emerald' is little more than a lightweight mystery tale, though it does capture the snobbish atmosphere and attempts at one-up-manship which were so much a part and parcel of English middle-class life in the Thirties. The drawing for the story when it was published in *Pearson's Magazine* in July 1934 – the same year *The Listerdale Mystery* was issued by Collins – illustrates this well. But what makes it memorable is, of course, Dame Agatha's choice of name for her hero.

Since discovering the story, I have learned that several Christie experts have commented on the similarity. Dennis Sanders, writing in *The New Yorker* in 1967, for instance, said, 'Agatha Christie's thrillers were for years compared, always unfavourably, with those of Ian Fleming. The irony: the meek self-effacing hero of "The Rajah's Emerald" is named James Bond.'

Mr Sanders and several of his colleagues believe that Ian Fleming read many of Agatha Christie's books – he admitted as much himself – and cannot help wondering whether he lifted the name from the pages of that short story rather than the spine of *Birds of the West Indies* by James Bond as he claimed .

Another American expert, Alan Morgan, wrote in *The New York Times* on 4 September 1982, 'Ian Fleming's sense of humour was well known and few people enjoyed a practical joke more than he. If he read "The Rajah's Emerald" isn't it just possible he played the biggest joke of all when he purloined the name of a whimp for his indestructible secret agent?'

Because both authors are now dead, the issue is obviously never going to be resolved, but I cannot help feeling there is some value in the argument. Fleming admitted he wanted a name that was 'suitably flat and colourless' for his hero, and even if the prompt was the book on West Indian birds, the seed could already have been there from reading 'The Rajah's Emerald'. In any event, Fleming would have had no qualms about his choice of James Bond because he had no idea of the success that was ultimately to envelop his creation.

The origin of the term 007 has been explained by Fleming as coming from his days at the Admiralty. But what about the story by the great English writer, Rudyard Kipling, entitled '.007' to be found in his collection of tales entitled *The Days Work*, published in 1898?

Again, we know that Fleming liked the work of the Anglo-Indian author, and though there is no suggestion of espionage or secret agents in '.007' – it is the story of a steam engine bearing that number – it is an unusual and memorable title.

Some members of the Kipling Society certainly think so, and there has been discussion in the pages of their *Journal* about the influence of this story on Ian Fleming.

'Is it not worthy of debate that the author of the James Bond novels found his special designation for his hero in Kipling's story, ".007"?' a Mr Charles Anderson asked in 1978. 'Although that ingenious little tale of a steam engine's admission into the Amalgamated Brotherhood of Locomotives is hardly the stuff of which spy stories is made, the thought is forever in my mind that it *might* just have been influential. I cannot think of any number that holds such mystery as seven and the addition of the two noughts seems to round off the designation perfectly.'

The sceptic may immediately say it is a very tenuous association, and I would have to agree. But Ian Fleming was a man with a nose for the unlikely and it *is* conceivable he may have found his unforgettable name and ideal designation in those two sources. The joke was then to throw people off the scent when fame stepped in.

The legend of Sherlock Holmes was built on conjectures such as these – and as James Bond is surely the modern equivalent of Holmes, why shouldn't he be the centre of similar light-hearted debate? I am sure Ian Fleming would have found it all enormous fun!

The Infamous Originals

The villains who confront James Bond in both the novels and on the screen are among the most memorable in modern literature and screen history. Five in particular have created enduring impressions – Le Chiffre, Dr No, Ernst Stavro Blofeld, Hugo Drax and Auric Goldfinger – and it is fascinating to discover that each have their origins in unique and mostly well-known characters. Three came from the pages of the favourite books Ian Fleming read in his youth, one from the reminiscences of another writer, and the fifth was based on a genuinely evil man who called himself 'The Great Beast'.

One of the major attractions of the first Bond book, *Casino Royale* – apart from 007 himself – is the villainous Le Chiffre, a fat, pasty-white, ugly man high on benzedrine, sadism and his insatiable appetite for women. His appearance and nature almost precisely match that of the notorious black magician and drug fiend, Aleister Crowley, known as 'The Wickedest Man in the World', whom Fleming met during his years working for British Intelligence. He was a man once met and never forgotten.

Crowley (1875–1947) whose philosophy was summed-up by the words, 'Do what thou wilt shall be the whole of the Law', and sometimes called himself 'The Antichrist' or 'Count Svareff', was born into a deeply religious family who believed every word in the Bible was literally true. The young Crowley rebelled against their Puritanism and by his teens was heavily into black magic, devil worship and drug taking – as well as the seduction of every impressionable young girl he met.

When he began openly to promote his ideas of 'Do what thou wilt' and 'sex magick' (the use of sex in magical rituals), Crowley was forced to flee the country and for a time ran an 'abbey' in Sicily which became notorious for the stories of sex and drug orgies which were said to have taken place there.

However, when Crowley returned to England just prior to the Second World War, he was an old and sick man almost wholly dependent on heroin. Yet his knowledge of the occult was undoubtedly vast, and it was because of this that Ian Fleming contacted him shortly after the unexpected arrival in Scotland of Hitler's deputy, Rudolf Hess, in May 1941.

As the whole manner of Hess's mission puzzled British Intelligence, they decided to

Aleister Crowley (right), the notorious black magician who inspired Le Chiffre in *Casino Royale*. Orson Welles (below) who played Le Chiffre in the 1967 version of *Casino Royale*.

play on the Deputy Führer's neurotic and highly superstitious nature. Perhaps someone with black magic powers could frighten the truth out of him? Ian Fleming suggested Crowley, having studied the 'Great Beast's' headline-making career for years.

Whether or not Crowley *did* confront Hess is a matter for conjecture. I have been told by thriller writer, George Markstein, that the two men were locked away together in a room for several hours, and such was the terror which the 'Great Beast' induced into Hess that he was never the same man again. Ian Fleming was fascinated by his experience of Crowley, and made full use of his appearance and character when he came to write *Casino Royale*.

As I mentioned earlier, the similarities between Dr No and Sax Rohmer's evil oriental, Fu Manchu, also seem obvious. Dr No is, of course, a member of SPECTRE: the Special Executive for Counter-Intelligence, Terrorism, Revenge and Extortion – the group of former members of SMERSH, the Mafia and other criminal organisations of which the awesome Blofeld is overall chief.

Christopher Lee as Scaramanga in *The Man With The Golden Gun* (1974).

Dr No's appearance and characteristics are rooted in Sax Rohmer's utterly ruthless Chinese master villain whose exploits excited and engrossed Fleming as a boy. Indeed, Fu Manchu as a man of untold wealth, enormous intellect and with the objective of world power as his aim, is in some ways the prototype of all Bond villains. Fu Manchu also has huge resources of obedient manpower at his command all over the world, and a very profound knowledge of the occult.

Sax Rohmer, whose real name was actually Arthur Henry Ward, developed an interest in the mysterious East and occultism while he was a young man, and for a time belonged to a secret order known as The Golden Dawn which also had Aleister Crowley among its members! Determining to become a writer, he joined a London newspaper and on an assignment in London's Chinatown came to hear of a mysterious figure called 'Mr King' who was said to rule all the criminal elements in the district and whose enormous wealth had derived from gambling, drug running and prostitution. When Rohmer caught a glimpse of 'Mr King' he described him as the 'embodiment of Satan'.

This terrifying figure become the model for Fu Manchu, the 'Devil Doctor' whom Rohmer introduced to the public in 1913 in *The Mystery of Dr Fu Manchu*. Later, Rohmer created Sumuru, the female counterpart of the evil Doctor, who, with her army of devoted female lieutenants, is hell-bent on enslaving all the world's most influential men.

Interestingly, Shirley Eaton, the girl who came to such a memorable end covered from head to foot in gold paint in *Goldfinger*, played the part of Sumuru in the American-International film, *The Million Eyes of Sumuru*, made in 1967. The links again between Sumuru and Pussy Galore's bevy of beauties are immediately apparent.

Sax Rohmer was like Fleming in that he had a passion for detail, and his books are sprinkled with exotic creatures and historically-accurate events. The Fu Manchu stories have also proved hugely popular at the cinema, with the American actor, Warner Oland, starring in the first series of pictures about the Devil Doctor made in the Thirties. The great horror film star, Boris Karloff, also played the part in *The Mask of Fu Manchu* (1932), as did Christopher Lee in five splendid modern versions of the stories made between 1965 and 1972.

The dark and towering Lee who became rather type-cast as the archetypal vampire, Count Dracula, retains fond memories of the Fu Manchu films – as he does of the one Bond film in which he appeared, playing Scaramanga, the million-dollar hit man who kills with a golden bullet, in *The Man With The Golden Gun*.

Christopher Lee says he was attracted to the part of Scaramanga because he is a kind of 'contra-Bond', an anti-hero of great stature able to deal with 007 on an equal footing.

'It was amusing for me to finally get a part in a Bond film,' he recalls, 'because Ian Fleming was actually my cousin and he always said I ought to be in one! In fact I would like to have played *Dr No* after all my experience as Fu Manchu; Ian told me all about him being modelled on Fu Manchu.

'But I think if had played the part, having seen that a very fine actor could make nothing out of it by virtue of the story, the direction or whatever, it's probably just as well I didn't. Dr No is a conventional, emotionless, straight-faced heavy. Joseph Wiseman was a marvellous actor, but he wasn't able to do anything because he wasn't required to.'

The books of Sax Rohmer inspired some of Ian Fleming's best villains – one of whom, Dr No, was described by *Time* magazine in 1958 as 'a sort of rich man's Fu Manchu'.

When it came to playing Scaramanga, Lee says that he was glad not to have had to pattern the role on the character in the book.

'In the book he's a great ox of a man. He's really just a thug who kills with a golden gun and there's nothing more to him that that. In fact, I think he's one of the least well-written characters in all Fleming's books. But the way the character came out in the script was infinitely superior.'

Christopher says he enjoyed working with Roger Moore – 'or Roger Bond as I called him' – and with the director, Guy Hamilton, who had a profound effect on his career.

'He got things out of me that no other director before had ever done – or even tried to do,' he says warmly. 'It was something I had never been able to show on the screen before. In Guy's own words he got the spook out of me. He got the Dracula out of me. I can be very menacing and heavy, but he got the lightness, the contrasts into the part so that you can hardly believe that Scaramanga is as lethal as he is. It was a very satisfying part to play.'

Ernst Stavro Blofeld whose sinister presence in the Bond films was first felt in *From Russia With Love* (or, to be more precise, his hands and the back of his head were all that was seen), and who then made the first of several appearances in *You Only Live Twice*, has his origins in Captain Nemo, the hate-fuelled rebel of Jules Verne's classic novel, *Twenty Thousand Leagues Under The Sea*. (Blofeld is, as a matter of record, the only Bond villain to have been portrayed on the screen by three different actors, Donald Pleasence, Telly Savalas and Charles Gray.)

Verne, as I mentioned earlier, was an amazing writer who is not only credited with being one of the 'Founding Fathers' of science fiction, but also gave the world a remarkable series of uncannily accurate prophecies. As a result he has proved influential on many of the twentieth century's best-known writers. In Fleming's case, it was the endless array of gadgets and fantastic machines in Verne's stories which captured his imagination, as well as Captain Nemo and another great 'inventor-criminal', Robur – 'Master of the World'.

Jules Verne was a writer who found the basis for his novels in the world around him – in particular the scientific world – and his great ability was to project developments in technology and aeronautics into their logical futures: creating along the way submarines, ballistic missiles, space ships and many similar inventions, now commonplace but mind-boggling one hundred and fifty years ago. Like Fleming, he believed in giving his fiction the ring of authenticity by packing in facts his readers would accept as the basis for even his most outlandish fantasies. When he couldn't be sure of the facts, he went to considerable pains to check them with experts who *did* know.

Raised in the French port of Nantes, it is perhaps not surprising that the sea should feature in some of his finest books, and *Twenty Thousand Leagues Under The Sea*, which appeared in 1870 and introduced Captain Nemo, has been called his crowning achievement. Critics have suggested that there is something of Verne himself in Nemo; the brilliant inventor and implacable anarchist with his rejection of all authority and dreams of starting his own kingdom. This objective is almost realised in the sequel, *The Mysterious Island*, which Verne wrote five years later.

The author picked the name for his character with care – Nemo meaning the nameless one, and like Blofeld whom he inspired, his shadow haunts the action of *Twenty Thousand Leagues Under The Sea* long before he appears in the dramatic aftermath of having blown a vessel out of the water with the armament of his futuristic submarine, the Nautilus.

Jules Verne's Captain Nemo was the inspiration for Fleming's Ernst Stavro Blofeld. This illustration (above) is taken from the first French edition of *Twenty Thousand Leagues Under The Sea* (1870). Of all the actors to play Blofeld, Donald Pleasence (left) has been the most memorable.

Captain Nemo has appeared several times on the screen, first at the hands of the great French film-maker, George Méliès, in a silent version of the novel made in 1907, and most recently by Walt Disney in 1954 with James Mason as an overpowering and coldly-calculating Nemo.

The sequel, *The Mysterious Island*, has also been filmed twice, with Lionel Barrymore as a particularly sinister Captain Nemo in 1929, and again in 1961 with Herbert Lom staying rather closer to the characterisation of the original book.

It is in another of Verne's famous novels, *The Clipper of the Clouds* (published in 1886 as *Robur Le Conquerant*), that we can find the inspiration for Hugo Drax of *Moonraker* and his nuclear rocket with which he plans to destroy London. Here again the French author was far ahead of his time in the description of a flying machine called the Albatross which can be alternately aircraft, submarine and automobile, and is capable of wreaking the most terrible havoc on those who defy its commander's wishes.

The commander in question is the enigmatically named Robur, a great inventor driven outside the law by his ambitions and what he sees as the blindness of authority to appreciate his genius. To be fair, he is a less obsessed creature in *The Clipper of the Clouds* than in the sequel, *Master of the World* (1904), when he has become a dangerous madman and issues manifestos to those who defy him in ringing tones such as these:

> TO THE OLD AND NEW WORLDS!
>
> 'With my machine I have undisputed power over the whole world and there is no human power which can resist me under any circumstances.
>
> 'Let the Old and New Worlds understand that they can do nothing against me and that I can do anything against them.'
>
> (Signed) 'Master of the World'

The words of Hugo Drax almost to a tee! And the Albatross is surely the forerunner of any one of half a dozen of the remarkable machines that Bond flies or drives or submerges under the water in his films.

Fittingly, too, Robur shares the same fate as Drax in an aerial conflagration which leaves him screaming impotently as his machine disintegrates all around him.

Filmgoers may well recall the 1961 film version of *Master of the World*, in which Vincent Price played Robur in his typical, larger-than-life style. His performance contained a lot of the mannerisms and grandiose gestures which the later Bond screen villains were to exploit with equal skill and effect. It is perhaps only to be regretted that Price himself has never been cast as one of those villains.

The fifth of the great Bond villains, Auric Goldfinger, is the favourite of many Bond fans. Fleming gained his inspiration for this character from the splendid writer, Phyllis Bottome (1884–1963) whom he met in 1927 when he was 19, while studying German and French in preparation for entering the diplomatic service.

Phyllis, the daughter of an American clergyman who had originally wanted to go on the stage but after suffering from a bout of TB had turned to writing, was a mesmeric personality with vivid dark eyes and a halo of white hair. Her husband was Captain Ernan Forbes Dennis, who had been severely wounded during World War I and after a period as an Intelligence Officer and Passport Controller in Vienna had settled in the Tyrol at Kitzbuhel to utilise his skill as a linguist. Together, the couple had seen a wide cross-section of people in the aftermath of the war, and this experience was to prove invaluable for Phyllis in her writing. (She had, in fact, had her first novel, *Life the Interpreter*, accepted when she was just seventeen, but it was in 1926 with *Old Wine*, about the decay of an Austrian family, that she attained wide-spread acclaim.)

Phyllis Bottome, the English novelist who inspired Ian Fleming to write.

The impact of these two people on Ian Fleming was considerable – Ernan developing his natural flair for languages and Phyllis, perhaps even more importantly, encouraging him to write. Years later, Fleming was to write to her: 'Looking back, I am sure that your influence had a great deal to do with the fact that I became a successful writer. I also remember clearly writing a rather bizarre short story for you which you criticized kindly and which was, in fact, the first thing I ever wrote.'

It was Phyllis Bottome who developed in Fleming his love of inventing imaginary happenings and peopling his stories with grotesque characters. Indeed, the central character of that first story he wrote was a certain evil lord of the manor, Graf Schlick, who delighted in crime and torture. Pretty and defenceless women were his favourite sport, but in Fleming's story Schlick came to a terrible end when he discovered that one of the girls he had raped was suffering from leprosy! It is certainly not difficult to see an embryo Bond villain in Graf Schlick.

Aside from encouraging the young man to write, Phyllis also excited his imagination with stories of the strange and remarkable people she had met during her life. Among these was the man who became the model for Goldfinger – Baron Hofflinger.

Goldfinger was described as a short, ugly man with a huge, round head, who had a passion for winning at cards and acquiring gold. Compare this with Phyllis Bottome's description of 'the mysterious Hofflinger' as she calls him in her biography, *The Goal* (1962): 'He was short, swarthy and with black eyebrows and a round, domed head. His passion was for horses (I found that the tips Hofflinger gave me were invariably correct) and diamonds. He had put everything he possessed into diamonds which he carried about with him concealed on his person or among his belongings. The Baron had a slow, sardonic humour, dressed impeccably, and knew only those things and people he wished to know.'

Fleming could hardly fail to be fascinated by such a larger-than-life character, and it is no wonder he inspired the remarkable Goldfinger.

Phyllis Bottome and her husband may even have been responsible for Ian Fleming writing spy stories rather than any other kind of novels. For Captain Forbes Dennis was full of tales from his days in Intelligence, and Phyllis also records in her biography that she knew a beautiful woman 'who was a leading secret agent playing a popular figure in American society.' In her book she speaks affectionately of Ian Fleming, and though she lived long enough to see his triumph as a novelist, did not survive to see the emergence of James Bond as a twentieth century legend.

A Licence To Write

It was perhaps inevitable after the death of Ian Fleming, and with the ever-growing popularity of James Bond, that the adventures of 007 would be continued by other writers. The makers of the films had already begun to elaborate the Fleming novels as they filmed them, and as the supply of original material inevitably dried up, the later movies could claim little more than the titles to be the creator's own work.

Before his death Ian Fleming had sold the copyright in James Bond to Glidrose Productions Ltd and it was therefore in their bequest to have the saga continued if they so desired. How not one but two writers, both of them major British literary figures, have kept the secret agent alive and kicking into the Eighties, is another interesting element of the Bond legend.

The story begins with Kingsley Amis, novelist, poet, playwright and bon viveur, not to mention one of the most vociferous fans of the Ian Fleming novels from the very beginning when some of the British literary establishment looked upon the stories as little better than second-rate thrillers containing a rather unsavoury amount of sex, violence and sadism.

Amis, now a much respected figure in British letters, was born in 1922, and followed a career as a lecturer in English at University College, Swansea and Peterhouse College, Cambridge until 1963 when he became a full-time writer. His reputation was made with one of his earliest books, *Lucky Jim* (1954), which won the Somerset Maugham Award, and confirmed with a wide range of books from poetry to political comment, humour to modern fiction.

A courteous if sometimes sardonic man, Kingsley Amis remembers clearly his discovery of the Bond novels in the Fifties when he himself was breaking new literary ground in his own books, and soon came to appreciate both their quality as stories and a conviction that there was more to them than was at first apparent.

'As I read the books the feeling grew that they were more than just simple cloak-and-dagger stories with a bit of fashionable affluence and sex thrown in,' he explains. 'On the contrary, they were just as complex and with just as much in them as more ambitious kinds of fiction.'

His belief that reviewers in particular were missing the point of the books was further underlined when he had the chance to meet Fleming at a publisher's party. Both men, in fact, were published by the same firm, Jonathan Cape Ltd.

'I was introduced to Fleming at a party,' he recalls, 'and I said to him, "Mr Fleming, it is very rare to meet an author to whom one can honestly say, 'I've read all your books and I enjoy them very much.'" And he replied, "That's very kind of you. Of course you know they're all true?"

'I was a bit surprised at this and said I had no idea they were. "Oh, yes," he went on, "If you go to that part of Moscow that I described in several of the stories – in particular *From Russia With Love* – and you go to that building on the Sretenka Ulitsa, you will actually find Colonel General Grubozaboyschikov and his friends – they are all there!"'

With this meeting still fresh in his mind – and more particularly the mounting wave of criticism of the Bond novels – Kingsley Amis decided, in 1964, to write what he thought would be a 'modest' essay of about 5,000 words in defence of Bond. He just did not believe people were buying the books by the million unless they were getting genuine pleasure from them and then coming back for more.

'I thought the books were being seriously misrepresented in the papers, and I thought I would write an article to set the record straight. I wanted people to pay attention to what Fleming actually *wrote*, not what he didn't write. I thought it would be a medium-sized magazine article, but I found it became a small book.'

The book became *The James Bond Dossier* which was published in 1965 and in it Kingsley Amis made his intention quite clear.

'I hope,' he wrote, 'I've sufficiently conveyed my admiration for what I think Ian Fleming did best. He has set his stamp on the story of action and intrigue, bringing to it a sense of our time, a power and a flair that will win him readers when all the protests about his supposed deficiencies have been forgotten. He leaves no heirs.'

Kingsley Amis also had a second meeting with Fleming as a result of this book.

'I decided to send a copy of the manuscript to him for his comments before I sent it to

Kingsley Amis, the James Bond fan, who first continued the saga in *Colonel Sun* (1968).

the publishers. He very kindly took me out to lunch and it was a most pleasant experience. And though there were quite a number of critical comments that I had made about the style of the books and that kind of thing, he had nothing to say on any of those.

'It was only on points of accuracy that he wanted to put me right. I remember that he said it was the Royal and Ancient Golf Club – not the St Andrews – and that Oddjob was *sucked* out of the cabin of the aircraft and not blown out. He had that kind of approach to accuracy.'

There is little doubt in hindsight that Kingsley Amis' fairminded, objective and engrossingly interesting study of Bond and his world made a lot of people re-assess their attitudes to 007. For fans it was a confirmation of what they had believed all along.

The book also clearly impressed the people at Glidrose Productions. And later when they began debating the idea of continuing the Bond stories, they agreed that Kingsley Amis was the ideal writer: a literary craftsman who was also an avowed fan.

'I had never even thought of writing a James Bond story myself,' Amis says, 'but right out of the blue came this invitation from Glidrose. The idea appealed to me and after some meetings I decided to go ahead. We also agreed that the book would appear under a pen-name, partly for my convenience to set it aside from my other work, and partly for theirs because they were already considering it possible that other writers might like to continue with sequels after me.'

One of the persistent rumours that Kingsley Amis has tried to dispel is that his book, *Colonel Sun*, was based on rough drafts that Ian Fleming had left at his death.

'It's a story that just won't lie down,' he says. 'In fact I still get letters from people asking if it's true that Fleming left plans for another book. In fact, I started absolutely from scratch. I supposed I should be grateful for the compliment those letters pay me in thinking that *Colonel Sun* is a worthy continuation of the series.'

Kingsley Amis decided to set his story in the Eastern Mediterranean because it was a place Ian Fleming had never taken his hero. 'Greece was also a place I had a standing invitation to visit from a very good friend and with his expert knowledge to guide me it seemed the logical thing to do.

'Luckily, too, it was an area in which the Russians were very interested, so that added to the plot. And though I don't really believe the West will get together with the Russians against the Chinese – the Chinese were nice and convenient.'

Kingsley Amis had also learned Fleming's lesson that it was important to start a Bond at a cracking pace and keep up the tension all the way through. Like Fleming, too, he found himself in trouble over a torture scene.

'There were people who objected to that,' he recalls. 'But I had taken a lot of care with it. I actually talked to a doctor and told him I wanted to do a torture scene unlike any other – which was a pretty tall order. But he came up with the solution. "Well," he said, "then it's got to be inside his head. That's what people are really afraid of – what they can't see."'

Colonel Sun proved a great success with the fans – starved for almost three years of a new Bond. But the critics were as hostile as ever.

'I wasn't that surprised, though,' says Amis. 'Fleming's reviews hadn't been that friendly either. They also accused me of the same thing they had done Fleming – that the writing was fascist.'

Since the *Dossier* and *Colonel Sun*, Kingsley Amis has written no further books about Bond, though his admiration for Fleming's work remains untarnished.

However, he does still write occasionally about his hero, and perhaps inevitably found a place for him when he wrote an essay 'My Favourite Sleuths' for the American *Playboy* magazine. Two extracts clearly demonstrate his continuing enthusiasm:

'All the sleuths we remember and revere and take into our private pantheon of heroes are figures not of realism but of fantasy, great talkers, great eccentrics, men who use inspiration instead of hard work, men to whom Venetian old masters mean more than police files and a good bottle of burgundy more than fingerprints. There is scope here for a scholarly footnote on the parallel with spy fiction: James Bond will still be around long after all the spies who came in from the cold, Ipcress-file-mongers and similar "real" secret agents have been forgotten.'

And later on, Mr Amis succinctly adds what he feels is the essence of Bond's success:

'In crime or spy fantasies the interest is partly a fairy-tale one, good versus bad in a rather basic way. James Bond would not mean so much to us if we were unable to feel that he was on the right side and that his cause was just. The toughies have no decent cause. Self-interest is all.'

The success of *Colonel Sun* convinced everyone concerned with Bond that there was a very substantial market for sequels, both in Britain and America, as well as a great many other countries where Kingsley Amis' book was published.

When Glidrose began looking for a new writer they drew up a short list of five authors and finally plumped for a man already expert in the spy genre and the creator of a secret agent he had unashamedly modelled on Bond. The man was John Gardner, an immensely likeable and highly professional writer who has been a regular best-seller on both sides of the Atlantic now for almost a quarter of a century. The suitability of their choice has been underlined by the fact that, at the time of writing (Spring 1986), John Gardner has written five Bond novels and is working on a sixth. Their titles, too, are surely redolent of Fleming: *Licence Renewed* (1981), *For Special Services* (1982), *Icebreaker* (1983), *Role of Honour* (1984) and *Nobody Lives Forever* (1986).

John, who was born in 1926, is the son of an Anglican priest and was for a time himself a curate. He has also been a professional magician and theatre critic before turning full-time to writing novels and autobiographies. Of his 007 novels he has said, 'I see Bond as a buccaneer, a romantic hero in the tradition of Bulldog Drummond. He still believes in Queen, country and his work.'

That is perhaps an over-simplification of John's contribution to developing and, more particularly, bringing Bond into the Eighties – while at the same time preserving the basic qualities that have made him such a universal favourite. But it equally illustrates his dedication to the legend.

As a child, John himself loved the works of writers like Sapper, E Phillips Oppenheimer and Dornford Yates as well as the adventures of the Saint and Slim Callaghan.

'I was an only child,' he explains, 'and therefore spent a great deal of my early years alone. I had friends certainly, but at home I was very much of a loner and became interested in a kind of secret life. This inspired me to examine the idea of organisations which exist in their own secret worlds and the kind of people who work for them. I suppose it was the first step towards my spy novels.

'However, I didn't discover James Bond until later when I was an adult. I happened to read *Doctor No* when I was confined to bed during a bad bout of influenza in 1961, and I was so hooked on it I immediately ordered all the other books from the local library.'

The influence of the books was to remain with him throughout his period as a journalist at Stratford-upon-Avon, and when he finally tired of writing about other people's work and decided to see if he could be creative himself, it was perhaps not surprising that he should try a spy novel.

'In the late Fifties most of us were Bond fans one way or another,' he says, running a hand through his thinning hair and pulling on a cigarette. 'And he was the influence for my Boysie Oakes novels, the first of which, *The Liquidator*, appeared just two days before Ian Fleming died. It was a mild send up of the Bond genre, but not of Bond himself as some people have accused me. Fleming's books were never meant to be anything more than kiss-kiss, bang-bang fantasies, and I get very annoyed when I hear writers of "the novel of espionage" talking down about James Bond.

'Although Boysie as a secret agent is everything Bond is not, if you take away the comedy and vulgarity you've got Bond plots underneath.'

It was, therefore, quite a surprise for John when he was approached to continue the series while living in Ireland in 1979. The memory of the arrival of a letter which started the chain of events still brings a smile to his face today.

'It was one of those letters that makes you do a double take. At first I thought it was just a hoax. In fact it was from a well-known reviewer of crime fiction who had been asked to contact me to see whether I would consider carrying on the James Bond stories.

'I was a bit reluctant at first, but when it was pointed out to me that I would probably find it fun to spend part of my year working on Bond as a change from my other work, I had second thoughts. It was also a challenge to my ability as a writer, and so I decided to accept.'

John had never actually met Ian Fleming, but had a vivid memory of seeing him on television not long before his death.

'I have always remembered him speaking then of his picture of Bond as a "blunt instrument for use by the government". Fleming said he was a man with a licence to kill on active duty, under orders, just as a member of the armed forces is under orders,' says John.

After coming to a basic agreement with Glidrose, John reread all fourteen of the Fleming books. He found that the passage of time had brought about some radical changes in his opinions.

'I was surprised by them,' he now admits. 'I found the sex nowhere near as vivid as we find daily in books – both literary and popular – or on our screens. In fact the original Bond is now fairly tame sex and I have kept it that way in my own stories. The same goes for sadism, though I have to admit that the torture scene in *Casino Royale* still manages to bring me out in a cold sweat. I have replaced this with mental violence plus of course the punch-ups and shoot-outs which are a natural part of the Bond drama. And as for snobbery – well I've never believed *that* to be true of the books anyhow! What some people took for that was actually just the use of brand names to illustrate a bachelor man enjoying a pleasant life style.'

But just familiarising himself with the Bond of old was not all John had to do. Glidrose were imposing very strict guidelines about his handling of their man.

'They wanted Bond to be lifted from where Ian Fleming had so untimely left him in the Sixties straight into the Eighties,' he says. 'He had to come back unaged, yet with all the knowledge and experience he would have had, had he lived through those years – for everyone knows that myths are ageless. They also wanted a little more humour, the technology of the eighties and a very definite Eighties outlook.'

In writing towards these ends, John decided to have Bond smoke less (the lowest tar level cigarettes from Morlands) drink only in moderation (champagne rather than martinis) and act as more of a gentleman and less of a chauvinist towards women. He also planned on introducing the same kind of gadgetry that had been such a feature of the films because of the vast technological advances made in the two decades since Fleming was writing. He felt it was inconceivable that in the 1980s a secret agent such as Bond would *not* be taking every advantage of all the electronic wizardry which is available.

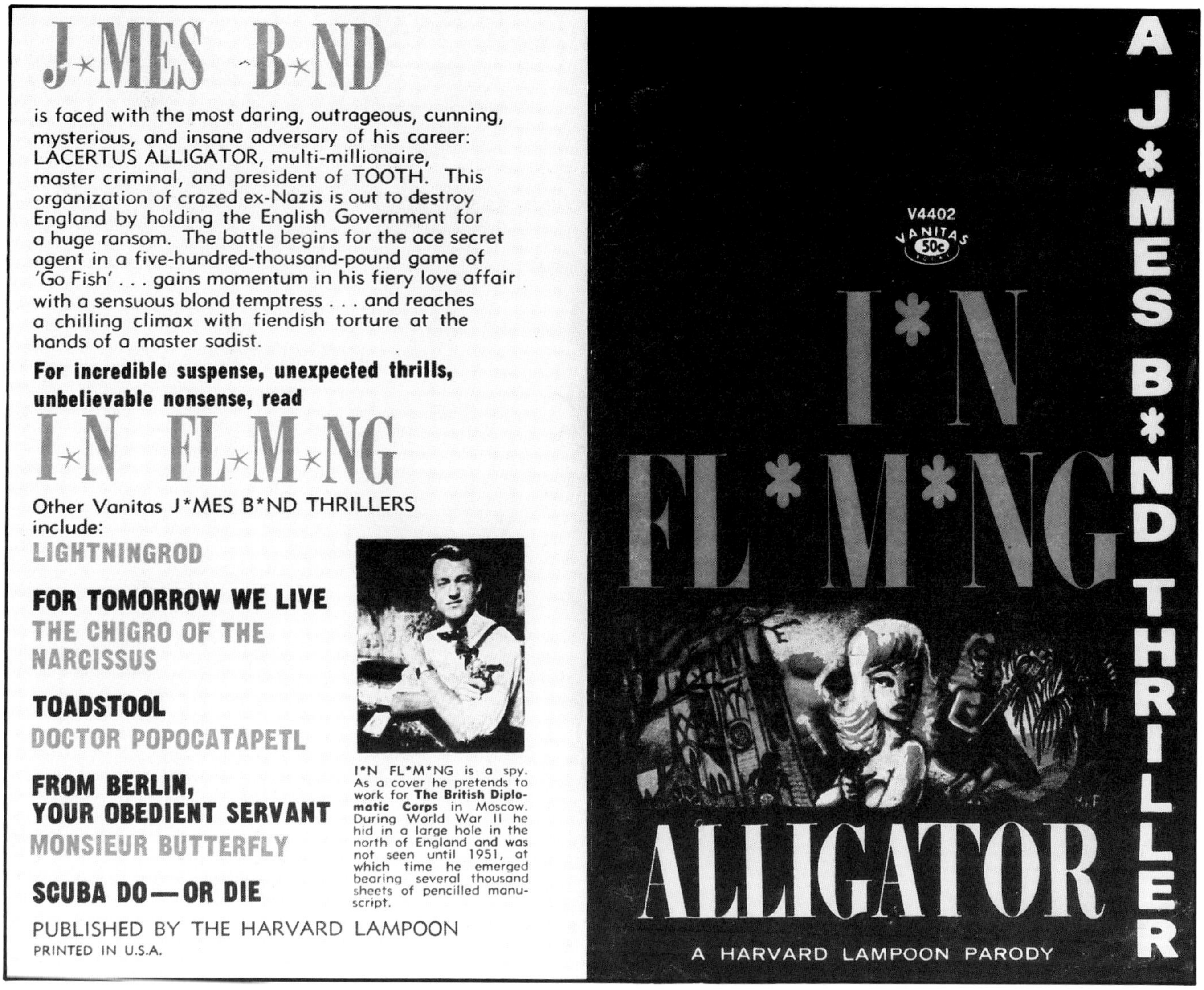

The famous Harvard Lampoon spoof of the Bond books published in 1962.

Perhaps most important of all, though, there was to be no diminishing of the larger-than-life villains whom Bond would encounter. That was something John wholeheartedly supported – for he had long felt these characters were often the best parts in the original Fleming novels.

Once he had the James Bond of the 1980s clearly in his mind's eye, John Gardner began on the series of adventures which will probably culminate – as far as he is concerned – with the sixth novel in 1987. A brief resumé of the five published to date illustrates the skill and imagination which he has brought to the new Bond. Though critical and fan reactions have varied enormously – as even John himself would expect – the books have unquestionably played their own part in the continuation of the legend.

The first novel, *Licence Renewed*, introduced both a major new piece of technology as well as a memorable villain. Anxious to put his own mark on the series, John made a controversial decision to change Bond's car from a Bentley to a Saab. (Many people mistakenly believe that 007 was an Aston Martin driver: this is purely because of the DB5 he has used on the screen – in Fleming's original stories he was always behind the wheel of a supercharged Bentley.)

'I wanted to put Bond into an Eighties car,' John says, 'and I felt he would be sensible enough to choose something that gave good performance, was safe without being flashy, and was made in line with pollution problems. After a lot of thought I plumped for the Saab 900 Turbo. I was, though, aware that there were those who believed I should have put him in a British car.

'Still, it was very satisfying when a number of Bond experts congratulated me and said it was the kind of motor Ian Fleming would have approved of. Indeed, I thought it worked well and I had a lot of fun with it for a time.

'But,' he goes on, 'in the three years of the first three books, Bentley brought out the Bentley Mausanne Turbo which they had been working on for ten years. As soon as I saw it, I knew that Bond would want one if he could afford it. I just knew his passion for Bentleys would make him want this safe, fast and luxurious motor car. So I gave him one!'

For the villain in *Licence Renewed*, John created an adversary of whom Fleming himself would have been proud, Anton Murik, Laird of Murcardy who plans to detonate six strategically located nuclear power stations thereby causing world-wide radioactive contamination unless his perverted demands are met.

In the second book, *For Special Services*, John re-introduced one of Bond's oldest adversaries, SPECTRE, now somewhat revamped and headed by the daughter of Ernst Stavro Blofeld, hell-bent on revenging her father who, of course, 007 dispatched to the great hereafter in *You Only Live Twice*. He also produced another famous daughter in Cedar Leiter, whose father, the resourceful CIA man, Felix, had been at Bond's shoulder on more than one occasion.

In true Fleming fashion John attempted to make the book as factually accurate as possible, and though he had been to Texas which provided the background for the story, he was forced to use his fertile imagination when describing the NORAD Command Headquarters in the Cheyenne Mountains of Colorado – as accurate information on this highly secret defence base proved impossible to obtain.

The third book, *Icebreaker*, is considered by many fans the most ambitious Bond so far – and certainly it is John's favourite as well as being the one he had most fun writing. The story brought Bond into uneasy partnership with members of the CIA, KGB and Mossad to combat a renewed Nazi movement headed by Count Von Gloda.

'The theme of the book was that the Nazis are always with us,' John explains, 'and that seems to be very topical what with the "Butcher of Lyons" and the others who have been caught in recent years. What made it such fun to write was that I had the chance to research it on the spot.

'I went up to the Arctic Circle and I went through everything that's now in the book. I drove fast in Saabs along icy roads and even had to be pulled out of a snow drift I

John Gardner with the Saab which he introduced as James Bond's new car to replace the Bentley.

HAPPY BIRTHDAY TO A SECRET AGENT (RETIRED)

It wasn't all bad for Bond. The Bentley had gone but he had his pensioner's bus pass

AT close range, the merciless grin was tormenting James Bond . . . No escaping it, any more than the savage pain skewering his scarred limbs.

Damn this rheumatism thought Bond, sitting up and fishing his dentures out of the glass beside the bed. An artificial smile was all he could manage on this milestone of a morning.

He was 65 today, and trust Fleet Street to rub it in! 'Happy bleeping birthday — I don't think,' he grumbled. Long widowed, Bond did a lot of talking to himself for lack of company.

Bond's radio alarm clock (disguised as an innocent hand grenade, it had been issued by Q and never returned) burst into life.

by SHAUN USHER

James Bond didn't bother to don his vital hearing aid. It would be more of the usual stuff: Whitehall leaks, another few sackfuls of secrets adrift from Cyprus, more egg on the CIA's face after falling for the umpteenth dud defector.

Over a sparse breakfast of muesli and dry toast — he shuddered again at previous folly such as lard-fried bacon served with endless patience by that bygone Scottish housekeeper, obviously an assassin for the Kremlin — the birthday boy confronted his future.

'Spoilt for choice,' he muttered sarcastically. Gone was the era of draught Dom Perignon; an excruciatingly dry martini would neither shake nor stir him. it'd see him off. The very thought triggered his dyspepsia.

Anyway, he couldn't afford it. Most of that high living had been on expenses. Official employment as a Civil Service principal officer paid around £12,500 a year and even with perks and covert bonus one didn't save much on that . . . Never mind Ernst Stavro Blofeld, inflation was the real killer.

These days he just scraped by. Couldn't bear to leave London, still the centre of the universe, and kept the Chelsea house by sharing it with tenants.

Mechanically Bond stamped on the floor in protest against the boom of reggae records from the room below.

The 1930, 4½-litre Bentley with Amherst Villiers supercharger, was a sad memory. After several MOT failures Bond had sold it to a jovial dealer who'd wanted him to take something called a Sinclair C5 in part exchange.

007 sighed, wishing he understood more of what people were talking about lately.

At least the pensioner's pass got him free travel on a Red Arrow bus stopping near Blades club.

Only Blades, desperate to cut overheads, had emerged with the Accountants and Actuaries' and the British Beekeepers: not the same place any more. Further, James Bond was three years behind with his subs.

Well, he brooded, he might just as well not exist. Those bounders Sean Connery and Roger Moore had pulled off the perfect disinformation exercise, passing themselves off as him and raking in the shekels.

Along with — he snarled silently dentures dancing — the ineffable Cubby Broccoli, who made the confounded films.

Infuriated, James Bond rammed in the hearing aid, snatched up his stick and hobbled downstairs. In time to hear the letterbox rattle, admitting a single envelope. Wary of danger he was relieved to see it was neither final demand nor summons for non-payment.

Tucking the stick under his arm, wheezing from the stairs, he ripped the envelope and withdrew an opulent ivory card with gilded edges.

'Happy Birthday and (Not Too Many) More of Them' it was inscribed in perfect copperplate. *'From those wonderful people who gave you SMERSH and SPECTRE.'*

Bond skimmed it away across the lino, just in time to dodge an explosion no more potent than a Christmas cracker's, a token whiff of poison gas.

His eyes misted, his back straightened, he felt not a day over. well, 63. The Establishment might have frozen him out and the general public be fooled by impersonators.

But James Bond was ten feet tall on knowing that *somebody* cared.

One of the numerous newspaper parodies of Bond that have been printed over the years. This appeared in the *Daily Mail* of 16 November 1985.

ploughed into. I had a spectacular and breathtaking ride on a snow scooter over open countryside and through woodlands following two absolutely mad Laps. They were trying to get me to go faster and follow them into impossible places – it was tremendous. Absolutely terrific! I think it was because I enjoyed it so much that I came back and roared through *Icebreaker*. I love that book.'

He is not so happy, though, with the fourth book, *Role of Honour* – although there are readers who have told him it is the best so far. He had, in fact, to write it under pressure and when not in the best of health. And also late in the day he found he had to drop an important section of the story.

'It was a lengthy sequence in which Bond played a very realistic computer programme game called "The Battle of Waterloo,"' he says. 'It was a strategic battle game and it *could* be done – I'd had it carefully checked out by programmers. Well, I'd spent a lot of time on this when I suddenly got a message from America saying I couldn't use it under any circumstances.

'Having lost that, I felt that the whole story was weakened, and I had to replace it with the Bunker Hill game which is played as a sort of role-playing game. It was very disappointing, because I thought with the original idea I had the modern equivalent of that famous game of golf in *Goldfinger* or else Bond's bridge match with Drax. I'd wanted to do something like that from the day I took over the series and it was a great shame when it had to be removed.'

The fifth book, *Nobody Lives Forever*, sees Bond with his defence mechanisms more sorely tried than ever before when the realisation dawns upon him that after all his years courting death, there is now a permanently fixed price out on his head.

The achievement of these five books has not been an easy one, as John is quick to state. 'Believe it or not, the Bond books are more difficult to write than my own work,' he says. 'With my books I can become completely immersed, identify with the characters and the book. But with Bond I can't.

'I have to stand aside, be careful with the plot, and conform at least with the spirit of the originals. I'm always conscious when I'm doing Bond that he is not *mine*. I have to keep a slight distance from him because he is somebody else's creation and not my own. I'm not God as far as he is concerned, but I *am* God when it's my own characters.

'But I do enjoy writing the Bonds and I'm very conscious of Ian Fleming looking over my shoulder and keeping the spirit of jolly James alive!'

John sees Bond as 'the Robin Hood of the twentieth century' who appeals to our collective sense of the myth. He even sees the plots as coming straight from myth, fairy tale and legend – typified by the story of St George and the Dragon.

'I never take myself seriously' he insists, 'but I always take work seriously. I'm not a writer, that is a label which belongs to men like Tolstoy. I am an entertainer – and Bond is pure entertainment. The books are for fun and enjoyment.'

Although John has indicated that his sixth Bond could be his last – I wonder if he is not in the same danger as both Sean Connery and Roger Moore who vowed they had appeared for the last time on the screen as 007 and then somehow succumbed to his magic and returned? John admits the possibility cannot be entirely ruled out.

'I don't think I'll be asked to do another cycle of stories,' he reflects. 'But who knows? If they're successful, if by any chance I manage to push it so that my Bond becomes completely acceptable to the fans, and if I was given a little more latitude . . . maybe. I'll just have to see.'

Whatever John Gardner decides, however, we should be in no doubt that the James Bond literary saga is by no means at an end. For myths like Robin Hood – as history shows – never die. . .

James BOND A CELEBRATION

PART TWO

Bond In Films

Casino Royale – The TV Gamble That Failed

In 1962 the first James Bond film, *Dr No*, starring Sean Connery, appeared in the world's cinemas, creating an image that has endured for a quarter of a century. But this was not the first time that 007 had appeared on a screen – for almost a decade earlier, in 1954, Bond had been featured on American television in a one-hour adaptation of the first of Ian Fleming's novels, *Casino Royale*. Yet today, this screen debut of the world's most famous secret agent is almost completely unknown.

Examined in hindsight, the TV version of *Casino Royale* provides another fascinating element in the creation of the legend of James Bond. For while the world at large thinks of Sean Connery as the first Bond, he was, in fact, only following in the footsteps of another actor who might so easily have become the star of a whole series of Bond productions.

The first Bond actor's name was Barry Nelson; a rangy, six-foot two-inch stage and screen star who portrayed him on CBS Television in October 1954. Nelson co-starred in *Casino Royale* with two other leading American film stars, the sinister-looking Peter Lorre, who played the villainous Le Chiffre, and the beautiful Linda Christian as Vesper Lynd – who was the very first of the now-famous Bond girls. Although, tragically, no copy of this TV production exists today because it was transmitted live, enough documentation and personal recollections remain for a comprehensive dossier to be assembled.

As is now generally known, Ian Fleming was optimistic as soon as he had created James Bond that the secret agent would be ideal for films or television. Indeed, he was convinced that if his character was going to achieve international fame and bring him substantial earnings it would be through either or both of these mediums – and he

The first James Bond – Barry Nelson who appeared in the CBS TV version of *Casino Royale* in 1954.

'I played Bond as an American, but I'm sure his eventual success came because he was so English' – Barry Nelson.

confessed as much to his friend and fellow writer, Roald Dahl, shortly after the publication of *Casino Royale* in 1953. (Dahl, as a matter of interest, was later to write the film script for *You Only Live Twice* in 1967.)

'If you get a chance of putting in a word with the TV tycoons for *Casino*, I shall be very grateful,' Fleming said. 'Money is despicable stuff but it buys Renoirs!'

Despite the light-heartedness of this suggestion, Fleming was quite serious, and his opinion about the suitability of Bond for the screen was shared by a number of film companies who considered adapting *Casino Royale*. However, only the Columbia Broadcasting Company in Hollywood came back to him with any kind of concrete proposal. They offered the fee of $1,000 for the right to make a one hour adaptation for their weekly TV drama series, *Climax!*

Though this offer was hardly earth-shattering – the value of the dollar at that time meant Fleming ended up with little more than £400 in his pocket – there was the carrot dangled before him that if the show was a success a Bond series *might* follow, and he would be well paid to write, or at least outline, the episodes. Fleming accepted.

The *Climax!* series for which *Casino Royale* was bought had its first transmission on 7 October 1954 and ran for almost four years until June 1958, thereby qualifying as one of the longer-running dramatic series on US network television during the 1950s. A Thursday night prime-time show going out between 8.30 and 9.30 pm, it followed very much in the traditional mould of having a host to introduce each story and sketch in any necessary details. For its entire run, *Climax!* was hosted by the famous TV veteran, William Lundigan, who was later joined by a co-host, the charming Mary Costa, in the summer of 1956.

The hour-long shows – interspersed, naturally, with commercials – were televised from CBS's facilities in Hollywood, and although put out live, both studio and outdoor facilities were used wherever feasible. As the show developed in popularity, pre-filmed segments were introduced, but to the end it remained a predominantly live show which regretfully was not taped for posterity.

Casino Royale was aired as the fourth story in the series, going out on the night of 21 October 1954. CBS deliberately turned the secret agent into an American, and also introduced several elements of comedy into the somewhat grim story of Bond's attempt to disgrace the unscrupulous and evil Le Chiffre.

Variety, the showbiz newspaper, in one of the very few reviews of the show, had this to say in its issue of the following week dated 27 October:

'Among the congested sweepstakes of the Hour Dramas put out on Thursday was *Climax!* which is yet to get into the money – despite the star-studded banners. As, for instance, last week's cloak-and-daggery *Casino Royale* fronting Barry Nelson, Peter Lorre and Linda Christian which and who drew laughs along the course by running with all legs off the ground.'

Barry Nelson, now a director and occasionally appearing on the TV, film and stage scene does not remember the show in quite such a flippant way.

'There were certainly moments of humour in the story,' he says, 'and we did diverge from the original story quite a bit, but there was still the great card-playing sequence in the Casino, and I don't recall a lot to laugh about when Peter Lorre was torturing me later to get back the money I'd won from him. He could make me shudder without saying a word! Linda Christian was, of course, a famous beauty and I doubt any James Bond since has had such a beautiful woman in his arms!'

Nelson is a tall and impressive man, with twinkling-blue eyes, hair that was once sandy-brown, and at his peak he was renowned for playing roles with what critics generally referred to as 'boyish enthusiasm'. He was born Robert Nielson, in Oakland, California on 16 April 1920, of Scandinavian descent, his father, Trygve Nielson, being a seaman.

His interest in acting began when he was at the Freemont High School in Oakland, and during his time at the University of California, he and two classmates also began to write a weekly drama sketch for a San Francisco radio station.

At the end of his second year at college, Barry took a leave of absence from his books to be the voices of a dozen characters in the 'Cavalcade of the Golden West' at the San Francisco World Fair. His earnings from this saw him through the rest of his time at University, and it was while he was playing the leading role in the Drama Department's

Production of *Macbeth* that he was spotted by a Hollywood talent scout. This lead directly to him being signed up by MGM and a start of a screen career.

After a small part in *Shadow of the Thin Man*, he filed a leading role in Mervyn LeRoy's 1942 production *Johnny Eager* and never looked back.

Barry was able to combine acting with his wartime service in the American Army (he was made a corporal in 1945), playing a leading role in the film and stage production of *Winged Victory* which he made for Twentieth Century Fox in 1945.

He fully established his name when he starred in several Broadway hits, including the Moss Hart play, *Light Up The Sky*, Garson Kanin's *The Rat Race*, and the highly acclaimed *The Moon is Blue* in which he played Donald Gresham. This was followed by an eighteen-month stint in London as the star of *No Time For Sergeants* and another Broadway triumph as a book publisher in Jean Kerr's *Mary, Mary*. He never quite forsook the cinema, however, and most recently has been seen in the hugely successful movie, *Airport* (1972).

Barry's talant also made him a natural for television and he has appeared in a number of TV series such as *The Hunters*, *Hudson's Bay* and *My Favourite Husband*.

It is perhaps surprising that for a man who was an expert boxer and wrestler in his early years, Barry should have played so many gentle characters and lovers on screen. Only in the CBS version of *Casino Royale* and more recently the NBC TV production, *World Premiere: The Borgia Stick* has he been cast in tougher roles. In *The Borgia Stick* he played an FBI agent and found curious parallels with the earlier role of Bond.

'Both guys had to be quick on their feet and take a fair bit of punishment before getting the job done,' he said. 'I enjoyed both roles because they were a change from the comedy roles I usually got. It made a real change to have to be dodging bullets instead of setting up laughs!'

Memories of the James Bond show are, naturally enough, fairly dim in Barry's mind, though he has watched the development of the extraordinary world-wide success of the films with more than average interest. He does not, though, feel any sense of regret that he has never been considered for the part of 007 on screen.

'I'm not sure my image would have been right,' he admits honestly. 'Sean Connery undoubtedly played a major part in creating the image of Bond that everyone could accept. I played Bond as an American, and I feel sure his success was established because he was so English – just as Ian Fleming had intended.'

Barry admits that there was no way the famous scene from *Casino Royale* in which the naked James bond is so excruciatingly tortured by Le Chiffre could be shown on television, and nor were the love-making episodes with Vesper Lynd considered suitable for prime time viewing!

'I guess you have to say that Peter Lorre was closest to the original story in the way he played Le Chiffre. I have to say I think he made a better villain than even Orson Welles who played the part in the screen story.

'And if anyone who saw our *Casino Royale* thinks that was a send-up of the original, then they should just take a look at that David Niven and Peter Sellers movie. If we'd done what *they* did to James Bond I don't think anyone would ever have heard of him again!'

By all accounts, Barry Nelson's estimation of Peter Lorre as Le Chiffre is accurate. For not only did Lorre have the physical characteristics to suit that sinister character, but brought a wealth of experience at playing bizarre roles to the part.

**Peter Lorre –
a memorable Le Chiffre
in CBS TV's *Casino Royale*.**

No Bond enthusiast will need reminding that Le Chiffre, the first and arguably most carefully detailed of all the villains, was described by Fleming as a man of 'gross physical habits' who looked like 'an octopus under a rock'. With his pale complexion, eighteen-stone bulk, and a touch of German in his humourless nature, he was a worthy first opponent for Bond – as well as introducing the reader to the Russian terror organisation, SMERSH, who control Le Chiffre and for whom he is desperately trying to recoup misappropriated funds of fifty million francs at the gambling tables.

Curiously though, Le Chiffre is introduced on the very first page of Fleming's book – and indeed appeared at the start of the Niven-Sellers film verison – Peter Lorre was not seen in the *Climax!* production until the crucial game of baccarat, after Bond has already escaped the bomb attack on his life. His shadow, though, was lurking off-stage from the moment the opening credits had rolled and Bond was shown getting his instructions to defeat the man who was known to be an enemy of the USA and in league with the Russians.

Peter Lorre, who died suddenly and rather tragically, in March 1964, was for many years one of the character actors most in demand for villainous roles in Hollywood films. An apt description of him in one of the pictures he made for Alfred Hitchcock in 1936 called *Secret Agent* referred to him as 'a happy little assassin with a taste for cold-blooded murder and warm-blooded women': this could just as equally be a description of Le Chiffre.

Lorre was born Laszlo Loewenstein on 26 June 1904 at Rosenberg, a little village high up in the Carpathian mountains of Hungary. He lived in this superstition-ridden area where vampires, demons and spirits of all kinds are believed to dwell, until his family moved to Vienna when he was six.

His fascination with the theatre and acting developed early – and was heightened all the more, he later said, because his family regarded the profession with complete distaste.

'My love of the theatre grew for the most perverse of reasons – it was forbidden fruit. My parents considered grease paint and stage doors the inventions of Satan.'

Despite this disapproval, as a child he sneaked into theatres whenever he could, and as soon as his schooling was over, ran away from home at seventeen and joined a touring company. Sought out and brought home by his father, Peter was put to work in a bank, but devoted all his spare time to a local theatrical group.

Finally, he made the break from family and bank and, after some years of hardship and almost starvation gaining experience on the stage, made a stunning debut in the world of films in 1931 when he was given the leading role of a child killer in Fritz Lang's movie, *M.* Lang later admitted that he cast Lorre in the part of the Dusseldorf monster because he saw him as 'the one actor in Europe who could portray the part satisfactorily and give it the proper shading of understanding and comprehension.'

The impact Peter Lorre had was indeed unprecedented, as a report in *Film Pictorial* of 1933 notes.

'No personality of stage or screen ever received so strange a reception from the public as Lorre after the release of his initial film, *M,*' said the account. 'He became the most hated man in Europe. As though he actually were the Dusseldorf murderer in person, people shunned him like the plague. He could not appear in public without causing every woman to grab her offspring and dash pell-mell for safety, or shriek in terror at his innocent approach. His conciliatory smile was taken to mean he was working himself into the mood for another homicide.'

People in the film business, however, were quick to appreciate just what a stunning performance the young man had given – Charlie Chaplin, for instance – a man not given

Peter Lorre in *Secret Agent* (1930) directed by Alfred Hitchcock whom Ian Fleming wanted to direct the Bond movies.

to fulsome praise of others – hailed Lorre ecstatically, saying, 'He is the greatest living actor' – and the result was that Lorre was soon in demand in Europe and America. In England, he worked for Hitchcock in *The Man Who Knew Too Much* (1934) and developed the role which was subsequently to become his hallmark, the ruthless professional killer, and he soon became known as 'Mr Murder'. Then he went to Hollywood where, after playing Raskolnikov in Josef van Sternberg's version of *Crime*

Linda Christian who played the seductive Vesper Lynd in the American television version of *Casino Royale.*

and Punishment, he began a series of thrillers built around the character of the oriental detective Mr Moto, as well as a number of horror movies and spy pictures.

His international reputation was fully confirmed in John Huston's *The Maltese Falcon* which earned him the epithet 'the man you love to hate'. The picture also, of course, contained an archetypal performance by Humphrey Bogart, and the two men became close friends – Lorre being one of the original members of Bogart's famous 'Holmby Hills Rat Pack' who met each night at the cocktail hour and broke up hours – sometimes days – later.

In the Fifties, Peter Lorre worked in television as well as in films, and his casting as Le Chiffre in the *Climax!* series was one of several notable performances on the small screen.

He brought the same dedication to the role that he did to all his work, and in reading the novel of *Casino Royale* before playing his part, noted that Le Chiffre took frequent sniffs from a benzedrine inhaler. In the script, it was merely said that the villainous agent smoked cigarettes – a habit Lorre detested. He insisted on being able to use the inhaler to allow for significant pauses while interrogating Bond; it proved an effective – and sinister – prop.

Peter Lorre demonstrated another of his remarkable attributes in *Casino Royale* – that of immersing himself into a role without vast amounts of make-up.

'No matter how villainous a role I play,' he once said, 'I prefer to use my own expressions rather than the make-up box. Underplaying a scene is also more effective than making a lot of noise. The audience find a villain far more sinister if he is quiet, and lets the expression in his eyes and the way he holds himself conjure up their fears. The littlest smile playing around the mouth can do more in close up than all the histrionics in the world.'

If Le Chiffre was one of Ian Fleming's most repulsive villains – and portrayed as such with consummate skill by Peter Lorre – then Vesper Lynd is also one of the most beautiful of his 'heroines' and was similarly played in the TV version by an equally suitable star: the stunning Linda Christian.

It remains one of the mysteries of the cinema why 'La Christian', the cool and statuesque blonde who exploded onto the screen in the late Forties did not become one of Hollywood's great stars. Certainly she played *femmes fatales* in several movies with great skill and was widely compared to Grace Kelly – yet history has marked her down as a playgirl who was more famous for her off-screen romances than on-screen performances.

Aside from her almost classical beauty, she was ideal to play the French girl, Vesper Lynd, who is seconded to Bond for his mission to defeat and disgrace Le Chiffre. Like a true Fleming woman she came from a multi-national background and was irresistible to men. The author's description of Mme Lynd underlines the perceptiveness of CBS's casting of Linda Christian (apart from the colour of her hair):

'Her hair was very black and she wore it cut square and low on the nape of the neck, framing her face to below the clear and beautiful line of her jaw. Her eyes were wide apart and deep blue and they gazed candidly back at Bond with a touch of ironical disinterest which, to his annoyance, he found he would like to shatter, roughly. Her skin was lightly sun-tanned and bore no trace of make-up except on her mouth which was wide and sensual. Her bare arms and hands had a quality of repose and the general impression of restraint in her appearance and movements was carried even to her fingernails which were unpainted and cut short. Her medium-length dress was of grey *soie sauvage* with a square-cut bodice, lasciviously tight across her fine breasts . . . Bond was excited by her beauty and intrigued by her composure. The prospect of working with her stimulated him.'

Linda was born Blanca Rosa Walter in Tampico, Mexico on 13 November 1923, the daughter of a Dutch oilman. Her father's profession took her all over the world and she has vivid childhood memories of Venezuela, South Africa, Holland and Palestine, where she first began her working life in the office of the British Censor who was based there. Initially, though, her heart was set on a career in medicine, until her evident beauty made her decide to try and break into films in Hollywood.

Linda's first film role was in 1946 in George Sydney's *Holiday in Mexico*, and she followed this with more substantial parts in *Green Dolphin Street* (1947) and *The Happy Time* in 1952.

In the years which followed she was to be seen on the arms of some of the most famous and eligible men in the world at that time; including Tyrone Power, Edmund Purdom, Ali Khan, Mike Todd and the famous international playboy 'Baby' Pignatti. She married Power and had two daughters, Romina and Taryn, and later became Edmund Purdom's wife.

Although her career was soon to dwindle in the Sixties in such forgettable movies as *The Beauty Jungle* (1964) and *How To Seduce A Playboy* (1966), her beauty remained eye-catching, and journalists were fond of calling her 'the last of the great playgirls with more romances behind her than the Queen has had free dinners' (Roderick Mann in the *Sunday Express* in August 1968).

She herself did nothing to discourage the stories. 'You know,' she told one interviewer in the late sixties, 'I've known a lot of men in my life, and I think I've learned something from them all. But it has made me very choosy, and that's a problem. Also, it's given me a terrible reputation. I've no doubt my reputation scares a lot of men.'

Linda's appearance as the first Bond 'heroine' undoubtedly set a standard for all the beauties who were to follow in her footsteps into the secret agent's arms and bed – though there was actually no bedroom scene for her and Barry Nelson on TV. And though the whole production had an element of comedy about it, her performance along with that of Nelson and Peter Lorre was noted in a brief report in the *Los Angeles Times* as 'solid TV fare for audiences who enjoy a spy romp.'

Like the book, the CBS version of *Casino Royale* ended with Bond vowing to 'take on SMERSH and hunt it down' – an obvious attempt to leave the way clear for other stories of 'James Bond, Secret Agent' if the public reaction was favourable.

While the story of *Casino Royale* had been in production, Ian Fleming had also been in contact with CBS in the hope that Bond might become the star of a regular series. As John Pearson has written in his biography, *The Life of Ian Fleming*:

'Now that he knew that Bond was in demand, the real question was how to make the most of him. As he realised, the big James Bond television deal with CBS offered an easy way out. It was James Bond he was selling to the Americans, not the books. He could have his sack of gold in return for a series of outlines for half-hour James Bond episodes on television.

'He found that writing these was child's play,' Pearson continues. 'He had finished six already, and these television episodes had another advantage. Without too much effort they could be turned into short stories, which is what he did adapting *Risico*, *From a View to a Kill* and *For Your Eyes Only* directly from the television outlines he had already prepared for CBS.' (These stories plus *Quantum of Solace* and *The Hildebrand Rarity* were later to form the collection *For Your Eyes Only* which Fleming published in 1960.)

Although Fleming was undoubtedly anxious for quite some time to close the deal with CBS, the television company – perhaps because of the luke-warm reception given to *Casino Royale* – finally decided against the project. It can now only be a matter for conjecture what *might* have been the future for James Bond if the series had gone ahead in 1958 . . .

Cubby Broccoli – The Film-Maker Who Loves Bond

Just as one man, Ian Fleming, was at the heart of the literary James Bond, so an equally inventive and determined man, Albert 'Cubby' Broccoli, has been behind the success of the 'Film Bond'. Initially half of a film-making partnership with Harry Saltzman who together bought 007 to the cinema screen, Cubby has since become the mentor and main driving force behind the incredibly successful series of movies that have now chalked up twenty-five years of unbroken box-office records.

To understand the success of these pictures – a success unparalled in screen history – it is necessary to know something about Cubby Broccoli himself, as well as his methods and philosophy where the making of the Bond movies is concerned.

One of the most remarkable facts that one discovers immediately about Cubby Broccoli, who is after all the producer of a saga which is basically about British ideals and attitudes as personified by James Bond, is that he is American. His success story is the archetypal American dream come true, and he is not at all like Ian Fleming – in either background or temperament – though the two men became friends and both their lives were changed irrevocably and for the better by 007.

Cubby was born Albert Romolo Broccoli on 5 April 1909, the oldest son of an Italian-American family living on Long Island, near New York. His name, in fact, comes from the broccoli vegetable, and he is proud of the fact that it was one of his uncles who first introduced the plant into America.

'They were hard times when I was a kid and we were a poor family,' Cubby reminisces today. 'My father, who was a civil engineer, had to work as a bricklayer in New York so the family could eat. I helped my uncle on his farm where he raised all kinds of vegetables – potatoes, peas, cabbages, asparagus, and, of course, broccoli. I'd help wash them, crate them and then take them to the market in Harlem on carts drawn by beautiful big bay horses with feathers on their legs.

'Trouble was often nobody would buy the stuff, and so instead of hauling it back again we'd dump it in the Harlem River!'

Recently, Cubby has discovered that his family had not always been farmers in the Calabria area of Italy from which they emigrated. They were, in fact, writers, politicians and historians in the north of Italy, and had been banished from the area about the year 1300 for political reasons.

The same restlessness which had brought his forebears to America also afflicted Cubby, and while still a young man he left the family business and became a coffin maker!

'I got this job as manager of the United Casket Company who made coffins,' he says. 'It was OK for a while, but just a bit morbid. Then I took a two week holiday and went to Los Angeles and everything changed. I stayed there.' (Cubby, incidentally, always likes to have a sly reference to this period of his life by including a joke about coffins or undertakers in every Bond film!)

Although Cubby had no real idea of what he wanted to do – and had no particular interests beyond a fascination with painting and sculpting (which continues to this day), he found the creative drive which is so much a part of Los Angeles, and Hollywood in particular, quite irresistible. But like so many young people drawn to the glamour of the film capital, work was hard to come by and he soon found himself forced to sell cosmetics and hairdressing materials on commission in San Francisco.

The partners who started the Bond saga, Harry Saltzman (left) and Cubby Broccoli viewing some early takes of a 007 movie.

'There I was in San Francisco,' he recalls, 'with no money, just this small room to sleep in, and the only companion I had was a rat who used to come on to the window sill every day. I really looked forward to seeing him. I fed him. He became my friend.

'Then one day I won a few dollars on the races. That was it: I said goodbye to the rat and took a Greyhound bus straight back to L.A.'

When Cubby returned to Hollywood a second time he was a little luckier. He found a job as a tea-boy and mail clerk at the Twentieth Century Fox studios. It was a start, and now with his foot in the door, his energy and enthusiasm soon got him a job as an assistant to the famous director Howard Hawks in 1938.

The Second World War intervened before Cubby could make his mark, and after five years in the Navy he returned to Hollywood and became an agent – representing Lana Turner and Ava Gardner among others – before in 1950 he decided to cross the Atlantic to Britain. Here he went into parnership with another resourceful film-maker, Irving Allen, to form Warwick Pictures.

'The incentive was Eady money – the government kickback given to home-produced films,' he recalls with a smile, 'and what we made was profitable crap! I think my favourite was *Zarak* with Victor Mature as an Indian brigand and Anita Ekberg with a ruby in her navel.'

Despite this slightly disparaging remark, Cubby and Irving Allen did make some successful pictures, particularly those with war themes like *Red Beret* (1953) and *The Cockleshell Heroes* (1955). One of their regular scriptwriters was an American named Richard Maibaum, and among their directors was Terence Young. Both were to be intimately associated with the success of the James Bond pictures.

High adventure stories appealed to Cubby Broccoli and by the mid-Fifties he was aware of waves being made by Ian Fleming's thrillers. He read the books as they appeared and became increasingly convinced of their potential as films. As early as 1957, he actually gave Richard Maibaum two of the books to read to see if they might be filmed.

Pressed for time on other projects, however, Cubby did not return to the idea of James Bond for some time. And when he did, he found that an option had been taken up by another film-maker with exactly the same idea: Harry Saltzman.

Saltzman was a Canadian, born in St John on 27 October 1915, who had spent his youth in Canada and the USA. His hankering after the entertainment business saw him gain splendid experience in vaudeville as well as in a travelling circus, before he crossed the Atlantic to France in the Thirties. Here he became a successful theatre entrepreneur until the war intervened.

After the war, Harry Saltzman returned to show business in America – in particular television – but in 1957 saw a new opportunity across the Atlantic and linked up with British director Tony Richardson to form Woodfall Films who became famous for their 'kitchen sink dramas' such as *Look Back In Anger* (1959) and *Saturday Night and Sunday Morning* (1961). Despite the success of these pictures, Saltzman grew tired of social realism and thought the time was right for the return of the big entertainment film.

His path crossed with that of Cubby Broccoli, and the two men formed EON Pictures. Their partnership lasted for nine films, until Harry Saltzman decided to sell his share of the operation to United Artists for £17.5 million.

'You could say that our parting was brusque,' Cubby Broccoli was reported as saying afterwards. 'But basically it was because Harry wanted to go into Technicolour and the manufacture of film materials – and I wanted to stay with Bond.'

During the setting up of the first Bond film, Cubby became friendly with Ian Fleming, and they remained in close touch for the remaining two years of the author's life.

'He was a very dear man, and a dear friend,' he says today. 'And very wise. I remember he told me, "You're going to have to update my stories eventually, because times change. Things happen. New innovations emerge. Just try to have the scripts written the way I have done in my early books." '

Cubby says that Fleming saw the films, *Dr No* and *From Russia With Love*, and also the rushes of *Goldfinger* – but had only an inkling of just *how* big 007 was to become with the public.

'He loved the films he *did* see and he loved Sean,' Cubby continues. 'But as the years have passed, the books have become largely redundant. They have had to be updated, rewritten, be made increasingly spectacular. Actually we have the right to go on making Bond pictures even when there are no more books to film. The flow need never cease.' (The Fleming Estate have already authorised several new titles.)

Cubby has kept a close watch on every Bond film right from its inception to the time it is complete.

'They are probably the only films written by committee,' he says. 'I sit down with the writer, director and executive producer and we decide what we want in the script. We have discussions, we have ideas. The final decision is made by me.'

He also often attends the shooting of the pictures, both in the studios and on location, and watches the cutting as well as overseeing the advertising and promotion.

'Bond is my life,' he says with studied deliberation. 'I get ideas for the films all the time. I scribble down ideas on the backs of old envelopes. Even if I'm on the toilet and get a Bond idea I grab a piece of toilet paper and write it down. And that idea, though it began on a piece of toilet paper, can cost millions of dollars to put on the screen.

'Bond films have been in continuous production since we began preparing the first one twenty-five years ago. While one film is in the studio another is already in the making in my head. With Bond I've got a tiger by the tail and while he's roaring ahead I'd be a fool to let go.'

This 'tiger by the tail' has brought more than just financial reward to Cubby Broccoli. In 1982 he was the recipient of the Academy of Motion Picture Arts and Sciences 'Irving G Thalberg Award' at the Oscar Ceremony in Hollywood. Then in January 1985, the Guild of British Camera Technicians presented him with their Lenham Award for 'loyalty and excellence in the British Film Industry'. Even when the stage at Pinewood (which was used for the Bond films) was burned down in 1984, it was re-opened the following year as the 'Albert R Broccoli 007 Stage'.

Cubby is also a popular man with both his stars and the technicians who work on the Bond pictures. Sean Connery and Roger Moore are among his most intimate friends.

'Do you know,' he says, 'there are a whole generation of filmgoers who don't even remember Sean as Bond? Of course he was the original 007 and – some say – the best. But it's just a difference in style. Both Sean and Roger have been marvellous in the part and I've liked working with both of them. They are also both better actors than most people give them credit for.

'And,' he adds quickly, 'George Lazenby wasn't the disaster everyone seems to think. No film can be a total failure if it takes 38 million dollars!'

Does he have any favourites amongst all the Bond pictures? 'My favourites are *From Russia With Love*, *Goldfinger* and *The Spy Who Loved Me*. I can't say there is a single one I'd want to re-do, although there are parts of *The Man With The Golden Gun* I'd change.'

Turning to the multitude of people who work with him behind the cameras, Cubby continues: 'I've got some very clever people working for me. But I don't have any geniuses.

'A genius is someone who costs you money. People are always saying that so-and-so's a genius. When they say that, I start worrying. I may not be the greatest producer, but what I know, I *know* – you know? Knowledge and luck are what you need. If you're not lucky, forget it. Deliver me from geniuses.

'I love working at Pinewood,' he adds. 'We started off there, and they're Bond-addicted and dedicated film makers. They know what we want and need.'

After a quarter of a century being steeped in James Bond, Cubby has developed seven basic ground rules for the pictures which he believes are essential for their continued success.

Sean Connery, the first James Bond, on the set at Pinewood filming *You Only Live Twice* in 1966.

Roger Moore, the third Bond, congratulating Cubby Broccoli after he had received the Irving Thalberg Memorial Award at the Oscar Ceremony in Hollywood in 1982.

Firstly, he says, it is important to *show* the audience something rather than talk about it. 'We have to take them on a free vacation to exotic locations. I loved those old-fashioned travelogues they used to show in cinemas. Well, today's audiences still do – as a background.'

Secondly, there must be a series of deliberate anticlimaxes when the audience thinks the show must be over when, in fact, it isn't. 'We call them "bumps" and there are about twelve or thirteen in every movie.'

Thirdly, each film should be preceeded by a mini film before the main titles, which is exciting and unusual in itself. 'Preferably with a new gadget or stunt,' says Cubby. 'The gadgets in the pictures also have to be real, and they must work and always be ahead of their times.'

Fourthly, get in as many beautiful girls as possible. 'They must be either looking admiringly at Bond, or with a challenge in their eyes, "So all right – try to get me."'

Five – the essential villain. 'He should be intelligent, articulate, foreign and with a cultured voice and smiling charm. The villain in Bond shouldn't need to go out and earn a buck – he has everything he wants but power: and his motivation is an extension of greed.'

Six – because the villain never does his own dirty work, he must have an assistant who is unusual, vicious, but never odious. 'Think of Jaws, Oddjob, Nick Nack the dwarf,' says Cubby by way of example, 'and the limp-wristed couple Mr Wint and Mr Kid.'

And finally, seven – the end. 'End on a laugh,' says Cubby, 'and Bond with a girl.'

Despite these formulas, Cubby admits that each new film gets harder and harder to make.

'It takes time to find interesting new set pieces, new ideas, new surprises,' he says. 'Yes, we find them, but it takes longer. For one thing there are so many imitators now. Some of them are excellent, too. I consider *Raiders of the Lost Ark* an imitator of our Bond series. I'm sure there wouldn't have been a Raiders if there hadn't been a James Bond. And I love the picture – Steven Spielberg did a masterful job.

'The costs also keep accelerating. The first picture, *Dr No* cost $1 million, and *Moonraker* in 1979 cost $30 million. It also becomes increasingly difficult to find places to shoot around the world. The political climates change so quickly.'

One place that he has not yet been able to film, although he would very much like to, is Russia. In fact, he has twice visited the Soviet Union (in 1975 and 1979) in the hope of getting permission to shoot, and came away convinced that the men in the Communist hierarchy had seen the Bond films.

But *would* it be possible to film 007 against the background of the Kremlin and the other images of his most implacable enemies?

'The Russians did invite me to make a film there,' he says. 'But when I said I'd like to make a Bond movie there, they said, "We're not ready for *that* yet!"'

Cubby has denied that there are any plans for a James Bond TV series – 'at least not while the films are still so successful. I don't see them playing out at theatres for some time yet because new generations keep growing up and meeting Bond and really enjoying him. People age, but James Bond does not.'

If Cubby has any regrets at all from his association with 007, it is that the series has proved so time-consuming that he has been unable to tackle other films projects. But one thing he has never become is bored.

'Never!' he replies with considerable emphasis when questioned on the matter. 'Quite the opposite. Bond keeps me alive. If I didn't make these pictures, I really think I'd become a vegetable. And I don't want to become a broccoli in fact as well as name!'

His Word Is Bond

Richard Maibaum – Script Writer

Richard Maibaum has written more words about James Bond's adventures than even Ian Fleming. To date he has scripted, or co-written, no fewer than eleven of the Bond films and will doubtless write still more in the years to come. His role-call is a virtual catalogue of the life and times of the secret agent: *Dr No; From Russia With Love; Goldfinger; Thunderball; On Her Majesty's Secret Service; Diamonds Are Forever; The Man With The Golden Gun; The Spy Who Loved Me; For Your Eyes Only; Octopussy* and *A View To A Kill.*

Richard met Ian Fleming before the author's death and cherishes the memory of that meeting and what the ailing but still witty author said to him.

'It was quite amusing, really. He said to me, "It's amazing, but your pictures are much funnier than my novels!" I don't think he understood that we were *trying* to make them funnier. They were a spoof in the first place, although always in a supposedly serious, dead-pan way. Because when the actor or the writer laughs, the audience never does. So what we have to do is spoof ourselves and quite rightly the audience enjoys the last laugh!'

Richard Maibaum is a silver-haired, rather grandfatherly man well into his seventies, whose genial disposition belies his fiendish imagination and mastery of witty dialogue. If the most successful films at the box-office owe a great deal to their scripts – as popular movie lore would have it – then the record-breaking Bond pictures owe every bit as much to Maibaum as they do to Ian Fleming.

It was in the 1930s that Maibaum began writing scripts for Hollywood from the quiet seclusion of a lovely home in Pacific Palisades, Los Angeles. The range of his scripts

Continued on page 105

Solid Gold! Sean Connery, the first screen Bond, as he appeared in *Goldfinger* in 1964.

(PHOTO: GEORGE RODGER, MAGNUM)

James
BOND
A CELEBRATION

(PHOTO: DAVID HURN, MAGNUM)

The superhero of the Sixties (left). Sean Connery on set, making the most highly-regarded Bond movie, *From Russia With Love* (1963).

(PHOTO: GEORGE RODGER, MAGNUM)

Twenty-one years as 007. A publicity shot of Connery for *Dr No* (1962), and Sean Connery photographed with his co-stars Pamela Salem (Miss Moneypenny) and Barbara Carrera (Fatima) while making his most recent Bond movie, *Never Say Never Again* (1983).

(PHOTO: FOX/KEYSTONE)

007 Mark I:
Sean Connery.
(PHOTO: BOB PENN, SYGMA)

007 Mark III: Roger Moore.
(PHOTO: N MORAN, SYGMA)

(PHOTO: FOX/KEYSTONE)

Roger Moore with Alison Doody, Fiona Fullerton and Tanya Roberts at Pinewood Studios prior to beginning work on *A View To A Kill* in 1985.

Roger Moore on location with one of the best Bond villainesses, Grace Jones, who played May Day in *A View To A Kill*.

(PHOTO: N MORAN, SYGMA)

The only Bond girl to give her name to a 007 story, Maud Adams as *Octopussy* (1983).

(PHOTO: FOX/KEYSTONE)

Bond meets Bond! Roger Moore and Sean Connery, who are great friends off-screen, toast the continuing success of the series.

(PHOTO: P LEDRU, SYGMA)

Continued from page 96

speaks volumes about his versatility: *Gold Diggers of 1937* (1936); *The Great Gatsby* (1949); *The Red Beret* (1953) and *The Day They Robbed The Bank of England* (1960). In the 1950s he became associated with the partnership of Irving Allen and Cubby Broccoli and moved to London where he has since written the majority of the Bond scripts.

The association with the secret agent is one that he has found both rewarding and challenging – and is one he sees continuing indefinitely. 'There's no reason why the Bond movies can't go on forever,' he says with quiet enthusiasm. 'Some characters like Robin Hood and Sherlock Holmes are immortal. Now to their ranks you can add James Bond!'

Richard was born in New York in May 1909, and already had the writing bug before he had left New York University to go to the University of Iowa.

'I wrote my first play when I was nine years old,' he recalls. 'It was about cowboys. At college I took up acting as well as writing, and in 1933 I joined the Shakespearean Repertory Theatre in New York. I also found time to write some plays and between the ages of twenty-three and twenty-six I had three plays running on Broadway, *The Tree*, *Birthright* and *Sweet Mystery of Life*.

'After that,' he says, 'I decided it was time I made some money. MGM in Hollywood beckoned with a contract, but I hardly got started before the war came along.'

'Hardly got started' is a modest assessment of these years when, among other movies, he wrote *They Gave Him A Gun* for MGM with Spencer Tracy, *The Amazing Mr Williams* for Columbia and the Ray Milland–William Holden film, *I Wanted Wings*, for Paramount.

Perhaps not surprisingly, when Uncle Sam called Richard Maibaum in 1942 he was attached to the Army's Combat Film Division where in the next four years he shot a great deal of outstanding war footage. When he was discharged in 1946 he had attained the rank of Lieutenant Colonel.

Returning to Hollywood he worked on a string of pictures for Paramount as a writer-director working with major stars such as Alan Ladd, Shelley Winters, Charles Laughton and Barbara Stanwick. In 1953, Richard became a freelance, and a year later met up with Cubby Broccoli.

He remembers the beginnings of the association vividly: 'I think the first time I worked with Cubby was when I adapted *Hell Below Zero* which starred Alan Ladd and Joan Tetzel. Then I came to Britain in 1954 and wrote *The Red Beret* which was Cubby's first film as producer. I also wrote *The Cockleshell Heroes* two years later, which Cubby produced with Irving Allen.

'It was funny, really. Here was I, an American who had only seen service in the US Army, writing about two very English military subjects. But they were very successful.'

A string of other action films for the Allen-Broccoli partnership continued until Cubby broke away from Irving and formed a new partnership with Harry Saltzman as EON Pictures to make the James Bond films.

Perhaps it was the very fact that Richard had succeeded so well with the two British war films that made Cubby Broccoli offer the Bond books to him for scripting.

'Cubby gave me two of the books to read in 1957 because he was thinking about doing them even then,' he recalls. 'Unfortunately, with all their inherent sex and violence, they

The most famous Bond fan, the Princess of Wales, meets Roger Moore and his wife along with producer, Cubby Broccoli, at a 007 première.

(PHOTO: FOX/KEYSTONE)

Richard Maibaum, the scriptwriter who has written more words about James Bond than even Ian Fleming!

just weren't producible at that time. But with the coming of the Sixties, attitudes began to change, and we decided to go with *Dr No*. It was pretty much of an experiment, though, the budget was relatively low – only $600,000.'

The actual making of *Dr No* taught Richard Maibaum and his associates an important lesson about the making of the Bond films: the importance of humour. Initially, the film was to have been a serious spy story, but the sardonic touches of Fleming's original story began to influence everyone.

'We certainly knew there was something different about *Dr No* from your average spy story,' says Richard. 'Like when Bond edges a hearse off a cliff and is then asked what happened and replies, "I don't know. I think they were going to a funeral." Well, now you know *that* was meant to be funny!

'Actually, *Dr No* told us what the audience liked, what they sparkled to. So when I wrote the second film, *From Russia With Love*, I think we crystallised the kind of thing that the Bond movies should be. That film was the one in which we set the style.

'In fact,' he goes on, 'I wrote that script in just six weeks. The others have taken considerably longer – but it still remains my favourite.'

For the third Bond picture, *Goldfinger*, Richard had a co-writer, Paul Dehn, and introduced stronger elements of both violence and sex.

'Well, yes, I suppose it was a *little* sexier,' he admits, 'but remember we still had the censors to contend with. For example, for the scene in the plane where Bond wakes up and sees gorgeous Honor Blackman, I first of all had him say, "Who are you?" She says, "Pussy Galore." And he says, "I know, but what's your *name*?"

On location in mysterious Istanbul in April 1963, Sean Connery and Terence Young's film crew at work on *From Russia With Love*, Richard Maibaum's favourite Bond movie.

'But I had to change that last line to, "I must be dreaming" – but it still got a laugh! Actually, we were only able to get away with Pussy Galore because that was her name in the novel. But it is true that in *Goldfinger* we were getting wilder. The whole business was becoming larger than life.'

Richard pauses a moment as his mind homes in on 1964 when he began work on the fourth picture, *Thunderball*.

'In *Thunderball* it really did become larger than life,' he says. 'The production became enormous, more fantastical; almost comic strip. And once we'd done that there was just no way of bringing them down. With *Thunderball* and its successor, *On Her Majesty's Secret Service*, the movies became documented fantasy.'

On Her Majesty's Secret Service introduced the second Bond, George Lazenby, and although Richard has strong reservations about Lazenby's performance, he does consider it, 'One of the best scripts I wrote and by far the best of Ian Fleming's novels.'

But another major factor was entering the production of the films at this time, as Richard explains. 'Our first four Bond films stemmed quite directly from the novels, although with some additions, of course. But with *Diamonds Are Forever* vast changes became necessary. Howard Hughes had to be kidnapped to build the satellite in the sky – kidnapped from an impregnable hotel suite. And incidentally it was Cubby who came up with the brilliant notion of using a look-alike to confuse things.'

After writing *The Man With The Golden Gun* in 1974, Richard was faced with *The Spy Who Loved Me* in which, he says, he had to invent *everything*.

'You see we weren't allowed to use the story by the terms of the contract, only the title. But that was just as well, really, because it was a terrible story. So in effect I wrote an original screenplay using the James Bond character.

'By this time, though, we knew the elements that made a successful Bond movie – the fantastic villains, the beautiful girls, the gadgets, Bond's wit and brutality, and the luxury syndrome. Those we knew were the things we had to have.

'But we still had to come up with a variation on the theme – and it's that variation which can be so difficult – finding new locations, devising new stunts, dreaming up new variations on the love story, a new villain and new things for the villain to do. After all, how many times *can* you destroy the world?'

Richard allows himself another laugh and then adds, 'At least in *The Spy Who Loved Me* we came up with a new motivation for him. The villain wasn't in it for the money.'

In his next scripting assignment, *For Your Eyes Only*, Richard conjured up a really new twist.

'It was the first Bond film in which the audience didn't know who the villain was. It could have been either Kristatos or Columbo, so that kept them guessing,' he recalls. 'In the other Bond movies you knew right from the start that the villain was Dr No, Blofeld, Goldfinger, Largo, Dr Kananga, Stromberg, Scaramanga or Drax – but in *For Your Eyes Only* it was different. You had to work it out for yourself who the baddie was.

'We had a problem in that *For Your Eyes Only* was a collection of five short stories and there wasn't much of a plot to any of them. I tried to use as much of his original dialogue as possible, but I think in the end there were only about twenty-five lines left!

Another exotic location, the Eiger Mountain, for George Lazenby in *On Her Majesty's Secret Service* which Richard Maibaum considers his best script. The girls are (back row) Helena Ronee and Zara, and at the front (from left to right), Anoushka Hempel, Julie Ege, Catherina von Schell, Joanna Lumley and Mona Chong.

Although *Octopussy* made in 1983 presented problems for Richard Maibaum, Roger Moore luckily didn't suffer any when filming took him to the very edge of the Iron Curtain to complete some scenes at Checkpoint Charlie on the Berlin Wall in October 1982.

'What we did was to take certain incidents and names of characters and make up our own story. And we also looked at current events in the newspapers for inspiration. Polaris nuclear submarines being kidnapped by the Russians – that sort of thing.

'*For Your Eyes Only* also got back much more to the physical fights that Bond used to have in the earlier films, like the struggle on the train with Robert Shaw in *From Russia With Love*. We consciously tried to get away from all the mechanical hardware and get back to people, which was what Cubby wanted. He has excellent taste and he didn't want any bloodshed. When the villain is hit in the face with a chain in any of the Bond films there's no blood seen – and that's how they differ from so many of today's other movies,' he added.

Octopussy, the title story from the posthumously published collection of two remaining Bond stories, presented similar problems for Richard when he scripted the movie of the same title in 1983.

'Ian Fleming was undoubtedly a master craftsmen with words,' says Richard. 'His stories were beautifully written, but some of them were unfilmable as they stood. Again with *Octopussy* we had to put our imaginations to work. Still, writing these pictures is very much a case of Walter Mitty for me.

'I'm a law-abiding citizen by nature and definitely non-violent. My greatest kick comes from being a professional, from knowing my job. I believe I have the experience to write a solid screenplay from even the barest details and that's the stage we've now reached with what original Bond material there is left.'

Most recently, Richard has worked on *A View To A Kill* with co-producer Michael G Wilson who was also credited for his script work on *For Your Eyes Only* and *Octopussy*. 'We work together like two collaborators always work,' Richard said of Wilson who has now become a close friend; 'we argue a lot!

Michael is, though, very receptive. He's the only man I've actually worked *with* on the Bond films,' he goes on. 'Other writers have come on before or after me, but never with me, until Michael. He has lots of ideas and we like each other, which always helps!'

One of the orginal ideas that Richard and Michael dreamed up for *A View To A Kill* was planned to be hugely topical. They would bring Halley's Comet into the story.

'We considered having the master villain Max Zorin manipulate Halley's Comet so that it came crashing down and devastated Silicon Valley,' he recalls. 'But in the end we decided that was just a little bit *too* fantastic. So we decided that as Silicon Valley lies between the Hayward and San Andreas Faults we would have him create an earthquake that would send the Valley into the Pacific instead!'

Richard says a story like that illustrates the problems he faces with every new Bond script. 'The plots have to be new and contemporary. They just cannot be small in concept – they must be of world-shattering proportions. The villains, too, have got to be ever-more grandiose megalomaniacs, but they must be intriguing and work within the Bond framework. We must also never forget that underlying element of sardonic humour.

'It just gets harder every time,' he adds with a smile, 'I get to the sets sometimes to see how it has all worked out. And I usually manage to be around when they're casting the beautiful girls!'

Richard Maibaum has been in the unique position of being associated with the James bond films for all of their twenty-five years and naturally has his own strong views on the actors who have filled the role.

'Sean Connery was absolutely perfect,' he answers without hesitation when asked for his verdict on the men. 'Apart from being physically a great specimen and good-looking, he had a basic irony about him. Also, he was a much better actor than most people thought. You believed all the physical stuff that Sean did.

'That's not true about Roger Moore, however, but Roger sensed this and played Bond in a different key. He made Bond more sophisticated: he didn't project the innate toughness that Sean had or the irony. Roger had cynicism – and there's a very real difference between irony and cynicism.

'Therefore we had to be more extreme with Roger in his films and find places for him to knock girls around and that sort of thing. We had deliberately to toughen him up.'

Richard prefers not to be drawn on George Lazenby's performance, though, as I mentioned earlier, he has a special fondness for the script of *On Her Majesty's Secret Service* which he rates one of the very best. He has still to form an opinion of the new actor, Timothy Dalton, bearing in mind the very special demands being made upon him by the vitual disappearance of any genuine original Ian Fleming material.

And with this in mind, Richard has been watching the development of Bond in the hands of the novel writers who have taken up his 'career'.

'The thing is, Ian Fleming was unique,' he says with quiet resignation. 'The only other writer who's literary style was anything like his was Scott Fitzgerald. Both had a love of detail which can help you build up something convincing on the screen.'

Views To A Triumph

Directing Bond

The success of the James Bond films undoubtedly owes much to the various directors who have made contributions to the series of pictures over the past twenty-five years, in particular four talented and highly individual men who have all put their mark on the saga and in their different ways helped to develop and expand the continuing story of 007. The men are Terence Young, Guy Hamilton, Lewis Gilbert and John Glen, and they provide a unique insight into the making of a legend.

Terence Young, who directed the first film, *Dr No* in 1962, its successor, *From Russia With love* in 1963 and the fourth in the series, *Thunderball* in 1965, has been called 'the father of James Bond'. There is much about this tall and distinctly elegant man and his character which makes comparison with the secret agent understandable. Writing in the London *Evening News* in June 1975, columnist William Hall echoed what a number of his colleagues had already said when he wrote, 'Young, who is a director, wine connoisseur and gourmet has been hailed as the closest thing in movies to James Bond himself. With a villa on the Riviera, his jet-set habits and the beautiful people who surround him – plus a five per cent share of the Chateau Lascombes vineyard – his lifestyle has inevitably been likened to his most famous screen hero.'

A brief résumé of his career underlines this assessment. Born in Shanghai in 1915, he has directed films in all parts of the world including Africa, the West Indies and even in the Arctic Circle. A natural athlete from his youth, Terence went to Cambridge University where he excelled at rugby, tennis and cricket. Although he obtained a Bachelor of Arts degree, he had already set his sights on a career in the film industry.

An introduction through a friend landed him a temporary job in a film studio during a vacation, and thereafter he devoted every holiday to learning the technique of writing for the screen. He eventually sold several scripts, and had just completed his first major assignment writing *The Night of the Fire* when the Second World War broke out.

Young served in the Guards Armoured Division and was twice wounded during his service with a tank force in Europe. His experiences gave him a profound understanding of men in action, and he put this to good use both when he returned to the business of script-writing and then later, in 1948, when he became a director. That, plus a meeting with the distinguished American playwright, Sherwood Anderson, who taught him the swift, punchy style that he later introduced in the Bond series.

'I learned everything I know in eight or nine days with Sherwood Anderson,' he explains with the kind of candour that is a feature of all his conversations. 'He was the greatest man I ever met. At the time I had a job as assistant to the British film producer, Alexander Korda. Sherwood was preparing a script and Korda sent me as his envoy. I had an idea I was supposed to fix up Sherwood's grammar and things like that. But almost at once, I was *his* pupil.

'I learned from him not to use up time and attention introducing characters and getting them started. He also taught me the immense importance of strong "go-outers" – which is the line you write to take someone off the scene in an unforgettable way. For example a girl says softly, "Oh, you really mean that my mother was never married to you?" – and off she goes. Just like that. You *remember* her.'

By the time Terence Young was asked to direct *Dr No* and in so doing turn James Bond into an international hero, he already had several highly successful action movies behind him, including *They Were Not Divided* (1950), *The Red Beret* (1953) and *No Time To Die* (1957). With the benefit of hindsight, he is in no doubt as to *why* the 007 pictures became so successful.

'It was a question of timing,' he says. 'I think we arrived in not only the right year, but the right week of the right month. We hit the audiences at *precisely* the right moment. I think the first picture was the most perfectly timed film ever made.

'What happened was that Ian Fleming's stories arrived in a dead, grey period. All the realistic "kitchen sink" dramas were weighing everything down. London was sinking under the weight of that deadly kitchen sink! It was getting to the point where people

The first 007 director, Terence Young – whose lifestyle might be likened to that of James Bond himself.

couldn't see anything outside their dismal interiors. Then we came along and they found something different – outside.

'When I made *Dr No* I was conscious of this, so I tried to make a picture in the mood of the vintage period of the Thirties cinema. Those pictures were played straight. We just added more cynicism and went a little further with the sex than was allowed in the earlier days.'

Terence Young pauses and carefully re-examines those crucial months of filming in 1962:

'I suppose I have to say I stumbled on the formula for the films,' he continues. 'I don't think when I took on *Dr No* I had a very clear conception of what I was going to do. The original Ian Fleming story was diabolically childish – like something straight out of a Grade B thriller. All Fleming stories are like that. He embellished them well, gave them a sophisticated veneer, but the story itself is infantile. The only way I thought we could do a Bond film was to heat it up a bit, to give it a sense of humour, to make it as cynical as possible.'

Young clearly remembers the impact this attitude was to have not only on the film – but the author as well.

'We started rather flatly with *Dr No*. Fleming was a bit shy at first, though somewhat arrogant. But he really was a superior sort of chap. At first he was just afraid we had taken the Mickey out of his book.

'Of course we didn't have many of the gadgets to begin with. Sure, I contributed to the gadgetry that came later – and to the decadence. That's the way it happens. You start off fairly simply, and then somebody thinks of something new, and you let it in. Pretty soon, you're hooked. You have got to have bigger gadgets, and better ones.'

Terence Young insists that his intentions for the films are self-evident right from the very start of *Dr No* 'Just look at the introduction to Bond,' he says. 'It's the take-off of the star build-up for every picture you've ever seen. Remember how it begins with that gun-metal cigarette case and lighter. Then the hand turning a card, and you see an arm and shoulder, and the woman on the other side. There are at least ten or fifteen set-ups without seeing Bond – everyone staring in admiration at this man who is winning all the time.

'Finally, the woman asks who she is to make the cheque out to. And you cut to the man for the first time as he lights his cigarette and says, "Bond; James Bond."'

This clever use of cutting is a feature of all three of Terence Young's Bond films, and apart from their impact on the public, he can also claim with every justification to have made a major contribution with them to cinema technique.

'Nobody ever cut pictures the way we did the Bond films,' he says with a gentle smile. '*Dr No* and *From Russia With Love* were an absolute breath of fresh air in the cutting rooms. Even the director David Lean, who's a great friend of mine and one of the best cutters in the business, used to come and watch *From Russia With Love* on the moviola while we were cutting it. He was cutting *Lawrence of Arabia* in the next room at the same time, and often used to say that he'd wished we could swap films. "This is fun," he said to me on one occasion, "this is real cinema!" '

And 'real cinema' *Dr No* and its successors were to prove – with the importance of Terence Young's contribution being acknowledged and underlined with the development of the legend through each passing year. Today he looks back on those early movies with a mixture of satisfaction and pleasure, though mingled with some criticism and regrets.

'I don't want to sound arrogant, but I do believe those early films were the best,' he says. 'Ever since *Thunderball* I think they have been repeating themselves – taking bits from the early movies that were good and using them again and again.

'It's sad really, for the series has ended up caricaturing itself. I mean Bond was already a kind of caricature thanks to his outrageous characteristics – and to parody is asking for trouble! After *Thunderball* the human elements disappeared, too, with gadgets and machines taking the place of people.'

Of the three films he made, Terence Young says *From Russia With Love* is his favourite – and also the best of the whole series.

'I think it shows Bond to the best advantage. The tone was set in *Dr No*, but completed in *From Russia with Love*. I have heard that during the filming of the other pictures, my successors have watched my films to see what they could find in them to cannibalise. Mind you, it was easier for those of us who started the whole thing!'

For all Terence Young's love of spoofing he does confess to a little unease about the violence that was unleashed in the early pictures.

'Nietzsche created a superman, and he never lived it down,' he explains. 'So did we. Bond can be amoral and violent, but we cannot.

'Of course he has a different appeal for women. They'd like to have someone like him pass through their lives once a week. He doesn't take sex too seriously, but that's all right with women. They're realists. They don't mind him brushing them off as much as they'd like to make you think.'

'In effect, he's a mixture of different things. He is not an idiot, but in some respects he appears to be a simpleton. In none of Fleming's novels is he seen going to the theatre or cinema or even reading. Perhaps he may consult a book about birds or some technical works, but his culture stops there. In other ways, of course, Bond is a man of extreme inventiveness and skill when it comes to getting out of trouble. I just think he is a limited man.

'It would be wrong of you to think I held him in contempt, though,' he is quick to continue, 'but he does lack a certain amount of balance. Anyway, we have definitely humanised him in the films for he had no humour in the novels. And how could I possibly dislike a man who has given me such a good livelihood?'

Terence Young also formed an excellent working relationship and close friendship with the first man to play Bond, Sean Connery.

'I actually first met Sean in 1957 when I was making *Action of the Tiger* which starred Van Johnson and Martine Carol,' he recalls. 'He was a rough diamond – but already he had a sort of crude animal force, you know? Like a younger Burt Lancaster or Kirk Douglas. The interesting thing is that Martine Carol, who was a very famous French actress at the time, said, "This boy should be playing the lead instead of Van Johnson. This man has big star quality."

'That movie was a *terrible* film, though,' Terence grimaces, 'very badly directed, very badly acted. But Sean was impressive in it, and when it was over, he came to me and said, in a very strong Scottish accent, "Sir, am I going to be a success?" I said, "Not after this picture, you're not. But," I asked him, "can you swim?" He looked rather blank and said, yes, he could swim – but what had that to do with it? I said, "Well, you'd better keep swimming until I can get you a proper job, and I'll make up for what I did this time." And four years later we came up with *Dr No*.

'Sean knew this was a big chance, and he made no mistake about it. But don't forget he was a damn good actor by then. He'd had stage success in the interim; and it was four or five years since *Action of the Tiger*. He'd matured, he'd become a better actor – and when the chance came, he was ready for it.'

'By the time we did *Thunderball*, Sean *was* James Bond as no one else will ever be. He had gained tremendous self-assurance and really knew how to wear those clothes which

The James Bond image being 'tailor made' on Terence Young's instructions.

are so much a part of the personality.

'I remember at the beginning I had to take him to my own tailor and my shirt-maker in Nassau so that we could create an image that was not his own. And after a time the clothes began to look really well on him. I was also the one who taught Sean to play golf. *That* was a mistake – because now he beats me hollow!'

Terence Young has been asked three times to return to direct other Bond films.

'I did in fact work on the scenario for *Goldfinger*, but left before it was finished. When I went, Sean also wanted to leave as well, though he was, of course, persuaded to stay.

'When I returned to do *Thunderball*, there were apparently plans to hold back *Goldfinger* and release it after *Thunderball*. But I took one look at the picture and said that would be a mistake. Although *Thunderball* was an enormous success, I don't really like it.'

He was also, he says, invited to direct *For Your Eyes Only* in 1981.

'They asked me because they said it was going to be the last in the series. I liked the idea because as I had made the first film I thought, "why not make the last?" It would also have been a marvellous opportunity to go back to the beginnings and do away with all the gadgets. However, when I introduced the condition that if ever Bond reappeared part of the profits should be given to the Red Cross I heard no more!'

Terence Young was most recently approached by Sean Connery to direct his "come back" film, *Never Say Never Again*, in 1983. 'However, Kevin McClory had his doubts about this because the story was too much like *Thunderball*.'

Despite his mixed feelings for the Bond saga, Terence Young remains a committed fan.

'I loved making the pictures and they made it possible for me to make other films which I wanted to do. I learned a lot about technique, too, and it is interesting the way so many people now film "à la Bond" – particularly in thrillers for television.

'Being a director puts you among the favoured people in the world, because we are paid to learn our trade, since you learn with each film you do. But equally you are in danger of becoming repetitive if you don't change direction from time to time. And I couldn't see myself making James Bond films for the rest of my life!'

Reflecting finally on the continuing saga, Terence Young says, 'I think that when Sean Connery went, that was the end of the original Bond. To me Roger Moore is an excellent actor who has carried the part well and not allowed himself to be completely swamped by the gadgets. But I don't think it is Bond he plays – but The Saint. A Saint dressed up as Bond, a lamb disguised as a wolf!'

Guy Hamilton, who was hired by EON to direct the third Bond film *Goldfinger*, in 1964, proved an ideal successor to Terence Young, and went on to make three more pictures in the series, *Diamonds Are Forever* (1971), and then Roger Moore's first two outings as the second Bond in *Live and Let Die* (1973) and *The Man With The Golden Gun* (1974). His major change to the established pattern of the Bond films was to introduce fantasy.

'In the early sixties, Bond was at the top of every school teacher's league for sex, violence and sadism,' Guy Hamilton explains. 'However, with *Goldfinger* we introduced fantasy, and then in *Diamonds Are Forever* we literally took Bond out of this world. The simulated moon sequence and the moon buggy were the farthest out Bond had been.

'You see it is a rule that the Bond films must have a GP [General Performance] rating as we know kids go to see them three and four times. Sex scenes have to be very carefully thought out. The Americans are particularly conscious of this angle. And though the US censorship is amazing, it's the parents who kick up rough. Using comedy can be very successful – but whatever Bond does, he must be perfect. He must be laughed *with* – but not at!'

Hamilton is a tall, laconic man with a mischievous sense of humour and not surprisingly takes a particular delight in making comedy films. His background and career is not unlike that of Terence Young, and in much the same way as his predecessor there have been Bond-like elements in his own life. As he said while working on *Live and Let Die*:

'The James Bond stories present a real challenge to a director. It is, briefly stated, a matter of creating and sustaining an atmosphere of belief in surroundings of utter improbability. To do this, I now realise, a director must have a touch of Bond in his system while bringing him to life on the screen.'

Guy Hamilton was born in September 1922 in Paris, where his British father was a diplomat. He was educated both in the French capital and at Haileybury in England. His father wanted him to become a diplomat, he says, but by the age of thirteen he knew that film making was the world for him.

'In those days the idea of being a film director was rather like wanting to run a brothel,' he says, 'and I was soundly spanked.'

Not deterred, he continued to nurse this ambition until 1939 when he was seventeen. His father then relented slightly and agreed that he could go into the film business for a year before going to Oxford University.

'He agreed primarily because the war was going to be over in six months,' says Guy Hamilton today, 'which shows you how well informed the diplomats were, what with the Maginot Line and everything! So I marched into the Victorine Studios in Nice and said I would like to be a film director. They said, "Start on Monday but you won't get paid." I said that was all right . . .

'The result was I got shoved into the accounts department. I licked wages packets all the week, because if you can count up to ten you can be a French accountant. I thought this was exploitation of child labour!'

However, Guy did come to appreciate that there was far more to a film studio than actors and actresses and directors – it gave him an insight into all the multitude of support jobs which are so essential to the successful making of pictures. When a chance arose to join a crew as a clapper boy, he jumped at it, and then advanced to holding a microphone boom. He was just on the point of being made up to assistant director when the Maginot Line crumbled before the Germans, and Italy entered the war. He and his mother escaped to Britain on an old collier that was also carrying the writer, Somerset Maugham.

Guy Hamilton decided to serve in the Navy and – in the same tradition as the secret agent he was later to put on the screen – became an Officer on a destroyer and served with distinction on runs to Norway, Murmansk and Malta. He also had the useful experience of transporting secret agents to the coasts of Norway and France in motor torpedo boats. Memories of these men were to prove invaluable to him as a film maker.

He was, however, able to further his intended career by making movies of the war for British Paramount News – and in 1945 joined director Carol Reed and thereafter helped in the making of several of his most successful films including *The Fallen Idol* (1948) and *The Third Man* (1949). In 1951 he joined John Huston as his first assistant and worked on the classic, *African Queen* (1951), before being given his own first chance at directing by the same man who had earlier launched Terence Young's career, Alexander Korda. The picture was called *The Ringer* (1952), and in the years which followed, Guy Hamilton proved himself a director of real skill and polish through movies like *An Inspector Calls* (1954), *The Colditz Story* (which he co-wrote in 1955) and *Man in the Middle* (1964).

Though Hamilton had also come to love making comedy films, it was the factual expertise which he found in Ian Fleming's novels which attracted him to Bond. He also shared a passionate interest in golf with Sean Connery and found this an ideal starting point to building up a relationship with the actor who had been so sorry to see Terence Young leave the productions.

'I knew right from the start that the standards had to go higher and higher,' he says in his precise and quiet way, 'because each Bond film has to surpass its predecessor. The films offer escapism so we have to endeavour to capture our audience at the very start, get them involved in the problems, and then take them off on a wild and glorious ride to the finish. The important thing is for everyone – the moviegoers and James Bond himself – to have a lot of fun.'

Guy says that because 007 is larger than life, this makes each film harder to create.

'The audience knows the rules by now,' he explained with a smile. 'They know what is going to happen. The question to be posed is, "How will Bond get out?" The film is part of the audience and it is therefore an exercise in audience participation. Timing is also vital. You must give the audience time to think it out – then they will say, "My God – he's in *real* trouble!" At which point the boy-genius escapes!'

Guy feels it is not difficult to become bored with Bond if changes are not regularly introduced into the plots.

'He's such a genius, isn't he? If he went under a car to put grease on it wearing a boiler suit that would be dull. But if he does it in a white dinner jacket, and then casually flicks away any spot of grease that might have got on it then that is – Bond.

'I don't believe that he should be too much of a genius, though. You must make him human – and believable. He needs to suffer a few indignities along the way. In *Diamonds Are Forever*, for instance, we had him about to lay a girl who is then thrown out of the window. And there was that terrible duo, Bambi and Thumper, who kicked him in the

Guy Hamilton, the second Bond director, who introduced fantasy into the series.

nuts and beat the shit out of him. But the audience were with him. They saw him as human after all.'

Guy Hamilton also appreciated that it was important for Bond to go to evermore exotic locations. Places far beyond the audiences' normal horizons.

'The great danger is to think that there is a formula for Bond,' he says. 'But there isn't. The only ground rule is that the films must be entertaining and the dialogue international. In other words – the scripting is good and dialogue is kept to a minimum. I once remember watching *Diamonds Are Forever* with a Japanese audience and they believed every word!'

Guy has never been anxious to talk about the respective merits of the two actors who appeared before his cameras as Bond. What he *will* say is that Sean Connery was an enormous pleasure to work with and could display a nice light touch as a comedian. Roger Moore he felt had tremendous problems trying to come to terms with the personality Connery had created, and wisely opted for his own calmer and more stylish version of 007.

'They both had to face up to playing someone who is perfect – and that's not easy! I mean, Bond can't even make love in an ordinary bed because everyone else does that. The water bed in *Diamonds Are Forever* was one way of getting round that. We even thought of having him do it in a balloon – but there's got to be a reason for him to be there. People are actually always coming up with marvellous ideas for situations for Bond, but so often there's no way of getting him out!'

Since his last Bond film, *The Man With The Golden Gun*, Guy Hamilton has watched the continuing success of the 'industry' and believes it can continue 'almost indefinitely'.

'You can go on making Bond films providing the people involved don't get fat and lazy. Everyone just has to keep coming up with bigger and better things for him to do, and still more exciting places to go. That was true when I made my last Bond in 1974 and it is every bit as true today. I mean, I can't ever see Bond in Blackpool, can you?' he adds with a final grin.

It was quite evident from Guy Hamilton's comments that a truly versatile and energetic director would be needed to continue the Bond saga into its second decade. In Lewis Gilbert, the producers found precisely the right man whose mastery of the epic set and high speed action were to characterise his three 007 films, Sean Connery's *You Only Live Twice* (1967), and Roger Moore's *The Spy Who Loved Me* (1977) and the spectacular space adventure, *Moonraker* (1979). Lewis remembers his association with Bond as one of almost total enjoyment.

'They were terrific fun to do,' he says, '*You Only Live Twice* was the first of the Bond films to use those huge, enormous sets. In fact, in the three films I did we probably had the biggest sets ever built. That's probably my only claim to fame, because nobody's had those kind of sets since, and they probably won't again, because of the incredible costs.'

Lewis Gilbert, the third director of the series, and the master of the epic set and high speed action.

As Guy Hamilton had hinted, Bond needed ever more exotic locations to hold his audience, and Lewis Gilbert was very well aware of the fact when he took over the helm.

'Of course there are still places for Bond to go,' he said. 'He hasn't been to Africa, for instance. But spectacle is where we are headed.'

Elaborating this statement later, Lewis said, 'We had to branch away from the early pictures. When I did my first Bond film, *You Only Live Twice*, there had already been four. To be the fifth film in the cycle was very difficult because you just couldn't copy the other four. Things were changing all the time and even then it was obvious that the series wouldn't last if we didn't change the format. Variation was needed all the time. So it was decided to go with more spectacle.'

Spectacle was something that the forthright Lewis Gilbert was well equipped to provide from a lifetime in the entertainment business which had begun for him as a child actor. Born in London in March 1920, both his parents and grandparents had a long tradition in vaudeville. Grandfather Gilbert had been a circus performer, and his grandmother had produced fourteen children all of whom went onto the stage under a variety of pseudonyms. Gilbert's parents toured the country as a song and dance act known as 'The Four Kemptons' and little Lewis joined them while still scarcely able to walk. At five years old he made his screen debut in a silent film, and until his middle teens he was rarely away from the stage.

'With my parents being in vaudeville it was quite natural for me to have been a child actor,' he reminisces, 'and during my early teens I was in a number of well-known productions including *Over The Moon* and *Goodbye, Mr Chips*. It was when I was seventeen that I got the break that set me on the road to directing – my real love.'

By the curious twist of fate that can be seen to link all of the first three directors of the Bond films, the man who gave Gilbert his chance was the legendary Alexander Korda.

'I was appearing in *The Divorce of Lady X* which starred Laurence Olivier when Korda noticed me,' Lewis says. 'He said I had promise, but I needed more training in technique and he would send me to RADA for lessons. It was a terrific gesture, but I already knew what I wanted to do. "I don't really want to be an actor," I said, "I would rather direct."

'To my surprise and delight he agreed – and made me third assistant director on Laurence Olivier's next picture at Denham, *Twenty-One Days*, which also co-starred Vivien Leigh. Funnily enough, when I went to dinner with Alex in the Fifties and he asked me how I got started he never realised I was that little boy he picked out on the set!'

For three years, Lewis was able to work as an assistant director for London Films, Associated British and RKO before the war intervened. He enlisted in the RAF, but after a short time his movie talents were noticed and he was attached to the US Air Corps Film Unit to shoot war footage and documentaries.

'That was a marvellous experience,' he says. 'There was no age barrier in the forces and you could make pictures when you were only twenty-two or twenty-three years of age. That hardly ever applied in civilian life because you'd be considered too young.'

The work was also to prove hugely influential on the future direction of his work. 'The scope we had with those wartime films was fantastic. It was just like shooting epics. We had all the time in the world. Money never seemed to be an object. We had everything at our disposal. If we wanted to film a great squadron of bombers taking off, we simply went out and did it. Imagine how much it would cost to film something like *that* today!'

Apart from training and propaganda films, Lewis was an assistant to director William Keighley on the famous film, *Target For Today*, before being invalided out of the service in 1944. He promptly returned to the film industry, and as it gradually returned to full production after the war he achieved his ambition to become a director, making his first feature film, *The Little Ballerina* (which he also wrote) in 1945.

In the years which followed he steadily built up a reputation as a director of great versatility, as comfortable with epics as sensitive love stories, and was renowned as a master of location shooting. Among his most successful pictures were *Reach For The Sky* (1956), *Ferry To Hong Kong* (1959) and the award-winning *Alfie* (1966). Having worked in front of the cameras as well as behind them, he also brought a very special knowledge to the problems engendered in either situation.

'I enjoy shooting action films tremendously,' he was quoted as saying while working on the Bond pictures. 'I suppose they bring out the child in us. For instance, you have a scene in which a guy edges round a street corner, there's a burst of gunfire, the guy staggers out clutching his stomach and falls into the gutter. They're marvellous scenes to shoot; if you ask yourself why you enjoy them you realise its because you remember doing exactly the same things when you were playing as a youngster!'

Turning specifically to the Bond films, he goes on: 'In the pictures characterisations are non-existent. Nobody's worried about what Bond did as a child or how his mother treated him – we don't even know if he had a mother! That's not what the Bond films are about. They're all action and fun,' which is why he packed the films with explosive devices, exotic locales, chase scenes and, of course, lots of lovely girls.

'The Bond films actually don't need as much direction as ordinary films because the characters are so well defined now,' he confesses, 'so with the exception of making up jokes and actually doing the action things, a director doesn't have to discuss who was his father and what was his relationship with him like, and all those aspects that are important in a serious film. As I have said, that is not what they are about.

'James Bond has become a kind of plastic character,' he continues, 'he's not a serious character, or even a serious man engaged by Her Majesty's Government. He seems to spend more money than the Government has in the way he lives! We know that the Secret Service are actually very anonymous and don't go around taking Concordes and private boats and things like that. They're actually poorly paid and lead very humdrum lives!'

For some members of the audience, the star attraction of Gilbert's first film, *You Only Live Twice*, was the awesome hollow volcano built by Ken Adam at a cost of £400,000. This was Blofeld's headquarters, complete with full-scale rocket, a helicopter pad and monorail system: nothing like it had ever been seen in the cinema before.

Such a huge construction presented special problems for Lewis Gilbert when it came to filming, as he remembers very clearly.

'Big sets certainly do present special problems,' he says emphatically. 'And indeed because of my three big Bond films I've probably filmed on more big sets than any other director in the world – in most films you're lucky if you get one big set.

'In *You Only Live Twice* the volcano was the size of a football field, while we had the super tanker in *The Spy Who Loved Me* and the whole of space in *Moonraker* – or so it seemed! The problem they and all the other big sets create is one of time – not time in shooting, but time in film.

'You see if you have someone walking across the set and it takes ten seconds, well, just multiply that by 500 times and you've got a film running for four or five hours! So the cutting has to be nipped along faster. Also, you're tempted with a big set to do more in it. You think to yourself, "My God, this has cost so much money I *must* try to justify it." '

Lewis Gilbert is very quick to pay tribute to Ken Adam for his work on the pictures and his contributions other than just design to them.

'In a Bond film a designer like Ken Adam is very valuable because he will often come up with a design that alters the story of the picture. Sometimes he will say, "Right, I've seen that. Why doesn't he fall down this flight of stairs – or instead why doesn't he fly through that trapdoor?" Ken's designs will sometimes bring a whole new dimension into the story. Yes, there's no doubt large sets are difficult to film in, but they're a definite contribution to a Bond film.'

In his second film, *The Spy Who Loved Me*, Gilbert had another headache to cope with.

'The problem was trying to get the image of Sean Connery out of the picture,' he explains, 'Because if you haven't got Sean, there's no use having his image. We had to do something to make Roger Moore's films quite distinct.

'What Sean did, really, was to make Bond in his own image – because he was not the Bond of the books. Of course he was a very sexy, attractive, macho man – he still is. He also gave Bond a cynical edge. When his Bond shot someone, they were really dead. Roger, on the other hand, is more like the character in the books. He also gets along on a

The spectacular set designed by Ken Adam for *The Spy Who Loved Me* opened by former British Prime Minister Harold Wilson on 12 May 1976, with Roger Moore and Barbara Bach in attendance. It measured 374 feet long, 160 feet wide and 53 feet high, and cost £350,000. The inside representing part of a super tanker and housing three nuclear submarines held more than 1,200,000 gallons of water and cost a further £600,000.

great deal of charm and friendliness. I don't think audiences ever believe Roger *really* kills anyone!'

A surprise success in *The Spy Who Loved Me* was the giant villain Jaws, played by Richard Kiel.

'Actually, he wasn't intended to survive that film,' Lewis says. 'It was put in at the last moment that he would pop out of the water. We had no way of knowing then what the public reaction would be – but it was a real piece of inspiration, for we got mountains of letters from people asking that he be brought back: which of course we did in *Moonraker*.'

Moonraker is a triumph of visual effects, and here Lewis Gilbert is quick to praise the man who masterminded this particular element, Derek Meddings.

'Whenever it came to special effects, Derek Meddings told us how it was going to be done because he's a real expert in that field. For instance most of the effects were done in the camera rather than against travelling mattes or back projection. Take the *Moonraker* scenes in space.

'We had three basic things: the world, the stars and the shuttle flying well above the Earth. So first of all Derek shot the Earth, then he would rewind and shoot the stars. Two months later he would rewind again and do the scenes with the shuttle. My shots would then be put into that, plus adding things like the laser beams. It was very complicated and had to be very carefully drawn on storyboards before we began. I sometimes think the technical people don't get enough credit for their contributions – for the one thing you can't have in a Bond film is *bad* special effects!'

Not only did the visual effects have to be good, says Gilbert, but also the stunts, and he particularly remembers filming the struggle between Bond and Jaws on cable cars high above Rio de Janeiro.

'Two things particularly stick in my mind,' he says. 'First the scene we had of Jaws jumping from one cable car to the other 2,000 feet up. Now that would be difficult on the ground and impossible in the air – even for the best long jumper in the world. And in actual fact the cable cars were thirty feet apart so we had to cheat and move them closer together. It was still hard, though, to make people believe someone could jump even twelve feet. So we secretly used a trampoline. We had Richard making the motion of a jump, then cut to a big stunt man coming down on a trampoline, and finally to Jaws landing on the other side.

'The other scene of Jaws and Bond sliding down on the cable had to be done with models – though not many people realised that at the time because it looked so real. To help create the illusion they were real I cut to Roger sliding down on a real cable. That was done in the open, but not very far off the ground. The insurance people are not keen on losing the star on a very expensive picture like that!'

Looking back on his three 007 pictures, Lewis Gilbert can allow himself a smile of satisfaction at most of the spectacular sequences he introduced and how they successfully moved Bond through the Seventies.

'A Bond film is really only an entertainment,' he summarises, 'and unless you look at it that way, you aren't going to get the maximum out of the film. They aren't series films, so we can change course half-way through, if need be. It can be made funny – or funnier – and even the ending can be changed. They are just not like ordinary films at all.

'I've always been something of a loner and tend to look for commercial projects that will entertain people. There's no greater thrill than to see a huge line round the theatre – I've had my share of Academy Awards, but that is the real reward. It's also enormously rewarding actually to sit in the audience and hear them cheering or clapping. You can only really know if your film has succeeded by the way the audience react. I honestly don't believe many people come out of a cinema after seeing a Bond picture not feeling happy.

'There has never been in the history of films a continuous series of movies that have all been successful like these,' he adds. 'It's an amazing tribute to Cubby Broccoli and all the others involved.'

The most recent director to be charged with sustaining and developing the unique series is John Glen. And like his predecessors he knew changes in the format were necessary – though he had the advantage over all of them of having been associated with the production team ever since the days of *On Her Majesty's Secret Service* made in 1969. The results of his work are now to be seen in the most recent trio of pictures, *For Your Eyes Only* (1981), *Octopussy* (1983) and *A View To A Kill* (1985), and with each the success at the box office has continued undiminished.

OHMSS, as it is generally known, is, of course, the odd-film-out in the series, having starred the 'once only' Bond, George Lazenby, and single-term director, Peter Hunt, the former script editor who made his directing debut with that sixth 007 movie. It was, though, Peter Hunt who brought John into the film and put him in charge of the second unit, filming the dramatic snow sequences in Switzerland.

It was John who filmed the exciting avalanche scenes and the break-neck schuss down the bobsleigh-run. And it was the quality of this work which was later to get him brought back into the series as editor and action unit director on Lewis Gilbert's second and third movies, *The Spy Who Loved Me* and *Moonraker.*

His familiarity with the saga was obviously a great factor in helping him settle on the major change of direction for Bond: a complete reversal of Lewis Gilbert's approach.

'We decided it was time for the films to return to the style of the first Bond pictures when they were straightforward thrillers,' John says in his quietly-spoken and thoughtful way. 'To put the emphasis back on *people* rather than gadgets and sets – though keeping the extravagance, the action and, of course, the "Bond Beauties". It was an idea that immediately appealed to me because *From Russia With Love* has always been a particular favourite of mine.

'It was also a fact that after *Moonraker* we really had gone about as far as Bond could go in that direction. Everyone agreed we'd got all the mileage possible out of the plots about guys trying to blow up the world. The Bond pictures have always prided themselves on being the originators of certain styles in the cinema, and although *Moonraker* appeared before the American shuttle had flown, once the space programme was underway, we knew it was time to get away from the hardware direction.'

John Glen, who was born in London in 1931, has shown an adaptability and inventive mind where films are concerned ever since he entered the industry in 1947. Films were his delight as a schoolboy, and his first job at Shepperton Studios in 1947 introduced him to film cutting. He fondly remembers his work on two of the studio's classics, *The Third Man* and *The Wooden Horse.*

John Glen, the latest in the line of James Bond directors, whose films have been highlighted by their glamour.

After a spell at Nettlefold Studios, he did two years National Service in the RAF, before a stint at Beaconsfield and then completed the circle by returning to Shepperton as a sound editor. Here he took up directing and from documentaries moved into television and worked on a number of high action shows like *Danger Man*, *Man in a Suitcase* and *The Four Just Men*.

The experience gained through this work was to prove invaluable when it came to perfecting the qualities of speed, economy and ability to handle big action adventure which are the prime requisites of any Bond director.

'I guess it is fair to say that Peter Hunt was the one who "discovered" me for Bond,' he says. 'He had seen my work on TV and invited me to go to Switzerland to help on shooting snow scenes for *On Her Majesty's Secret Service*. I met Cubby Broccoli there for the first time and found what a great guy he is. He's the real expert on what makes the Bond films tick.

'I didn't do any more work for them for about eight years until Lewis Gilbert brought me into *The Spy Who Loved Me* to make another snow scene. This was the pre-credits sequence where Bond skis off the top of a cliff and after falling thousands of feet suddenly opens a parachute with a Union Jack on it. Lewis also got me in for *Moonraker* to do another parachuting sequence. That was the opener where Bond is pushed out of a plane and manages to save himself by grabbing one of his attacker's parachutes while they are still in mid-air.'

It was in 1978 when he was working on another action film *The Wild Geese* – which also starred Roger Moore – that John learned all about the free-fall parachuting that made this highly successful manoeuvre possible.

'I knew nothing about free fall when I came to that picture, but when I saw what could be done it made me want to have another go. And so when the *Moonraker* sequence came up, we got in touch with a group of free-fall parachutists called Big Sky. It was amazing the things we were able to do using a camera stuck on top of one of those men's helmets.

'I think the whole sequence took about three weeks, and although the stunt men *did* wear parachutes under their jackets the result was very realistic. Curiously, the easiest bit of all to film was the dangerous-looking moment when Bond puts his hands by his side to swoop down on his enemy. For, in fact, that's how free-fall parachutists normally accelerate and decelerate by putting their hands backwards or forwards!'

It was John Glen's creation of these outstanding cinematic moments that were crucial in making Cubby Broccoli decide to give him his debut as a director on *For Your Eyes Only*. But as he remembers, the decision nearly proved a disaster.

'We had a horrendous first week on a beach in Greece with everything getting stuck in the sand, and I got three days behind,' he recalls, a look of horror still coming over his face. 'To make matters worse it seemed as if all the top men at United Artists were sitting around on the beach watching me fall behind and calculating that by the end of the second week I'd be six days behind – and so on – and at that rate it would take a year to shoot the movie!

'But Cubby was a rock. He told them to count to ten and give me a chance. He's such a good guy and backed me up so strongly that we were all busting a gut to keep the thing on the rails so as not to embarrass him. In the end we rewarded his good faith by keeping within the budget, even though shooting did take a few days longer than originally expected.'

John Glen also enjoyed working with his star, Roger Moore.

'He's the great mainstay of the films,' the director says with evident admiration. 'His humour is different from Sean Connery, though – I don't think anyone would disagree with that. Mind you, we have to be very careful with the Bond humour – it's a very finely balanced thing and you must try and make sure you don't go too far in any particular direction – comedy, slapstick or whatever.

'One works towards a "Bondian" humour rather than, say, the style of humour in the "Carry On" films. But sometimes the line is very thin and you have to pull back from a situation which you think is just too bizarre; but on the other hand, life itself can be bizarre!'

By the time John Glen came to work on *Octopussy* in 1983 he felt far more comfortable in his role as director and is quick to praise his back-up team. His own experience as a second unit director was also invaluable in keeping to a tight schedule.

'It's easy for me to break a schedule down into segments,' he explains. 'It's actually the reverse of editing. Like taking the composite and breaking it back into its parts. Working with a storyboard artist I can estimate in advance the duration of individual shots.'

John is particularly proud of the fact that he brought in his third Bond film, *A View To A Kill*, at $30 million dollars – $5 million below budget. And that's despite sometimes having had as many as six units working simultaneously.

'Take the case of second unit director Arthur Wooster who shot the car chase sequence along the bank of the River Seine from a succession of very early morning shoots lasting no more than two hours,' he says. 'That was the only time the Paris authorities would allow. So Arthur and his team had to be well prepared. They practised everything on an aerodrome outside Paris and then had to set up by the Seine in the dark in order to be ready to start shooting as soon as the light was good enough. You only have to watch the finished picture to see how well they did it.'

John believes that the spectacular sequence featuring the Golden Gate bridge in San Francisco was the most difficult ever attempted.

'It was certainly the hardest Bond film,' he believes, 'the filming with the Golden Gate and Zorin's dirigible was incredibly difficult. Although only about five per cent of the sequence was actually filmed on location, not one shot was wasted. To complete it we had to build a scale model of the bridge on the Pinewood lot together with a model airship forty-feet long!

'It's very hard shooting in big cities nowadays,' he adds. 'I think that over the past twenty-five years audiences have become more involved with films, more demanding. They no longer accept just anything – a film really has to be very authentic and extremely good to be acceptable.'

As a member of the Bond production team who has 'moved up the ranks', John Glen has enjoyed the challenge of his central role of late – and hopes to be part of the team for future films. For like all those who have been associated with Bond both past and present, he is convinced 007 still has many adventures ahead of him – with new directions and still more varied plots very much a part of this.

'I'm sure James Bond is going to be around for a long time yet. He's a very unique character, and I'm sure the public will go on enjoying him as long as we don't cheat them. We spend a lot of money making the pictures – and the money is there on the screen for everyone to see.'

John allows himself a little smile and then adds finally as if he has suddenly thought of a new direction for the indestructible secret agent, 'Of course we could always start *remaking* the films. We could have *Dr Yes*, for example! I hope I'm around for whatever *does* happen for I'd like the chance to make five Bonds. I just don't think I would *ever* get bored with them.'

And that is surely a sentiment that every James Bond fan around the world would echo.

The Wizard Of Bond

Ken Adam – Production Designer

Among the many unique achievements of the James Bond films, few have been more visible than the sets which have formed the backgrounds to the most lavish of the pictures in the series. Writing about this particular element of the movies in July 1979, the *Daily Express* columnist, Judith Simons, expressed the consensus of opinion when she wrote: 'It's not just daring 007 and his glamorous girls who make the James Bond films such satisfying escapism. Equal credit goes to a behind-the-scenes-man, Ken Adam, creator of those amazingly lush settings and incredible gadgetry.'

Ms Simons went on to describe Ken's contributions to what was then the latest of the Bond films, *Moonraker*, including a massive, three-tier space station and the 'Bondola' – a Venetian gondola which converted into a motor launch and hovercraft – and she added, 'These latest products of Adam's imagination are worthy successors to the Aston Martin car in *Goldfinger* which among other tricks fired machine guns from its bumpers and ejected an enemy thirty feet in the air from the passenger seat . . . the giant tanker holding three submarines in *The Spy Who Loved Me* . . . and the SPECTRE headquarters in the base of a volcano in *You Only Live Twice*.'

This opinion was underlined by *Film Comment*, which said in January 1982: 'The Bond films represent something unique in contemporary film – the progression of one production designer's work in an ongoing series of increasingly popular films, growing from a tentative talent into a protean artistry. Like William Cameron Menzies and every other great production designer, Adam is a collaborative craftsman, facing self-doubt, super-budgets, creative battles, and the chance of colossal failure – and emerging remarkably unscathed as he enters his thirty-sixth year in the film business.'

Not for nothing, then, has Ken Adam been called a 'miracle worker' and the man

Ken Adam, the 'Wizard of Bond' and designer of some of the most lavish sets ever seen on film, pictured here with his wife.

'with the knack of making even the most potent Hollywood star subordinate to his sets.'

Ken Adam is a dark, stocky man, intense but very polite and with a slow German accent. He has to date worked on over fifty movies in a career spanning almost forty years. Yet it is his contribution to the Bond series which may well write his name large in film history.

Ken's great skill is to put onto paper the grandiose fantasies which have proved the centrepieces of many of the most successful Bond pictures, and it is fascinating to realise that they are in an almost direct line of descent from the primitive fantasies created in the UFA studios in Berlin, when he was growing up in the Twenties.

He was born Klaus Adam into a prosperous middle class family in Berlin in February 1921. From an early age he demonstrated a talent for art and his wish to become a painter was encouraged by his parents – until the Nazis came to power and the whole Adam family fled to London in 1934. Tragically, soon after their arrival Ken's father died, and his mother opened a boarding house for refugees to raise the money to send her son through a course for architects and civil engineers at the Bartlett School of Architecture.

When the Second World War broke out, Ken was eighteen and he decided this was not the time to try and launch an artistic career. Although he was also too young to be naturalised, he nevertheless joined the Pioneer Corps and in 1941 obtained a transfer to the RAF where he learned to fly.

Ken later had the distinction of becoming the only German to fly with the RAF as a fighter pilot, serving both in England and on the Continent with the 609 WR Squadron. In 1946 he was demobbed, and went straight into the film industry as a draughtsman. Two years later he became an assistant art director and his facility with languages and remarkable ability to visualise scenes for production companies made him much in demand.

Highlights of his early career in the film business were work on *Captain Horatio Hornblower* (1951), *Helen of Troy* (1954) and the Mike Todd extravaganza, *Around the World in Eighty Days* (1956) in which he had a foretaste of the demands to come in the Bond movies when Todd asked him to design a space rocket literally over-night. Although Ken admits he knew nothing about space travel then, he came up with a three-stage rocket which delighted the American showman. For his contribution to *Around the World in Eighty Days*, Ken later received an Oscar.

It was in 1959 that he became a production designer – at the same time abandoning his architectural style of designing, in favour of the felt-tip pen sketches which now flow from his studio in Knightsbridge to become reality in the hand of countless studio riggers, carpenters, plasterers and painters. One of his most memorable early contributions was the vast war room set for Stanley Kubrick's *Dr Strangelove* (1963).

It was in 1963 that Ken became a part of the world of James Bond when he was brought into the project by Cubby Broccoli. The challenge the larger-than-life stories presented to him were irresistible.

'I have always leaned towards the theatrical because I feel very often you can create a reality which is more acceptable to an audience but doesn't copy reality,' he explains, drawing on a cigar. 'I had read some of the Fleming books which I liked so it seemed to me a rather exciting undertaking.

'Mind you, I don't think I've ever had to do so many sketches for films as I have done for the Bond pictures over the years. The thing is I can really let myself go on them because there are no rules. And the story is normally the weakest element. I just don't have to be as disciplined as I am on other pictures.

'Of course the strength of the Bond films lies in a profusion of sensations and maintaining the suspense,' Ken goes on. 'That is what the audience wants in entertainment. Their novelty also lies in the variety of gimmick-gadgets that act as pacemakers for the plot. By gadgets, I don't mean just the SPECTRE boardroom or Goldfinger's electronically-controlled home. I also mean the giant rockets in *You Only Live Twice* that swallowed up the space vehicles and brought them back to the hideout in the crater.'

Though that volcano is arguably the most famous of all Ken's contributions to the Bond saga – it is without doubt the biggest – he talks of other creations with equal pleasure. The thought that he began as a one-man band on *Dr No* with a budget of just £35,000, and six pictures later had sixteen assistants and a budget ten times larger also brings a smile to his face.

'Right from the start of the James Bond pictures, though, I was working on bigger sets than I had ever done before,' says Ken. 'I was also trying for a slightly tongue-in-cheek, slightly ahead-of-contemporary concept, and when it worked it became more important with each succeeding film.

'Looking back, I was pleased with the way *Dr No*'s underground apartment with the fish tank came out. But the set I was keenest on of all was the big tarantula room with the circular opening in the ceiling. I thought that was simple, but ominous.'

Ken remembers that he struck up an immediate rapport with director Terence Young who, he says, identified himself very much with Bond.

'When shooting began in Jamaica, Terence and I had some preliminary discussions about how we visualised the film,' he recalls. 'Because time was short, I went back to the Pinewood Studios and got on with designing the sets while he continued filming. When they came back they were really faced with a *fait accompli* – but I'm glad to say they all liked what I'd done.'

The second film, *Goldfinger*, went more smoothly for Ken because of the lessons learned while making *Dr No* – and it also proved a major trend setter by introducing Bond's famous Aston Martin car and the amazing Fort Knox set.

'I had a great deal of difficulty talking Aston Martin into letting me have one of their cars,' he says, 'but once I got it, the rest came easy. I'm a sports car freak myself, you see, so all the ideas for the gimmickry and gadgets were no problem. They were just my own dreams! But I have to pay tribute to the work John Stears put into the special effects, because it's one thing to come up with ideas but quite another to make them *work*!'

Ken also had some initial problems with the Fort Knox set because the interior of the building is designated highly secret.

'I was allowed to look at Fort Knox from the outside but not inside,' he remembers. 'But I had a pretty good idea what bank vaults looked like so I used that as my starting point. Mind you I knew that gold is never stacked more than two-foot six-inches high because it is a very heavy metal. But I felt the audience would want to see it piled high – which is why we went for the forty foot stack which is quite impractical and unrealistic.

'Still, I have since received letters from people all over the world asking how we were able to shoot in Fort Knox. They believe what they want to believe,' he adds.

The third picture, *Thunderball*, also broke new production ground with its underwater scenes.

'It was a spectacular idea right from the beginning,' Ken says. 'There were the exotic Bahamas locations, the Vulcan bomber, the hydrofoil "Disco Volante" and the bomb carrier. All this – and underwater scenes, too. The only two sets on which I tried to outdo these locations were M's conference room where I used tapestries to conceal the secret charts, and the SPECTRE conference room with its disappearing seat.'

You Only Live Twice which followed introduced the biggest and most complex film interior ever built in Europe. Ken's famous volcano was 400 feet in diameter with a 70 foot diameter sliding roof; it towered 126 feet above the backlot at Pinewood and was spacious enough for a helicopter to fly inside. It cost £350,000 to build and was described by director Lewis Gilbert at the time as 'the most fantastic, most spectacular, most expensive and most ingenious toy Bond has ever been given.'

The volcano which served as the super-modern Japanese headquarters of SPECTRE was both a triumph and a nightmare for Ken, as he vividly remembers.

'When we went to Japan to scout for the locations mentioned in Ian Fleming's story we found they just weren't there. So we had to improvise, and when we came across this volcano on Kyushu we thought, "Wouldn't it be fün to have our villain inside a volcano?" '

Fun it might at first have seemed, but the result was one of the most traumatic periods of Ken's career in films.

'The nightmare part was suddenly realising that I had designed something that had never been done before in films and was bigger than anything that had ever gone before. I kept waking up at night wondering whether or not the whole thing would work.

'You can surround yourself with construction engineers, but that doesn't help. They may be qualified to build the Empire State Building or the London Hilton – buildings which are a part of their trade and which follow construction patterns – but we were building something for which there were *no* terms of reference and which no one had any previous experience of. That can be a little nerve-shattering to realise!

'But on the other hand, the volcano was also a designer's dream. To be given the freedom to plan something so fantastic as that was a challenge no one could resist. And to see your drawings and ideas taking shape and becoming reality in steel and concrete and plaster was the most incredible feeling. It was like seeing your own baby grow and become a superman,' Ken says.

The volcano set at Pinewood for *You Only Live Twice* which Ken Adam designed in 1966 and which remains unsurpassed to this day for sheer size and effect. Photographed with Sean Connery are (left to right) Lois Maxwell (Miss Moneypenny), Akiko Wakabayashi (Aki), Karin Dor (Helga Brandt) and Mie Hama (Kissy Suzuki).

Only the interior was to be filmed, but still the materials required were awesome:

Two hundred miles of tubular steel. Seven hundred tons of structural steel. Half a million tubular couplings. Eight thousand railway sleepers for the working platform and approach road. Two hundred tons of plasterwork. And more than 250,000 square yards of canvas for waterproofing – enough to cover Wembley Stadium football pitch nine times! In all 250 men worked seven days a week for almost three months to build the structure.

Although the volcano was clearly visible from the main London to Oxford road three miles away while it was being built, the operation was cloaked in secrecy despite an average of 200 phone calls a day from the public enquiring as to just *what* was going on.

Ken Adam who knew only too well what was happening, almost worried himself sick.

'All I could think was, "Am I going crazy to take on a million dollar set?" I know I suddenly broke out in eczema all over the place. It was certainly nerve-racking – but ended up working extremely well, I think.'

That is without doubt a most modest assessment of perhaps the most spectacular backdrop ever seen in a film. That and the sixty-six-foot rocket modelled on an Atlas missile, as well as the helicopter which made such a dramatic entrance into Blofeld's vast hideout.

It was perhaps inevitable after such a spectacular set that *On Her Majesty's Secret Service* would be something of an anticlimax, and, although Ken Adam was involved in some of the initial location work, he was quite glad when the picture was postponed for a time, and he switched to designing the film of Ian Fleming's children's story, *Chitty, Chitty, Bang, Bang*.

By the time he came to work on *Diamonds Are Forever*, Ken was aware that any intentions of basing the stories on the original novels had all but disappeared.

'By then everything was larger than life,' he says, 'although still very much tongue-in-cheek. There was still a basis in reality for *some* of the things I did, though, like the penthouse and the moonscape.

'Willard Whyte's penthouse was based on the one used by Howard Hughes. Cubby Broccoli had been a friend of Hughes' and told me all about it. It was, though, more operatic than realistic.

'As far as the moonscape was concerned I tried to bring a mood of absurdist reality into it, especially with the lunar-vehicle chase sequence. I did, though, make full use of the photographs taken by NASA on the moon.'

The next film in the series on which Ken was involved was *The Spy Who Loved Me* – which once again presented him with a not insubstantial problem: that of designing the interior of a supertanker which could swallow three Polaris submarines!

'It boiled down to a logistics problem,' he says in hindsight, 'involving a 1,250 foot tank and a lot of scaling down. I created a cathedral effect within the tanker, then I tried to create various levels which would make interesting compositions and at the same time be functional.

'I had no desire to repeat what had happened on *You Only Live Twice* where I ended up with a workable but ultimately wasteful free-standing set. So I designed the tanker interior in terms of what could remain for use after the film was finished. And that's how the James Bond 007 Stage at Pinewood came into being. Instead of building the set inside an existing stage, none of which were big enough anyway, we built the stage over and around the set.'

Moonraker, the last Bond picture on which Ken worked as production designer, was not only the most expensive at $30 million, but also appropriately the biggest and most complex he had ever worked on. The space station at the centre of the story was also a masterpiece of design.

'I did my research for that at NASA,' Ken recalls, 'looking at the designs they had in mind for the real thing. However, because Stanley Kubrick had already used the wheel idea which they favoured in his film *2001*, I used my imagination and expressed things in my own terms. Something else that bothered me about the wheel shape was that it would be rather like shooting inside a bicycle tyre.'

Ken pauses a moment, obviously reflecting on what proved a crucial decision. 'The space station I finally came up with did, nevertheless, use a NASA idea. This was one composed of a number of cylindrical sections bolted together in space. But as I thought this would look rather boring on screen, I designed the station like a mobile, in a completely irregular form, so that once it began to rotate, the audience got a different composition from each angle.'

The film was also rich in Earth-bound locations, and Ken recalls that there were four separate film units shooting around the world at one particular time.

'We shot combinations of real locations, full-scale mockups, partial mockups and miniatures in a number of sequences and thankfully they all cut together well,' he says. 'We had to shoot most of our interiors in Paris where there was very little stage space. So as soon as we had finished with a set it had to be struck and a new one built in its place. This meant we had to go on location a lot. In fact, on *Moonraker* we shot more location interiors than on any previous Bond.'

It is no surprise to learn that a man of such talent and imagination as Ken Adam is today much in demand in the film business – and despite all his other achievements, his work on the Bond series can be seen to have been a vital element in the amazing success story. From the comparatively modest sets of *Dr No*, through the gigantic volcano of *You Only Live Twice* to the out-of-this-world space station of *Moonraker*, Ken has played a crucial part in giving shape and form to the fantasies which are such an integral part of the world of 007 on the screen.

One of the many NASA pictures that Ken Adam used when designing *Moonraker*, a visualisation of a future space colony such as Hugo Drax built.

James

BOND

A CELEBRATION

The James Bond Files

The men and their assignments

1962–1987

007 FILE ONE:

Sean Connery

'A Man For All Missions'

The path which was to lead Sean Connery to super-stardom as the first cinema Bond can be traced back to a significant period of his life when he was working on a Scottish newspaper.

Today Connery lives far from the noise and grime that was then the newspaper industry in both Scotland and England. He enjoys a life-style which surely Bond himself would appreciate when off-duty, living with his wife, Micheline, in well-protected privacy in a low-roofed Andalucian villa, the Casa Malibu, which is sited on the beach at San Pedro de Alcantara on Spain's beautiful Costa del Sol.

The former fishing village is not far from Puerto Banus, a glittering resort much favoured by the European jet-set, but largely ignored by the Connerys. Marbella is the major town closest to hand, and itself also the epitomy of the Bond lifestyle, while further east is Torremolinos, the sprawling, eyesore tourist resort. Only by driving south past Estapona towards Gibraltar does one find more of the real Spain which attracted Sean Connery here to find a haven from the pressures of the film world almost twenty-five years ago.

Despite the changes that tourism has wrought on this area, the Connery villa has remained carefully unostentatious so as to avoid the unwelcome attention of sightseers or journalists.

It is undoubtedly Connery's haven and he leaves it either to film or else play golf at one or other of the numerous golf courses in the area. For if this remarkable man has one great passion beyond his family it is golf, and, as those who play with him will tell you, he plays it with highly competitive skill.

He is also the consummate professional when it comes to his work – be it acting or organising his business affairs. It is an attitude which has been built up from the experience of a life which began in humble circumstances in Edinburgh and which could so easily have been thrown into the realms of unreality by the phenomenal success of Bond.

Sean, who has piercing brown eyes and deeply tanned features, talks in a quiet, unmistakable Scottish burr and with measured self-depreciation.

'I got into acting because it was very convenient really,' he explains. 'I was in Edinburgh working in the machine room of the *Evening News* when I read about auditions being held for the musical *South Pacific* which was to open in London. So I decided to go down to London, practised for two days, sang a sailor's shanty, and got a part.

'It was a pretty good deal after slaving in that machine room. A few hours work a night for three months at the Drury Lane Theatre in the West End and then a year on tour around Britain. I would be what was then considered relatively well paid, and I also got to see the country. It wasn't until I began touring, though, that I seriously decided to make a career in the theatre.'

The only thing that bothered Sean about taking this step was the fact that he was also good at football and might just have been good enough to make a career in the game. It was another actor in the company who helped him to make the decision.

'I chose acting through the influence of an American actor, Robert Henderson, who was in the *South Pacific* company,' he recalls. 'He said to me, "If you're thinking of being a football player, it's a bit late." I was twenty-three at the time so what he said made sense. "I should seriously consider being an actor, if I were you."

'Well, I thought about what he said and then spent hours discussing the difficulties with him. Once I had made up my mind, he gave me a list of ten books to read in order to get a background in literature. I remember they included two books by Thomas Wolfe, *Look Homeward, Angel* and *You Can't Go Home Again*, Tolstoy's *War and Peace*, *Finnegan's Wake* by James Joyce and Proust's *Remembrance of Things Past* – which I thought would put me in an early grave!'

It was a daunting task for the poorly-educated young man, christened Thomas Connery, who was born in the tough and impoverished tenement area of Fountainbridge, Edinburgh on 25 August 1930.

'My education was pretty much of a wipe-out because of the war,' he says today. 'Mind you, I never thought of myself as underprivileged, because I had nothing to compare my situation with. I started to work when I was nine, delivering milk in the morning before I went to school. It was probably good training, because when I finally left home, I was already formed in terms of taking care of myself. My folks were not too concerned about how I was going to do.'

Though happy memories of his childhood are not plentiful, Sean did love football, reading comics and going to the Saturday morning matinées at the local cinema. His particular favourite was, appropriately, one of the 'super-heroes' of the inter-war years, Flash Gordon, played on the screen by Buster Crabbe.

In 1943, when he was thirteen, young Thomas Connery quit school. 'I had no qualifications at all for any job, and unemployment has always been very high in Scotland anyway, so you take what you can get. I was a milkman, labourer, steel bender, cement mixer, coffin polisher and printer's devil – virtually anything.'

In the hope of better things, he signed on for the Royal Navy when he was seventeen, but apart from developing an ulcer which got him a medical discharge after three years, his only mementoes of life at sea are two now-faded tattoos on his right forearm which read 'Mum and Dad' and 'Scotland Forever'. He had, though, developed a considerable physique and this got him work as a lifeguard as well as a male model.

'I worked as a model at the Edinburgh School of Art for which I used to get a bit over a pound an hour. You posed for forty-five minutes at a time. It wasn't nude; you wore a pouch. It was very arduous – but good discipline.

'I've always been athletic,' he goes on. 'I ran while I was in the Navy, boxed, lifted weights and played soccer. Nowadays I play tennis and golf. Do you know, during the war, my parents thought about evacuating me to Australia. If I'd gone, I might well have led an entirely different life – I'd probably have been a tennis player!'

Sean also put his physique to use when he entered and won the title of 'Mr Scotland' in 1953. He followed this by representing his country in a 'Mr Universe' competition in London, but though he didn't win, it was unconsciously his first step towards acting. The first stirring of any ambition developed when he landed the part of an American serviceman in *South Pacific*. This same show provided the christian name by which he is now internationally-famous.

'I'm not quite sure where it came from,' he says, 'because as a child I was called "Big Tammy". But Sean was the name I decided on when they asked how I wanted to be billed in the show; Thomas Sean Connery. But they said that was too long. I didn't know if I was going to stay as an actor so I dropped the Thomas, and Sean Connery it's stayed ever since.'

It is wrong to think – as many people have done – that when Sean was picked for the role of James Bond in 1962 he was a complete unknown. In fact, he had gone through an arduous apprenticeship in both repertory theatre and on television before breaking into films. He puts the facts – *firmly* – like this:

'I'd been an actor since I was twenty-five – but the image that the press put out was that I just fell into the tuxedo and started mixing vodka martinis. It was nothing like that at all. I'd done television, theatre, a whole slew of things. But it was more dramatic to present me as someone who had just stepped off the street.'

Among this 'slew of things' had been a memorable performance in 1956 as a broken down boxer, Mountain McClintock, in the BBC TV production of *Requiem for a Heavyweight*, and following this a completely different role as Count Vronsky opposite Claire Bloom in another BBC production of the classic *Anna Karenina*. More stage productions and film work in *No Road Back* (1955), *Time Lock* (1956) and *Hell Drivers* (1957) may not have been particularly earth-shattering, but they *did* help him learn the technique of acting as well as appreciating the value of good scripts.

'Initially, it's words that draw me to a project,' he says, reflecting today on those years of hard-won experience. 'The toughest thing, mind you, is to find good dialogue. There are many fine story ideas, all utilised on TV, radio, plays and films. What makes some stand above others is dialogue and characterisation. I've found that when solid characters are conceived in solid situations, their dialogue seems to come easier.'

Unfortunately, however, his next film was to be sadly lacking in either quality – though it was to provide his first meeting with a director who was to prove crucial in his career. He was Terence Young, and in 1957 he directed Sean in *Action of the Tiger* with Van Johnson and Martine Carol.

Four years later – years in which Sean had matured as an actor and widened his range in both Shakespearean productions as well as a six-month engagement in the West End in Jean Giraudoux's critically-acclaimed play, *Judith* – the two men were to be re-united when Sean was selected from a host of names to play James Bond in the first film, *Dr No*. (As a matter of record, when the London *Daily Express* ran a poll among its readers to find a suitable James Bond, his name was high up the list of over 250 actors who were

007 Mark I:
Sean Connery.

Sean Connery makes his first public appearance as James Bond at the première of *Dr No.*

nominated.) Now, the career of Sean Connery was destined to reach heights beyond anything he might have dreamed of.

Sean makes no bones about the fact he approached the project with some trepidation.

'I had only read two of Ian Fleming's books before filming began, and I wasn't all that in sympathy with the character,' he says. 'In fact, I thought to myself that I probably wouldn't even *like* Bond if I met him on the street. I'm referring to the way he was conceived in the novels, of course.'

What helped Sean get to grips with his character was meeting Ian Fleming. Though at first glance the tough-looking Scot with his thick brogue might have seemed an unlikely actor to be cast as the sophisticated agent, the two men took an instant liking to each other and Fleming was happy to encourage the actor he soon came to believe a better choice than his own first choice, David Niven.

'The thing was,' Sean says, 'I found Fleming much more interesting than his writing. He was terrific company, with a tremendous knowledge of the world. He spoke German, French and Russian and told me all about the times when he was working for Reuters in Moscow.

'Anyway, I was able to discuss Bond with him. You know, Fleming was a terrific snob, yet once you got past that, he was really a very nice guy, quite shy, very intelligent, highly original and most curious. But he had a snobbishness that he wrote into Bond in the novels. It was the lack of humour about himself and his situation which I didn't like about the character.'

Yet Connery was desperately keen to make his mark in the film business and threw himself into the part.

'It was the fact that I'm naturally cool by nature that helped with the part,' he says. 'I use as much of myself as possible to make the role work. Basically, in any part I play I begin from the reality of the situation. Then I try to extract humour from the character because, for me, those aspects are much more interesting and revealing – and harder to play – than all the melodramatic stuff. The dramatics take care of themselves if you get it right. The humour you have to find.

'As to Bond the man, one must always use the *humanity* of his character. We have to start with him as a man, because however original the gadgets are, it's the human being, with all his human instincts who has to overcome the obstacles, isn't it?'

There were plenty of obstacles for Sean as he grappled with portraying Bond to Terence Young's satisfaction. In an effort to give *Dr No* added authenticity, he asked to do some of his own stunts. One of these – in which he had to drive a sports car between the tyres of a giant construction crane – nearly brought his career and his life to a very premature end.

'I was damn lucky to get out of that alive,' he says. 'When we were rehearsing the scene I drove at about five or ten miles an hour to see if I could go under the crane. There was about four inches to spare.

'But when we were shooting the scene, I was doing nearer forty to fifty miles an hour. Suddenly I realised the car was bouncing two feet up in the air and my head was sticking out of the car! Amazingly, the last bounce came just before I reached the crane and the car went down and under. If it hadn't I'd have been killed for sure!'

Though Sean can laugh at the memory today, he adds with a wicked smile, 'If I remember correctly, going under the crane was Cubby Broccoli's idea. Maybe he'd paid very heavy insurance beforehand . . !'

Sean also worked hard – though with less danger to life and limb – at Bond's voice and manner.

'Because I'm Scottish I stress certain words differently,' he says. 'The Scots, for instance, say, "How are *you*?" while the English say, "How *are* you?". I hate the poetry-voice; the poetry should speak for itself.

'So because of my word-stress I was able to get away from the original Bond character and take the sting out of those bad-taste jokes that crop up in the films. Terence Young and I worked hard on the character to get in some humour: it certainly isn't in the books I've read.'

The incredible impact which *Dr No* had on audiences is well-known – though it was to prove just a taste of things to come. The Bond bandwagon was soon rolling.

In 1963, Sean was back before the cameras to make *From Russia With Love* – again directed by Terence Young.

'That is my favourite of the films,' he says. 'I liked the story very much and I think it had more credibility than *Goldfinger* and *Thunderball*, which were quite fantastic. And, of course, as the films got bigger and more expensive, they became more involved with hardware than people.'

Once again on *From Russia With Love*, Sean had a narrow escape from disaster.

'It was certainly the most dangerous of the Bond films I made,' he reflects. 'You remember the helicopter chase among the hills of Scotland? Well, we found out a bit too late to do anything about it that the pilot was not very well trained. If you look at the film you'll see how perilously close the helicopter swoops at me. And let me tell you that was not a camera trick – and nor was it planned!'

The third Bond picture, *Goldfinger*, had such a tremendous impact in America, says Sean, that he remembers being told of one New York cinema that ran the film constantly for twenty-four hours a day. Finally, the place had to be closed for half an hour so that the ankle-deep popcorn could be swept up!

'I particularly loved the sequence in which we crushed that Lincoln Continental in a wrecking yard,' he remembers. 'That was a real car, you know, and when we drove into the Miami wrecking yard the foreman just couldn't stand it. It's understandable, I suppose. After all, to own a Lincoln Continental is part of the great American dream. And there we were, squashing one flat. "Goddam sadists!" the man shouted!'

Thunderball again re-united him with Terence Young – and revealed that despite the fact Bond had now made him an internationally-known and very wealthy star, he was growing a little weary with the part.

'My only grumble about the Bond films,' he told film columnist Roderick Mann in February 1965, 'is that they don't tax one as an actor. All one really needs is the constitution of a Rugby player to get through those nineteen weeks of swimming, slugging and necking. It must look easier than it is, though. I keep getting fan letters from Japan praising my "tender gait".'

For the first time, too, Sean indicated that he felt the films would go on whether he wished to play the role or not.

'I'd like to see someone else tackle Bond,' he also told Roderick Mann. 'I must say, though, I think they'd be crazy to do it. There was talk of Richard Burton doing one, and I said he would be out of his mind. It would be like putting his head on the chopping block. Whatever he did he couldn't make the films more successful than they are!'

He also told another columnist, David Levin in May of that same year, 'There is all this talk about my image – whether or not I'm really like Bond and rather rude and aggressive. What am I supposed to do about it? Go around wearing a sign saying that I have played the classics on stage and read a great many books? Really, I am detached from the success of the Bond films. I am concerned about the money I earn from them, naturally, because I think I should get every penny I am entitled to. But when I have finished a film – any film – I think it has a life on its own and there is nothing I can do about it.'

Looking back on that period today, Sean says, 'At the highest time of the Bond films – such as when I was filming *Thunderball* in the Bahamas – I worked fifteen consecutive nights shooting from 6.30 pm until six in the morning. And then I'd go back and try to have some free time to sleep, but the hotel was full of journalists and photographers. I'd get messages, telephone calls. And I was left to handle everything. Soon, I was beginning to think of James Bond as a Frankenstein monster.'

Looking back at those days it is easy to sympathise with Sean. James Bond was suddenly the biggest craze in the world. Apart from all the spin-offs from the films, there were also innumerable rival film and TV secret agents, books and advertising featuring 007, and an almost limitless range of toys and souvenirs.

What Sean later called 'the last straw' came when he made *You Only Live Twice* in 1967.

'The trouble was the films were getting progressively longer to make and that made it more difficult to even consider other work,' he says. 'And it *is* important for any actor to play diverse roles. The final straw was *You Only Live Twice*, the second to last Bond I did. That took six months of my time – and that on top of two or three postponements. I could never give a firm date to anyone else and that meant I missed out on other parts I wanted to do, all because of Bond.'

Despite these problems, Sean agreed to appear in the role a further time for Cubby Brocolli after the ill-fated interlude with George Lazenby.

'I did *Diamonds Are Forever* mainly because it was on my terms. I was involved in the writing, the ideas and where it was going right from the start. There were also heavy penalties built into my contract about delays. Interestingly, it was the first one I ever started and finished on time!' he says.

Interesting, too, is the fact that Sean was able to command the then unheard of fee of $1.25 million plus a percentage for his appearance – and promptly donated his salary to a charity he had set up in Scotland in the hope of easing the conditions in which he had grown up: the Scottish International Educational Trust.

With *Diamonds Are Forever* behind him, the world reluctantly believed it had seen the last of Sean Connery as secret agent 007. Until 1982 and the announcement he was to play the part again in a film most appropriately called *Never Say Never Again*. The background story to this movie in fact went back almost a decade to 1975.

'It was in the January of that year that Kevin McClory came to see me and said he had the rights to do another story on a similar theme to *Thunderball*,' says Sean. 'I told him I wasn't interested in playing Bond again, but when he said would I co-operate in some way because of the experience I'd had, I thought about it and agreed. I was also intrigued because Len Deighton was going to work on the script and I have a lot of respect for him.

'Well, the three of us did a screenplay and put all sorts of exotic events in it. You remember the aircraft that were disappearing over the Bermuda Triangle? We had SPECTRE doing that. There was also this fantastic fleet of planes under the sea – and they were going to be used to attack the financial nerve centre of New York by going through the sewers of New York – which you *can* do – right into Wall Street. There were going to be mechanical sharks in the bay, a take-over of the Statue of Liberty and the main line of troops on Ellis Island. All that sort of thing.'

Sean says there was even talk at one time of trying to involve his successor, Roger Moore, in the picture as Bond, with himself playing 'M'! Another possibility was that Connery himself should be the director of what in Hollywood circles was being described as 'Star Wars Under Water'!

Unfortunately the project – initially to be entitled *James Bond of the Secret Service* and later *Warhead* – ran into legal problems, and Sean bowed out. But somehow 007 would not go away. When the legal entanglements were finally resolved and yet another approach was made to him in 1980, he was in a mellower frame of mind.

'I thought about it for a long time,' he says. 'Then I talked it over with my wife, Micheline. She encouraged me and said, "Why not? What would you risk? After all these

A second 'comeback' for Sean when he drinks to success before filming *Never Say Never Again* with co-star Klaus-Maria Brandauer in September 1982.

years it might be interesting." And the more I thought about it, the more I felt she was right. Micheline also thought up the title. I liked it immediately. It was romantic and pre-empted all the bullshit I knew would be written about my coming back to Bond.'

Right from the start, Sean insisted that the picture was to go for quality rather than expedience, and the story was to take priority over the gadgetry. He wanted outstanding actors alongside him, too, and was delighted with the performances of Klaus Maria Brandauer as Largo, and beautiful co-star Kim Basinger who played Domino.

One scene with Kim reminded him that he had not only come full-circle by re-playing Bond. 'It was the tango I danced with her in the Monte Carlo casino,' he says with a smile. 'It took me right back to my beginnings as a dancer in the chorus line of *South Pacific*!'

Sean was naturally concerned how the public would react to *Never Say Never Again* – not only at his return in the role, but the whole question of the place of secret agents in the Eighties.

He explains what he means by this. 'I've been asked many times what place there can be for a man like James Bond in today's highly computerised world. Yet not so very long ago in London there was a Bulgarian official who was murdered by a jab from the poisoned tip of an umbrella. And there are people gunned down on the steps of the Dorchester Hotel. With all this happening in real life, you can't tell me there's no place for a man like Bond.'

He also felt there was no reason against his playing Bond as an older man. He believed the younger generation who had not seen his earlier Bonds might well be fascinated.

'I'm over fifty now,' he says, 'and there's nothing particularly daring about playing your age on screen. I've done it before in *Robin and Marian*, and *Murder on the Orient Express*. It's absurd to cling to what you were in your youth. But,' and his face breaks into a wide grin, 'I suppose Bond will follow me wherever I go!'

Sean is never very keen to talk about his two successors as Bond, but has been demonstrably fair to both without the slightest hint of jealousy.

'Poor George Lazenby never really had a chance,' he says, 'he just didn't have the experience for the part – even though I believe the director Peter Hunt was quoted as saying that he had taught Lazenby all that I knew! In three months he couldn't do a good job because you have to have technique and get the character right.

'In the case of Roger Moore and I there have been a lot of unfair comparisons. I don't want to make them. Roger plays Bond his way and I played him my way. One newspaper ran a comparison and was particularly flattering to me and unjust to Roger. I don't appreciate that kind of flattery.'

And he adds, 'I met Roger in London while I was making *Never Say Never Again* and suggested we squash the rumours and speculation about rivalry by posing together and issuing a statement. He naturally agreed. After all we're friends. In a sense, though, it's a no-win situation, because we both lose because we're being set up against each other.'

Sean is convinced that Bond is now bigger than any single actor and is truly one of the enduring figures of our times – as the character's success over the past quarter of a century has shown. As the man who pioneered 007 on the big screen, does he, finally, have any idea just *why* he should have proved so popular?

Sean Connery's answer in that unmistakable brogue is spoken with the conviction that has been the hallmark of his own life.

'It is the basic theme of the stories,' he says, 'how one person wins through, however high the odds against him and no matter whether they are mechanical, geographical, sexual or whatever. That one person – James Bond – has to resolve the problem. And in a much smaller way that is what we all strive for in our everyday lives, isn't it?'

007 FILE TWO:

George Lazenby

'The Trials of Bondage'

Like Sean Connery, the man who was the second James Bond today lives quietly in a beautiful though far from ostentatious home overlooking the rolling, ocre-blue Pacific Ocean at Santa Monica, California. The sea, it might be said, offers the peace of mind any man who enters the frenetic and dangerous world of 007 would find essential to escape to. And this is certainly true in the case of George Lazenby, the Australian actor asked to follow in Connery's footsteps, and to whom history has been less than generous. In fact, almost totally hostile.

Though it is beyond dispute that the newspaper critics were universally damning of Lazenby as Bond, with the passage of time an ever-increasing number of fans and even several critics have revised their opinions – perhaps too hastily made in a general mood of hostility – and there is today a solid body of opinion that has advocated the six-foot two-inch, strikingly handsome man being recalled for a further tour of duty as 007. Should such a call be made, there is only one major problem: George Lazenby's aversion to the idea of ever playing Bond again.

When one examines the facts of his single excursion into the world of the secret agent in *On Her Majesty's Secret Service* in 1969, it is not hard to understand why.

'I cannot deny that I had a lot of problems making the Bond film,' he says today in a voice which still maintains a hint of his Australian birth, 'and that I created some of the difficulties myself. But the truth is I didn't know what I was doing and nobody told me. I was just plucked from the world of advertising and thrust into the role of a superstar. Overnight I became what they call a Class A celebrity. I felt very insecure.'

There is no excess of self pity in George's voice when he talks, and indeed he has learned to face up to hard knocks all his life.

'The curious thing was that a woman astrologer I consulted in Wimbledon before I even got the part told me almost word for word what was going to happen,' he says, the memory momentarily darkening his chocolate-brown eyes. 'She told me that I would be famous, that I would run into problems, that I would be ill, and that I would have a two year struggle to get back into the profession in any kind of way. Everything she predicted came true.'

Today, with the security of his marriage to his American wife Chrissie, and their children Melanie, thirteen, and Zachery, twelve, George can look back on his life – and more particularly – his period of 'Bondage' with dispassion.

George Lazenby was born on 4 June 1939 in Goulburn, New South Wales, and showed a thirst for adventure as a youngster by restlessly exploring the wild Australian bush around his home which had once been the haunt of the outlaw bushranger, Ned Kelly. George's father was a keen hunter and by the time the boy was thirteen he used to accompany him on hunting expeditions. Notwithstanding this, his early ambition was to be a motor mechanic.

'My dad was a railway man and although we didn't ever have much money, I always knew that I was not cut out to be poor,' he says. 'Hell, by the time I was twenty-two I was driving a Mercedes and earning £200 a week as a car salesman in Canberra. I reorganised the whole method of selling and increased the profits by thirty per cent, so they made me manager over all the guys who had been there twenty years.

'I used to go up to Sydney for the weekend and blow the lot. I'd hire the best suite in the best hotel and just have a spree. One weekend, I remember, I spent £700!'

If such an attitude of mind showed a certain irresponsible streak, it also revealed a driving ambition to get on in life, and in 1964 he decided to come to England to further his career.

'But things weren't so easy when I got to England,' he says. 'I went through all my money on the boat coming over and ended up in Earl's Court in a room that wasn't even a bed sitting room. It had a bed in it, sure, but you certainly couldn't sit there as well.

'A job was a necessity so I got into a cab and asked to be taken to the heart of the car sales yards in London. That bothered the driver a bit, but he took me to Finchley Road and after a bit of chat I got a job at £10 a week with an extra £3 for each car I sold. Once I'd got a bit of experience I moved on to Mercedes Benz where I got £30 a week and £30 a car.'

Among the numerous secondhand car dealers who are still to be found along Finchley Road there are still those with memories of the brash young Aussie who was destined to become James Bond. But not because of his debonair good looks – for at that time he was, by his own admission, something of a slob, overweight, with long hair and an appalling taste in clothes. The very antithesis of 007, in fact.

'Then one winter I went on this skiing holiday with a girl I was keen on,' he recalls, 'and I decided to get cleaned up for it. I had my hair cut properly, bought a few decent clothes and the mountains did the rest. When I came back to London I had a tan and I'd lost my gut.

'Everything just seemed to happen from there on, although I'd never thought of myself as good-looking. The girls started to notice me and then this fashion photographer named Chard Jenkins to whom I tried to sell a Mercedes said I should become a male model!'

George wrinkles his lazy, almost hypnotic eyes at the memory of those days. 'To begin with I thought modelling was a lot of nonsense, and all it would do would be to

007 Mark II:
George Lazenby.

George Lazenby and his co-star in *On Her Majesty's Secret Service*, Diana Rigg. Their relationship was often stormy.

give the four boys I shared a flat with a bit of a laugh. But that was until the fees started to come in from jobs, and I realised it paid a lot better than selling cars.'

Success, in fact, came quickly and soon he was much in demand advertising petrol, cigarettes, and cosmetics – all of these culminating in a television commercial for Fry's chocolates in which he starred as a benevolent provider of sweeties for children called 'Big Fry'. Overnight, it made him a household name and pushed his earnings to over £25,000 a year.

'After the "Big Fry" commercials every photographer in town wanted me and I never had a spare moment,' he says. 'Finding even the time for a haircut was a problem. But I happened to be getting one in Mayfair one day and who should be sitting in the next chair but Cubby Broccoli. I didn't know that at the time, of course – but that was where he first saw me and thought of me as a possible replacement for Sean Connery.

'When my agent rang to say they wanted me to test for Bond I was absolutely stunned,' he recalls. 'I'd never acted before and didn't think I stood a chance. But I played a fight scene and made love with a girl and they told me I'd got the part.

'I went to see the director, Peter Hunt, and he took one look at me and said, "You're the new James Bond – but we will have to convince them in America. Oh, by the way, what's your name?"'

In fact George had to put in four strenuous months of testing before the Americans were convinced he could play 007. He also had to oppose vigorously a plan to change his name.

'I told them no,' he says. 'That's who I am and that's who I'm going to continue to be. And it's the same with my accent. That stays, too.'

Making the $6 million dollar *On Her Majesty's Secret Service* was a daunting task for

George. For not only was he following in a very successful actor's footsteps, but Connery had brought a wealth of stage, television and film experience to the role. It was to prove far more daunting, in fact, than he had ever imagined.

Today, George Lazenby still walks with the same kind of catlike tread that he brought to his Bond, but there is a worldly-wise look in those brown eyes which was not there then.

'You must understand one thing,' he says, again measuring his words. 'Before the Bond film I'd never met an actor in my life. No, that's not true: I did meet Jane Fonda once. I was a model – and a male model isn't exactly society's idea of the perfect dinner companion; you're not invited anywhere. Then, overnight, people are told I'm to be treated like a superstar. So of course it went to my head and I became hard to handle. My brain was reeling.'

Before work began on the film, George read some of the Fleming books, viewed the Connery movies, and gave some thought as to how he was going to play the part. He knew right from the start what his major problem would be.

'Audiences need a lot of imagination to be able to switch from one person to another after the other chap has put in five films,' he says. 'In fact it takes a few films before people can put the *other fellow* to the back of their minds. I don't think now it would have mattered who they had put in *On Her Majesty's Secret Service* – he would have had the same problem. Especially if he hadn't acted before!

'So with this in mind I just set out to do the best I could. Though I had never met him, I admired Sean Connery and because I wasn't then an actor I thought my best chance would be to try to play Bond as he had done. And despite what they say, I don't think I was that bad in the part.'

George pauses a moment and then goes on, 'One thing I did want to be was loose, and play the character loose. But right off Peter Hunt kept telling me to walk like Prince Philip and talk with more reserve. I mean that wasn't acting. That was *his* idea of James Bond!'

As the frustration built up in George Lazenby, he says he let off steam in other ways.

'The trouble was I lived Bond *out* of the studios as well as in,' he reflects. 'I had to have a Rolls Royce to go around in and women just threw themselves at me if I stepped into a night club. I couldn't count the parade that passed through my bedroom. I became hot-headed, greedy and big-headed.'

Perhaps most damagingly of all, George fell out with his co-star, Diana Rigg, and producer Cubby Broccoli.

'I'm sorry that things between us worked out the way they did,' George says today. 'We all make mistakes and I made mine. But I don't recall the petty grievances or paranoid statements Diana accused me of. What may have been petty to her was much bigger to me because I was only a beginner. And as for paranoid statements they were all part of somebody trying desperately to co-operate and become a good actor.'

Diana Rigg, for her part, has since preferred to remain silent on the whole subject of the film. George, however, retains an affection for his co-star and an admiration for her talent as an actress.

'I remember her parting words on the film set: "One day we will sit down and talk about it all." What she meant was when I had grown up. After that I believe I did,' he says.

George is equally honest about the decline in his own career which followed all the problems making the Bond film – though it was, of course, a great success at the box office.

'Although I had been offered a contract for another film, I refused to sign it,' George says. 'I thought I knew better: I thought I could make my name with the film and then be taken up by other producers. And that way I wouldn't get locked into the Bond image. Well, it was a crazy decision. Things didn't work out that way, and what made it worse was that people thought I'd been kicked out and were reluctant to use me. There was a vendetta against me. In some places, there still is.'

George was so upset by this turn of events after the heady success of getting the Bond role that he left London and went to Spain.

'There I hit the bottle hard,' he says in a voice grown quiet, 'and one night I just blacked out. I came round to a circle of frightened faces. They told me I had stopped breathing for about ten minutes. They thought I was dead. It was absolutely terrifying. When I recovered, I found that the experience had changed my whole life.'

It has not been easy, though, for George to find work as an actor. He has appeared in a handful of films including the much-praised but never widely released *Universal Soldier* which he made in 1971. Dilys Powell, for instance, called it 'a notable performance', but George remembers it more fondly for being where he met Chrissie Townson, now his wife. He has also appeared in a number of TV productions in both Britain and America, including one of BBC's prestigious 'Plays for Today', *The Operation* in 1973 in which he played a high-powered real estate tycoon.

It is a little known fact that he also very briefly reprised the role of 007 in March 1983. 'It was for a spoof Hollywood television film *The Return of the Man from UNCLE*,' he explains, 'but just a cameo part. But it does prove what they say – it's hard to get away from that man Bond!'

George also works occasionally in American TV commercials, and of late has developed a quite separate business in California buying, renovating and selling old houses. He finds time, too, for his old love of mechanical things and likes to take part in motorcycle races in what he calls 'the old timers' class.

Now forty-eight, he still yearns for a return to big time movies. 'I haven't worked for any of the major studios since Bond,' he says. 'I'd love to win a big acting role again. But who's going to give me a shot?'

Whether George gets his 'second chance' or not, there are those who have reassessed his performance as 007 and found it far from deserving some of the caustic comments that were poured upon it. And they are quick to refer to the verdict of that doyen of film critics, Alexander Walker, who wrote in December 1969, 'The truth is that George Lazenby is almost as good a James Bond as the man referred to in his film as 'the other fellow'. Lazenby's voice is more sauve than sexy-sinister and he could pass for the other fellow's twin on the shady side of the casino. Bond is now definitely all set for the Seventies.'

Such words may have a poignant ring about them for the man in his beachside home in Santa Monica, but his decision to stay clear of the world of Bond is, I believe, final. He may have committed one of the most extraordinary acts of self-destruction in movie history – as one newspaper called his refusal to sign that Bond contract – but he is today a changed and likeable man.

'In some ways maybe my life is better than either Sean Connery's or Roger Moore's,' he says with a philosophical smile. 'They are Bond for ever. I was the no-go Bond. Now I can play any character I choose. I'm just hoping that character will come along.'

007 FILE THREE:

Roger Moore

'From Saint To Winner'

The change in Roger Moore's life as a result of playing Bond is every bit as dramatic as those of his predecessor's – though far closer to Connery than Lazenby. He lives in Switzerland in a nine-bedroom villa overlooking one of the most fashionable gathering places in the world, Gstaad. It is as much Roger's haven of privacy as Connery's villa in Spain, and has the added attractions of a swimming pool and trout farm. In the winter the nearby mountain slopes provide some of the finest skiing in Europe, and the Moores are great entertainers of their many friends in the show business world.

Roger has lived in this popular resort since 1978 with his wife, Luisa, and their almost grown-up family of Deborah, in her early twenties, Geoffrey, nineteen, and young Christian, thirteen. It was Geoffrey, in fact, who finally convinced Roger that he should play the role of James Bond.

'When the part was offered to me I asked my son who he preferred: James Bond or me,' Roger recalls. 'Geoffrey said, "Don't be silly, Daddy. James Bond, of course." So how could I turn it down after that?'

In fact, Roger could well have been the *first* James Bond, for there is little doubt that it was a close-run thing between him and his long-time friend, Sean Connery; it was only because he was fully booked with work that he could not finally be considered.

'It's not true that I was approached to play Bond before Sean,' he says, raising those unmistakable and expressive eyebrows. 'I was on the short-list with Connery, Patrick McGoohan and I think Richard Johnson. But I was already committed to *The Saint* anyway, so there was no way I could have done it.

'I think it's unfair to speculate what the films might have been like if I'd taken the role then. Sean's pictures were very successful so you can't say what would have happened. I think he was absolutely right for the part at that time. It's never been my intention to copy him.'

When Roger first took on the role and was asked what would be different about his 007 from that of Sean Connery, he would answer with a wicked smile: 'White teeth!' Today, he is less flippant:

'I try to take a sardonic approach to my portrayal of Bond,' he says, 'as though I'm sharing a joke with the audience.'

Unlike Sean who once complained of being 'bottled in Bond', Roger says he has suffered no personal or professional identity crisis by associating himself with such a popular role for so long.

'I don't see what there is to worry about,' he says, 'I've been typecast for most of my life and I'm still busily employed on the verge of being sixty . . .'

Roger George Moore was born on 14 October 1927, the son of George Alfred Moore, a police constable at Bow Street who acted as a draughtsman preparing the plans of crime and accident investigations, and Lily, the daughter of an Army Sergeant Major. The couple, both in their early twenties, lived in a modestly comfortable apartment in Streatham, and Roger had none of Sean Connery's struggle to escape from a poor background. He has, though, had to work hard to acquire the elegant manner and impeccable accent that has made him such a distinctive James Bond.

Roger was an only child, and spent a happy and contented childhood being educated first at Hackford Road Elementary School and then Battersea Grammar school. His father had formerly been a physical training instructor, and taught Roger to excel at swimming.

When the war interrupted his schooling in 1939, Roger was evacuated and spent periods of time in Chester, Amersham and Worthing. During this time he began to show a real aptitude for art, and when he left school at fifteen in 1943 he got a job as an animator making films for the war effort. It was Roger's first introduction to the world of films and was to prove more influential on his life than he could ever have imagined.

By a curious twist of fate, a visitor to the studios one day was a certain Lieutenant Colonel David Niven, already a well-known actor and then involved in making propaganda pictures. It was an unlikely first meeting for the two men – both of whom would one day star in films together as well as portray very different versions of James Bond.

Roger's time at the cartoon studios was short-lived, however, for he made an error over a film and was sacked. Perhaps it was a fortuitous error, for Roger is rather inclined to feel that if he had not lost his job then, he might well have made a career as an animator rather than becoming an actor.

As it was, a friend suggested the tall (six-foot two-inch) blond-haired, broad-shouldered young man with his clean-cut features and light blue eyes should perhaps try for work as a film extra. After successfully landing the part of a spear-carrying soldier in *Caesar and Cleopatra* (1944), Roger was recommended to take a three-year course at RADA by the film's co-director, Brian Hurst.

During his three terms at the Academy he also got in some more experience as an extra and began to develop both the accent and pleasant manners which were to become his hallmark. When he did his National Service and was posted into the Combined Services Entertainment Section, he earned the nick-name 'The Duchess' for his immaculate appearance.

While at RADA, Roger had fallen in love with an attractive blonde named Lucy

007 Mark III:
Roger Moore
and Tanya Roberts.

Woodard, an ice skater who appeared professionally under the name of Doorn van Steyn. In 1946, when he was just nineteen, the couple married. Their time together, however, was beset by professional and financial difficulties as they both struggled to establish their careers, and the marriage soon foundered.

Roger only managed to secure a few minor roles as an actor, and had to supplement his income with jobs as a waiter, dishwasher, street salesman and a male model. In this capacity he was featured in a number of knitting books, modelling jerseys and sweaters. The debonair good looks are there for all to see, though, in the rare copies of these leaflets which still exist and are much coveted by fans.

In 1952, Roger met one of Britain's best-known popular singers Dorothy Squires and the couple were soon in love. A year later his first marriage was dissolved.

Roger Moore's fortunes improved somewhat when he started travelling to America with Dorothy Squires, and there his charm and good looks won him roles both on the stage and screen. He appeared in *The Last Time I Saw Paris* (1954) with Van Johnson and Elizabeth Taylor; *Interrupted Melody* (1955) with Eleanor Parker; and then later that same year found himself on a set with the Army gent he had first met in the London animation studio, David Niven. He played a swashbuckling soldier in a picture called *The King's Thief*.

This historical drama proved a foretaste of his first television series, *Ivanhoe*, which he returned to Britain to make in 1956. This 39-episode series proved immensely popular with younger viewers in both Britain and America, but has left something of a bitter taste in Roger's mouth. Frankly, he prefers not to talk about it.

From a knight of old, Roger was next cast as a cowboy and the year 1961 saw him making the prophetically titled western, *Gold of the Seven Saints*. From this he went into two more television series, playing a slippery fur trapper in *The Alaskans* and then Beau Maverick in the peak-time favourite *Maverick* – perhaps the first of his screen appearances to give him the chance to show a little of his skill at tongue-in-cheek humour.

That same year also took him to Rome to make a less-than-promising picture called *The Rape of the Sabines*. But though the film did little to further his career, he met and fell in love with another member of the cast, a dark-haired and strikingly attractive Italian girl, Luisa Mattioli. 'As awful as it may sound, I think I fell in love with her at first sight,' Roger says today.

It was to prove a turning point in his life, for after what proved a rather painful and litigious divorce from Dorothy Squires, he and Luisa have created a happy and sound marriage.

In May 1962 Roger's career finally took off when he was cast to play the title role in ATV's production of *The Saint* based on Leslie Charteris' famous books about a debonair crime fighter, Simon Templar. It was to take up six years of his life, and make him wealthy and internationally famous.

Roger talks about this turning point in his life with understandable affection.

'Although I had said I never wanted to make another television series again after *Maverick*, I couldn't resist the chance to play *The Saint*, he says. 'I'd read the books when I was a youngster and they'd left such an impression on me that I even tried to buy the rights myself after doing *Ivanhoe*. But Leslie Charteris wouldn't sell then.

'I remember when Lew Grade offered me the part. He said, "I think we should grey him up a bit – he looks too young." But in fact I've never greyed up for anything! Right from the start, though, we set out to try and make *The Saint* look very attractive and glossy, with a certain panache. Obviously we were successful because the show ran for such a long time. I think we did it very well.'

Roger Moore as the 'Saint' in the TV series that made him a household name before he became 007. He is seen here in an episode called *Death Penalty* with Wanda Ventham.

Roger particularly enjoyed playing Simon Templar for the opportunity it gave him to really develop his natural talent for humour and the sort of controlled and seemingly effortless action which was to be perfected when he came to play the third James Bond in 1973.

As an actor, Roger has always tended to underestimate his ability and is much given to saying that he is 'basically just a lump of meat on the screen' – but this cannot detract from the fact that aided by *The Saint* and now James Bond he has become one of the best known – and best paid – British film stars in the world.

Still, though, he likes to tease interviewers with statements such as, 'When I was doing *The Saint* I had two expressions; as Bond I've managed to work up to four.'

However, when he can be encouraged to talk more deeply about his films as 007 – and with seven appearances he has now done one more than Connery – the real nature of his character and the work he puts into his acting becomes evident. He is, in fact, a shrewder and more thoughtful man than his screen roles might suggest.

'I have to be honest and say that Ian Fleming's books have never been my favourite reading,' he says. 'I looked through a few of them when I was first given the role – but there's nothing about Bond in them.

'Sean had, of course, established a number of characteristics in the role, and I wanted to change some of these to make the part my own. For instance, his Bond ordered vodka martinis, while mine never does – although over the years other characters have begun ordering them for me! I have also tried to put more accent on humour and less on sex. I want to get fun out of the part and let the audience know that if they want to scream hysterically, they can.'

Roger says his attitude to Bond is that he is a completely unreal person.

He explains, 'I mean here you have this secret agent who's recognised by every barman in the world and they know that he takes his drinks shaken and not stirred. It's crazy. What sort of secret agent is that? So you know that it is a spoof already before you start.

'I don't like to play him as a true blue hero,' he continues. 'There's always a moment of doubt in Bond's mind. I mean, if I save the girl, I may get killed doing it. So I always let that go through my mind and then say, "Oh, to hell with it. I've read the script. I know I'm going to live!" '

Interestingly, Roger – just like Sean Connery before him – also had a very close encounter with death when making his first picture in the series, *Live and Let Die*, which commenced filming in America in October 1972. He can smile about the experience now, but it was obviously terrifying then.

'It happened in New York when we were filming a car chase along FDR Drive,' he remembers. 'About three miles had been closed off, and all the other drivers were stunt men or women and were strapped in their cars. I was in the back seat of my car, not strapped in.

'My driver was hit by a bullet, but his seat belt kept him upright and our car began hitting one car after another with me in the back trying to grab the wheel. The dead man still had his foot on the accelerator and we were bouncing off cars right and left.

'Now, they shot this scene six times and my backside was twitching at an alarming rate by the time we'd finished. If we had hit anything that would have made us stop my head would have gone clean through the window. I would have come back a lovely subject for Jimmy Saville's "clunk-click" safety commercials!'

The entire schedule making *Live and Let Die* proved hectic for the new 007.

'You know I didn't say a word of dialogue for the first three weeks of shooting,' he says; 'it was all action. I had a nerve-racking time going fifty foot through the air in a speedboat and then I had to walk over a row of crocodiles. It's difficult to train those creatures, in fact, and all the trainer could do was to get them into a shady spot and put their food there. Then while they were feeding on chicken I walked over the top!'

The second Bond film, *The Man With The Golden Gun*, established Roger Moore as an international star as well as a completely individual and new-look secret agent.

'We were not making films like Sam Peckinpah,' says Roger, 'there is very little blood in the Bonds and we don't lay the violence on with a trowel. But you've got to remember that there are some countries where they even ban the Tom and Jerry cartoons for their violence. We fill the pictures up with a lot of jokes – that's what makes the violence acceptable. Cubby Broccoli once called it sadism for the family.'

Roger enjoyed this film because it reunited him with Christopher Lee playing the villain of the title. The two men had previously shared a dressing room when both had small parts in the Jean Kent film *Trottie True* (1949) about romance in a music hall. Roger also had two beautiful co-stars in Maud Adams and Britt Ekland – who both later reported being charmed by his intelligence and dry wit. Maud Adams, in fact, reappeared with Roger in the later film *Octopussy*.

Philosophising on the sex scenes in the Bond films, Roger has this to say:

'Actually, there has always been less sex in Bond than people think there is. The notion of sexuality in the films really stems from Ursula Andress coming out of the water in *Dr No* wearing a bikini which by today's standards would be a golfing outfit. Sex in Bond is suggested, but never suggestive.'

Playing what scenes there *are* is not necessarily all that much fun despite making them with some of the most beautiful women in the world, as Roger also reveals.

'They always seem to pick the coldest day of the year,' he smiles, 'and usually a Monday morning when the studio's been shut all weekend, and the heat's been turned off, so you're freezing cold. And you've always got sixty to a hundred people standing around – including electricians up on the rails looking down. 'There's very little romance about it. If you can get really excited about doing *that*, you should be starring in blue movies!'

The Spy Who Loved Me, the third in Roger's series, remains his favourite to this day.

'I can't really say why,' he says, gazing reflectively into the distance. 'I think perhaps we reached the right level of humour. Certainly all the right elements came together.'

By the time this film was made in 1977 Roger was clearly comfortable in the role of Bond.

'I found him to be a curiously unemotional man,' he says with hindsight. 'But then emotion isn't called for in an action adventure film. I did have to use a little in *The Spy Who Loved Me* because of the reference to Bond's wife who died.

'It's a major mistake for an actress to marry Bond because she knows she must get killed off quickly. In the same way a girl must never go to bed with Bond in the first two reels because she knows she'll be dead before very much longer. That's the little piece of justice being meted out by Cubby Broccoli. The heroine who gets Bond always has to wait until the end before she can safely get him between the sheets.

'It's that kind of predictability that the audiences like about the Bond films,' he adds. 'It's exactly the same as a child wanting to hear a bedtime story, and if you change a word or leave out a few lines because you think they've fallen asleep – or you're bored and want to get off to bed yourself – then look out! We all want the comfort of sameness.'

Roger also enjoyed making *The Spy Who Loved Me* because it was 'filled with fun, glamorous lunacy and incredibly ingenious spectacles'. These special effects were, though, to prove as nothing in comparison with the next picture, *Moonraker*, which catapulted both him and 007 into space.

The seven months of 1978 it took to shoot the picture in locations as far apart as Pinewood, Paris, Venice, Rio de Janeiro and Guatemala were physically draining on Roger, and he still recalls today the exhaustion he felt after completing the costly $30 million epic.

'All the Bond films are intensely physical,' he says, 'but there's never been one like *Moonraker*. Now you never have to go mad learning the script, but once the action begins . . .

'In twenty-eight weeks working I only had three days off. I really don't want to find myself ever again up the Amazon climbing up and down waterfalls or struggling through the jungle for five kilometres – and on foot – to get to the next location. If you worked a horse that hard, you'd be prosecuted.'

Roger recalls that a lot of journalists visited the filming – almost four hundred of them. 'It got to the point at one stage where I literally had to excuse myself from writers and TV crews to go and do the next scene.'

If ever he had needed any convincing as to just how successful his Bond had become – *Moonraker* certainly left him in no doubt. The boy from Streatham who had set out to be an animator was now the prime mover of what some critics had called the 'most successful movie comic strip of them all.'

For Your Eyes Only proved a less demanding film for Roger, and reintroduced some of the old elements of a traditional thriller that had been the feature of the early Bonds until the arrival of the mass ranks of gadgets.

'I enjoyed the skiing for that one,' says Roger, 'and although we didn't travel to as many locations, I still came in for a fair bit of battering. In fact I usually do. Do you know at the end of every Bond film I'm always a mass of bruises, and it takes me about three months to heal up!'

He remembers the sixth picture, *Octopussy*, as much for the title as the stunts he was called upon to undertake.

'The title caused a lot of concern in America,' he says, smiling broadly at the memory. 'They understood only one meaning for the word "pussy" and it was certainly not what Ian Fleming meant when he picked the title. I think it was only because it had been Fleming's title that we were able to use it.'

Once again in this picture Roger continued to make the role of Bond lighter and more amusing.

'Bond must never be taken too seriously,' he chuckles and another story springs into his mind. 'I remember doing a scene where the girl and I had broken down in the desert and we had to set out on foot in full evening dress.

'Well, it wasn't the most pleasant of tasks and when they asked for another retake I quietly unfastened my waist-button and zipper. As we walked off into the sunset my trousers slowly slid down until they were around my ankles. You can imagine the effect that had on the crew. I'm sure we could have got away with using it in the film – it looked *so* funny!'

Roger also tells another delightfully *risqué* story about that other great Fleming name, Pussy Galore.

'Some years ago when I was playing "The Saint", I appeared with Jimmy Tarbuck at the London Palladium. He asked me if I was friends with Sean Connery who was then playing Bond and Patrick McGoohan who was "Danger Man" on television. I said that I was.

'He then asked whether "The Saint" and "Danger Man" and Bond ever went out for an evening together. I said that we did. Then Tarbuck asked, "And Pussy Galore?" To which I replied, "Well, we don't go looking for it!" '

Roger admits he finds it amusing whenever people comment on how immaculate he always looks on the screen.

'In fact I'm forever having to take my clothes off when we're filming,' he says. 'All that jumping around in dinner suits – and Bond never sweats. I spend all my energy changing shirts!

'It's so incongruous if you think about it. Bond running around in strange climates wearing a white dinner jacket and looking impeccable!'

And so to the seventh of Roger's Bond movies, *A View To A Kill* – and his last. Filmed in 1985, it also coincided with a personal tragedy when his much-loved mother, Lily, died after suffering a stroke at her retirement home in Frinton-on-Sea in Essex.

As ever, though, Roger applied himself to the task of bringing Bond to the screen with his customary style and panache. It was not until after work had been completed that he announced in January 1986 that it would be his last appearance as 007. He had said that before, of course, but this time it was final.

'I've had a lot of fun playing Bond,' he told the press, 'but it was jolly hard work. Just think of all the dangers I won't have to face again. No more jumping out of helicopters, dodging giant spiders and snakes, bending down to kiss all those beautiful women! No, this really *is* the end. I'm moving on.'

As a new era in his career opens before him – for Roger has no intention of retiring from acting despite his enormous wealth – he can look back objectively on what he has achieved. Predictably, he is modest about the acclaim he has earned.

'I always wanted to have a career like Rex Harrison who was an actor who made movies,' he says. 'It didn't work out that way – I'm a movie actor. The longer I am away from the theatre the more nervous I am about going back. I should get out and exercise my legs, but I'm so exhausted by the time I finish a picture, I don't want to go and rehearse a play – I'd much rather enjoy myself.

'I'd be a sitting duck, of course. The critics would love to think, "Here's a bloody movie actor on the stage – let's have a go at him." Then I have the habit of working on films where, if someone drops a hammer, I stop. I could see myself in the theatre stopping every time someone went to the toilet. If circumstances financially said I had to get off my bum and do a play, I would have done it.

'But they never have,' he adds, 'it's a double-edged sword. Bond doesn't win awards, except perhaps for the song and special effects. It's the same as with Steven Spielberg – the films the public really like never get the awards. I can't understand that.'

Roger is in no doubt that although Bond is now behind him, he'll never be completely free of the man. Driving through France recently he had a vivid illustration of that fact.

'I had just sneaked into this parking space ahead of a Frenchman,' he says. 'The man got out of his car, waving his fist, obviously ready to hit whoever had stolen his spot. Then he took one look at me, clutched his forehead, and groaned, "*Alors! C'est James Bond.*" He leapt into his car and drove off at a terrific speed!'

On a visit to England a little while back, Roger took his wife and daughter, Deborah, on a drive to revisit the area where he was raised in Streatham. It was a salutary lesson as to just how far he had come.

'I passed a corner tabacconist and told them how I used to debate whether I'd buy five Weights cigarettes and walk half-way to town, or else go without the cigarettes and take the bus all the way.

'But in retrospect I enjoyed it all – money or not. I like earning money, but I don't respect it,' he adds.

Like his three predecessors, Roger has no doubt that Bond still has a very bright future ahead of him as one of the great favourites of cinemagoers all over the world.

'I replaced so many other actors in *my* career, it should be a fairly simple matter to replace me,' he says. 'All the guy will have to do is get up early, say his lines and not trip over the furniture.'

For a moment Roger pauses, he chuckles quietly and then adds in that voice which has delighted all the millions of Bond watchers:

'And, of course, he'll have to be prepared to answer questions with a smile on his face when he's asked how *his* Bond compares to Roger Moore's!'

007 FILE FOUR:

Timothy Dalton

'The Hero From The Heights'

The choice of 38-year-old Welsh-born stage and film actor Timothy Dalton as the latest James Bond followed six months of intense speculation. When Timothy's name was finally announced in August 1986, it came as a major surprise to 007 fans all around the world who had endured months of waiting and the sifting of yet another large field of 'possibles'. The hottest favourite of all had been debonair Pierce Brosnan, the star of the TV series *Remington Steel*, who was earmarked as Bond by Cubby Broccoli but was unable to accept the offer because of his contractural obligations to the American private detective series.

The choice of Dalton, a craggy, six-foot one-inch tall, classically-trained Shakespearean actor, drew immediate comments about his similarity to Sean Connery. Unlike Pierce Brosnan who many saw as being in the same suave mould as Roger Moore, Dalton with his dark-brown hair, blue-green eyes and deeply dimpled chin – not to mention his slightly sardonic air – was undoubtedly a throwback to the first 007, and Sean Connery was the first to applaud his selection.

'Tim Dalton is a very good choice,' Sean said en route to Hollywood on 8 August. 'I haven't worked with him but I know him and I think he'll be very good. And he's the right age to play Bond, about thirty-eight – just like me!' (Sean is now fifty-six, though he was thirty-three when he first played 007.)

Timothy Dalton was himself filming on location in Puerto Rico with Brook Shields for a movie called *Brenda Starr*, when the announcement of his new role was leaked to the press, so it was some weeks before the Bond ballyhoo caught up with him.

Nevertheless, he was quick to reveal his pleasure at being offered the part, although he knew it would irrevocably change his life-style.

'I'm really delighted about it,' he said. 'The joy and excitement James Bond brings to people throughout the world is very, very special. I'm looking forward to the challenge of playing him.

'But I have to say that following in Sean and Roger's footsteps is a daunting task, especially handling all the publicity. I'm a very private person, you see, with nothing mysterious to hide, who likes to do his work and do it well and then get away from it all and go fishing. There is no Pussy Galore, no jet-setting, no champagne or caviar – even a dry martini, shaken not stirred – in my life!' he added with a smile.

The appropriateness of the choice seemed to be immediately confirmed not only by the tests Timothy made in Hollywood, but also by the fact he had already played three of the greatest lovers in English literature, and was highly attractive to women, and admired by men for his stunt work.

Landing the coveted role came as almost as much of a surprise to him as it did to everyone else after the months of speculation and constant newspaper headlines. Initially, Cubby Broccoli had hoped to announce the new Bond at the 1986 Cannes Film Festival in May. This proved impossible, but Cubby was less than amused by one newspaper story claiming that he had cancelled a £1 million launch party for the new star, 'because of fears of terrorist reprisals over the US bombing of Libya.'

Cubby retorted bluntly, 'EON Productions wishes to go on record that the decision to cancel the presentation of a new James Bond was made before the recent political crisis as no actor has yet been selected.'

Cubby and his associates had, in fact, as on the previous occasions, been working through a very extensive list of possibles for the role. Aided, of course, by the press and fans all over the world. Strong cases were made not only for British actors, but also Americans and even Australians.

One of the strongest contenders from down under was Mel Gibson, who had shot to international fame as Mad Max. Fellow countrymen, Andrew Clarke and Bryan Brown, were also on the list.

A fourth Australian, Finlay Light, a former model and TV commercial actor (shades of George Lazenby), was actually reported to have landed the role on 27 April. He was said by the British newspaper, the *Mail on Sunday*, to have signed a ten-year contract for the next five Bond films which would take him from obscurity to become a multi-millionaire. Light himself was quoted as saying, 'The Bond contract is pretty good. I think it will work out fine for me.'

But the idea of a Bond who might drink Foster's Lager rather than Martinis was promptly denied by Cubby Broccoli.

American actors who appeared on the lists of possibles fared no better. Tom Selleck, the star of TV's *Magnum*, was listed as a 3-1 likelihood in March 1986, just a whisper (or moustache) ahead of John James, the soap opera star who first appeared in Dynasty and was then given a starring role as Jeff Colby in the spin-off serial, *The Colbys*.

As the months passed, however, it became increasingly evident that Cubby Broccoli shared the view of many newspaper and magazine readers who felt that Bond could not be played by anyone other than a British actor. 'Keep Bond British' was a frequent plea to be read in the columns of the press.

Among the British actors who were strongly supported were Michael Caine (yet again), Lewis Collins, of *The Professionals* TV series, and Ian Ogilvy – a curiously prophetic suggestion as he had taken over the role of The Saint from Roger Moore. Ian, though, denied the idea shortly afterwards.

'I could well be the only actor in Britain to state that he is *not* going to be James Bond,' he said in June.

Ian was then appearing in the television series, *Robin of Sherwood*, which happened to star Sean Connery's son, Jason; perhaps not surprisingly, the youngster's name was also put forward as a possible 007.

'He would be a continuation of the real Bond, his father Sean,' one supporter wrote. 'Jason is the obvious choice for Cubby Broccoli.'

Cubby didn't agree, and so in the first week of August after months of speculation, Timothy Dalton was confirmed as the fourth James Bond with a four-picture contract. His debut film, it was announced, would be *The Living Daylights*, scripted by Richard Maibaum and Michael Wilson, for release in 1987 to coincide with the silver anniversary of the series. John Glen was again signed to direct the movie on location in Austria, Morocco and Gibraltar as well as on the traditional Bond stage at Pinewood studios – with a budget set at a new record figure for the series of $35 million.

This latest 007 film is based on the Ian Fleming short story of the same title – and is a happy choice for the anniversary year as it is Anne Fleming's favourite among all her husband's writings. Not that she was a great admirer of the secret agent, as is generally well known.

'I was never a James Bond addict because I didn't care for the violence,' she told the showbiz 'Bible', *Variety*, in an interview in December 1965. 'I don't think my husband took Bond seriously, either, in fact he probably came to think of him as a Frankenstein monster towards the end. I think he got hypnotised by the character and became its prisoner.'

These same words have haunted the various actors who have played Bond on the screen – but were no deterrent to Timothy Dalton when he made a secret test for the role. Cubby asked him to show that he could play both a love scene and be a killer. Ironically, the scenes were taken from the Lazenby movie, *On Her Majesty's Secret Service* – but according to EON executive, Jerry Juroe, Tim passed with flying colours.

'I don't know why we chose scenes from that particular Bond picture,' Juroe said afterwards, 'but Timothy showed he had every quality we were looking for to take over the role. The one thing that impressed me was his incredible and believable likeness to the Bond character.

'When we studied his screen test every one of us believed he could have been a former commander in the British Navy. He behaved as though he had the ability to be a spy and he looked as though he wouldn't think twice about killing somebody coolly and cleanly. It was a pretty impressive screen test,' Juroe added.

In fact, Timothy Dalton with his athletic body and finely chiselled features has been impressing people on the stage and screen throughout most of his twenty years as an actor. He is certainly no stranger to big budget movies and although outstanding reviews and award nominations are nothing new to him, the kind of international celebrity that being 007 will bring him undoubtedly is.

Tim was born in Colwyn Bay, North Wales on 21 March 1946, one of five children of an advertising executive. His background was 'faintly theatrical', he says, in that his grandparents were noted music hall performers, and an earlier relative had been a variety headliner at the turn of the century with the young Charlie Chaplin.

'My grandfather, having started on the halls, later took to running a theatre in Bath,' Tim explains. 'He was also one of the very first agents – when he was on tour he used to photograph other acts on the bill with him and then carry the photos from town to town recommending people to theatre managers who in those days didn't have much idea of what was going on elsewhere.'

James BOND

007 Mark IV: Timothy Dalton.

Taking on the mantle of James Bond is another remarkable step in the career of Timothy Dalton who has already played three of the greatest lovers in English literature: Romeo, Rochester in Jane Eyre; and Heathcliff in *Wuthering Heights* (1970), from which the still (bottom right) is taken. The newspaper story from the *Daily Express* and the cartoon from the *Star* of 8 August 1986 were typical of many which greeted Timothy's casting as 007.

CONNERY, THE FIRST 007, GIVES THUMBS UP TO NEW-BOY TIM

That's my Bond!

And he's right age!

By GARTH PEARCE, Showbusiness Editor

THE ORIGINAL James Bond nodded his approval yesterday to the latest choice as agent 007 and said: "At least, he's the right age!"

Sean Connery, the first man to get the licence to kill back in 1963 in Doctor No, passed judgment on the new boy—38-year-old Timothy Dalton, named for the glamour role just 24 hours before.

Connery: Yesterday

Sean said: "I think they have made a very good choice. I haven't worked with Tim but I know him and I think he will be good.

"He's certainly the right age to play Bond, about 38—just like me."

Sean, who in the later Bond films had to don a toupee to cover his thinning hair, made that remark with a twinkle in his eye. He's really 55, though when he first played Bond he was 33.

Yesterday Sean, flying from London to Chicago to play a cop in a TV gangster series, said: "I am finished with Bond. I came back to do 'Never Say Never Again,' but I think it's never from now on.

Fishing

In Florida the new man was talking about himself and preparing for his Bond debut while filming with Brooke Shields.

He begins shooting the new 007 film, the Living Daylights, next month.

"I'm a very private person with nothing mysterious to hide who just likes to do his work and do it well and then get away from it all and go fishing," he said yesterday.

There's no jet-setting, champagne and caviar or the best tailor in town for Tim.

He's a 6ft 2in blond, blue-green eyed Shakesperian actor who admires the professionals iin his trade.

"As for me, I've never been out of work since I left drama school, which is very fortunate. Life has not been a struggle. And as for my private life, that is my private life," he said.

Despite his longing for the quiet life, the man with the £1 million Bond contract has long had a winning way with women which 007 would admire.

And just like the super-spy, he never kisses and tells.

He has had an off-on relationship spanning 15 years with Vannessa Redgrave—which is currently ON.

She is 10 years his senior and there have been storms and separations.

During one, Timothy grew fond of East End model and novelist Patsy Booth, who is five years older.

"It's bad news, I'm afraid—they've got a new 007"

The new 007, Timothy Dalton, charming one of his previous co-stars, the ageless Mae West, in *Sextette* (1978).

His own interest in acting came dramatically at the age of sixteen when he saw an Old Vic production of *Macbeth*. At school in Belper, Derbyshire he threw himself enthusiastically into acting, and also became a member of the local amateur dramatic society where he followed a fine performance as Sergius in George Bernard Shaw's *Arms and the Man* with the title role in a production of *Billy Liar*.

In 1964 Timothy's evident talent was recognised when he was among a select group invited to join the Michael Croft National Theatre, and with the company he made his professional debut in a small role in Shakespeare's *Coriolanus* at the Queen's Theatre in London.

There followed two busy years of study at RADA before he was given his first lead as Malcolm in the National Youth Theatre's 1966 production of *Little Malcolm and His Struggle Against the Eunuchs* at the Royal Court. Following this Timothy was offered a contract by the Birmingham Repertory Theatre and played several classical roles, then, in 1967, he made his TV debut in the series *Saturday While Sunday*.

That same year, aged just twenty-one, he was catapulted into the world of movie making when he was offered the role of King Philip of France in the epic production of *The Lion In Winter* which starred Peter O'Toole and Katherine Hepburn.

'I've been very fortunate all my life really,' he says today. 'I've never been out of work since I left drama school which is remarkable for an actor. My professional life has not been a struggle like it has for so many others.'

Timothy does not say that with any sense of false modesty, for he would also admit to having made some erratic choices with the roles he has played in his rise to stardom. Indeed, a couple of years ago, the film critic Sheridan Morley wrote about him:

'Few actors of thirty-six can look back on a fifteen-year career which has encompassed a film debut at twenty-one in *The Lion in Winter*, a long-standing affair with Venessa Redgrave, star turns in *Cromwell* and *Wuthering Heights*, a stint in *Charlie's Angels* and a role as the sixth of 91-year-old Mae West's husbands in her farewell movie *Sextette*, to say nothing of three classical years with the Prospect Theatre and another three with the RSC back in the early 1970s. Like O'Toole who got him the job in *The Lion in Winter* and like Olivier into whose *Wuthering Heights* footsteps he followed, Dalton has always lived dangerously on both stage and screen.'

It was in 1970 that Timothy played the menacing figure of Heathcliff in the American-financed *Wuthering Heights*, and instead of being compared to Sir Laurence Olivier found himself hailed as a new star of the screen. He had not seen the 1939 version in which Olivier had starred, and certainly didn't believe in 'looking over my shoulder to see what someone else had done.' That way would get him nowhere in life, he believed – a philosophy he now intends to employ when playing James Bond.

After the release of *Wuthering Heights* in America, Timothy found himself described by one of the critics there as 'the greatest acting find in the last decade' and he was said by another to have 'the looks which could well bring back the era of the matinée idol.' The film's director, Robert Fuest, went even further. 'Tim is no carbon copy of anyone,' he said. 'There was Brando. There was James Dean. Then along came their imitators. But Tim is no imitation. He is a new "original".'

And just to cap everything else, the London *Evening News* carried a gossip column note, 'It has been reported from a show business newspaper office in Los Angeles, that the female staff, who wouldn't usually flick a false eyelash if most superstars walked in naked, still haven't come out of their swoon since our Timothy Dalton paid a quick visit!'

Timothy was, though, rather embarrassed by such fulsome praise. 'This absolutely isn't me,' he protested. 'I think the Americans must have gone completely mad!'

Although he obviously hoped that the role might lead to the kind of success that had since been accorded to Olivier, Tim was determined to keep his feet on the ground and so for two years worked only on the stage.

'It's important for me to work in the theatre from time to time,' he said. 'But I'd still like to do one film a year. You've got to be true to yourself – as long as you've got a good reason for doing what you're doing, then it doesn't matter what it is. You die your own death. You live your own life.'

Timothy returned to the screen in another spectacular costume drama, *Mary Queen of Scots*, playing Lord Darnley, the weak and dissolute charmer who marries the Queen, played by Vanessa Redgrave. This meeting on screen was the forerunner of two more pictures together for the couple, as well as the start of an off-screen relationship.

In the ensuing years he continued to mix film, stage and television work, and in 1975 actually had a foretaste of the world of espionage when he appeared in the Dirk Bogarde movie, *Permission To Kill*, in which Bogarde played an utterly ruthless British secret agent empowered to bribe, blackmail and murder in order to complete his mission. Tim was cast as Charles Lord, a homosexual British Embassy official, whom Bogarde had compromised by photographing him in bed with another man. It was Timothy rather than Bogarde, however, who won the better reviews, Virginia Dignam of the *Morning Star* praising his performance as a 'cool, wise-cracking undersecretary tragically tied up in his own red tape simply because he happens to fancy little boys instead of little girls.'

In 1979, Timothy also put in a 'strong, funny' performance as the adulterous first husband of Agatha Christie, in the controversial film made about the famous eleven days in 1926 when the great crime novelist went missing, The picture, called *Agatha*, starred Vanessa Redgrave in the title role and Dustin Hoffman as an American journalist. The picture and Timothy Dalton's association with it provides another interesting coincidence as far as the 007 legend is concerned because, as I mentioned earlier, Miss Christie was the first writer to create a literary character named James Bond.

By 1984, Timothy could safely be said to have completed his 'apprenticeship' in readiness for playing Bond, when he appeared as the third of the three greatest lovers in English literature. With Heathcliff and Romeo already behind him (Tim had appeared as the tragic lover in 1973 as one of several roles for the Royal Shakespeare Company) he completed the trio when he was cast as Rochester in the BBC TV serial of *Jane Eyre*.

However, for his next role, and in contrast to dying for love, smouldering with passion or sweeping women into his arms – which have been a feature of many of his roles and earned him something of a reputation as a romantic hero – he appeared in ITV's £4 million adaptation of the Robert Louis Stevenson classic *The Master of Ballantrae*, and for once left his co-stars Michael York and Richard Thomas to fight over the beautiful Finola Hughes. What he particularly enjoyed about the film, though, was performing his own stunts.

'I had to dodge explosions on battlefields and plunge into raging torrents,' he recalls. 'And in one scene Michael York and I had to canoe through some rapids and tip out into the foaming water. We were very nearly swept away because the current was so strong!'

With this experience of the epic movie, the demands of the screen lover, and his expertise at dangerous stunts, Timothy is well equipped to play Bond. And he also happens to have very definite opinions on both women and the attitude of 007 towards them.

'Bond is a welcome change after being cast so many times as the mystery lover,' he told Corinna Honan of the *Daily Mail* after signing to play the part. 'I'm single. I'm not married and I'm not a pouf!'

He went on, 'Actually, I'm an unromantic male chauvinist. It's the natural role of the man that he should be boss. You can't have a democracy of two. I want things my way, but it doesn't preclude having things the woman's way – if that's what I want.

'I think that somewhere instinctively within a woman she wants a man capable of looking after her – you'd be a pretty useless man if you had to have a woman looking after you. If I wasn't running a relationship and being a man, I wouldn't be fulfilled.'

Timothy Dalton in fact matches his dark, brooding good looks with outspokenness, a keen sense of humour, and refreshing honesty. He has a great enthusiasm for his craft and revels in the challenge of each new role that comes his way whichever medium it may be in. And if he should dislike personal publicity, he also has the resources and level-headedness to handle it in a role which he knows has always attracted enormous public interest. When he made his breakthrough as an actor all those years ago playing Heathcliff, those qualities were noted by one critic, William Hall, who believed they probably held the key to his eventual emergence as 'a very hot property indeed'.

That prophecy now seems certain to be fulfilled as the new James Bond continues the greatest success story in cinema history.

The Bond Girls

Another essential part of the Bond legend – some may even call them *the* most essential part – are the girls who have emerged seductively from the pages of Ian Fleming's books and come dazzlingly to life on the cinema screen.

Over the years these lovelies have proved as vital to 007 as his gadgets, his boss 'M' or his armourer 'Q', even Miss Moneypenny – though her views on some have been less than printable!

Part of the success of these girls undoubtedly lies in the deliberately provocative names which Fleming dreamed up for them: Honeychile Rider, Pussy Galore, Mary Goodnight. That, and the inspired choice of the beautiful actresses selected for the parts during the last twenty-five years.

The Bond girls have been as varied as they have been lovely. Some have helped him, others have betrayed him. Some have tried to kill him, others have died for him. Some have been compliant in his arms, others calculatingly deadly. But *all* of them have loved him.

All have been women, too, not girls and not too young – for as Cubby Brocolli has explained, 'Otherwise it becames rape. Bond's ladies must stay in the background and must give the impression of being experienced with men. They must be strong but elegant. And *something* has to happen when you look at them.'

Sean Connery who set the pattern for his predecessors once defined the core of the relationship between 007 and his ladies: 'Bond is never in love with a girl and that helps,' he said. 'He always does what he wants and women like that. It explains why so many women are crazy about men who don't give a damn for them.'

Terence Young, the first of the Bond film directors, has also offered this view, 'They have to have beauty, smashing figures and more than just Hollywood toothpaste sex. They must have innocence, but be able to kill a man without showing any guilt.'

Though these ladies now have a world-wide band of admirers, there have still been people who have attacked them. Indeed, over the years they have been a favourite target of extreme feminists and hard-line communists. The Russian newspaper *Pravda*, for instance, once denounced them as the exploited victims of capitalism and said that James Bond moved in a world 'where rape and outrages on female honour are considered gallantry.'

Such attacks notwithstanding, playing a Bond girl has made international stars of a number of actresses and brought the names of all of them to widespread public attention.

During a quarter of a century, uncounted thousands of beautiful girls have sought the parts – but only a few have been chosen. In fact, the years are scattered with the names of stars who *might* have entered the world of 007 but for one reason or another did not. Talented ladies such as Julie Christie – who might have been the very first Bond girl – or Faye Dunaway and Koo Stark.

What remains undisputed, though, is that no actress is ever quite the same after playing a Bond girl. And talking to them today it is fascinating to discover that their memories of the films remain vivid – though not *always* affectionate . . .

There are those who believe that Ursula Andress, the Swiss-born beauty who played Honey Rider in the first film, *Dr No*, was the sexiest Bond girl of all. Certainly her emergence from the waters of Crab Key wearing only a bikini with a knife on her hip was one of the most stunning entrances in cinema history – and perhaps accounted as much for the successful launching of the series as Bond himself!

Interestingly, there is only one major difference between this scene and that in Fleming's original book. There Honey was naked – and one wonders how the scene might be shot if *Dr No* was remade today.

'Oh, I'm sure Honey would come out of the ocean naked – full frontal,' the still strikingly beautiful Ursula Andress smiled mischievously when asked the question at a party in March 1986 to celebrate her 50th birthday. Also present at this landmark in her career was none other than Sean Connery himself, for the two have remained firm friends ever since the days that film made them both international stars. Ursula became one of the sex symbols of the Sixties, and is remembered in the mind's eye of a whole generation of men for that dripping white bikini.

'It was one of those cases where a brilliant scene from a book was put right onto the screen,' Ursula recalls, 'though obviously I couldn't appear naked. One thing they did have to change, though, was the book's ending. There poor Honey was left staked out naked on a hill at the mercy of some giant crabs. Instead, I got a boat ride into the sunset with Sean!'

Ursula's astonishing success created an immediate problem for Cubby Brocolli when he came to cast for the second Bond picture. 'It wasn't easy to find another Ursula,' he was quoted as long afterwards as 1976. 'I only wish I could.'

Ursula Andress also appeared as Vesper Lynd in Charles Feldman's version of *Casino Royale* made in 1967, with David Niven and Peter Sellers. Her memories of this picture are, though, far from happy. 'I was in a daze the whole time,' she says. 'There were script changes being made every day and I was never quite sure who I was supposed to be – or who anyone else was for that matter. I think I was the world's wealthiest spy!'

In fact Ursula's role was just that, and she had to hire Peter Sellers, the world's greatest baccarat player, to outwit Orson Welles, the world's most merciless gambler, in order to steal from him some microfilm which showed a number of double agents in compromising situations.

'I'd worked with Peter before so I enjoyed the scenes with him,' she recalls. 'I had to test his mastery of disguise by photographing him in various costumes, and he play-acted so much we both kept cracking up!'

This was not surprising when one scene called for her to smooch with him on a couch and breath seductively into his ear, 'I'm going to take you at 500 at F11.'

Peter Seller's response was equally memorable, 'That's the nicest thing anybody ever said to me.'

'And I'm afraid that's about the nicest thing I can remember about *Casino Royale*!' she adds.

Ursula Andress (left) who has twice appeared as a Bond girl – in *Dr No* (1962) and *Casino Royale* (1967). Daniela Bianchi (above) who played Tatiana Romanova in *From Russia With Love* (1963). Honor Blackman (below), Pussy Galore in *Goldfinger* (1964).

The second Bond film, *From Russia With Love*, was a far cry from such lunacy, and though a little more complicated than Fleming's original book, was faithful to the basic storyline. The film introduced the second Bond girl in the shape of a sexy Italian blonde named Daniela Bianchi who played the SMERSH recruit, Tatiana Romanova, initially set to trap Bond but ultimately succumbing to his charms.

It was a daunting task for the 21-year-old Italian, for not only had she to follow Ursula Andress, but also bring to the screen a character Ian Fleming had described as resembling Greta Garbo.

'I was a high fashion model in Rome and had made a few nondescript Italian films when I was asked to test for *From Russia With Love*,' Daniela recalls today. 'The picture certainly made my name – but all I got offered afterwards were crime, mystery and espionage pictures. I became stereotyped and then a bit disillusioned.'

During this unsettled period, Daniela met and fell in love with a ship owner. 'When I knew I was going to be a mother I had to reflect on what kind of life I was going to lead,' she says. 'I loved my work and I knew that one part of me would regret giving it up; but I'm sure I made the right choice.'

Today, twenty years after her retirement, Daniela still enjoys watching her old movies whenever they appear on Italian TV. 'Recently I saw *From Russia With Love* again,' she says. 'I was amused. "Look at that! How could I have been so awful?" I said to my family who were watching with me.'

This verdict is not, however, one that is shared by a great many Bond fans, who believe *From Russia With Love* to be arguably the best of the entire series.

The third Bond girl was the memorable Pussy Galore of *Goldfinger* – the first to be played by an English actress: the dynamic 37-year-old Honor Blackman, who came to the role in 1964 already well known as Cathy Gale, the leather-clad heroine of the hugely successful TV series, *The Avengers*.

It was to prove a very different kind of role for Honor as she realised on reading Fleming's description of his heroine: 'She had pale, Rupert Brooke good looks with high cheek-bones and a beautiful jawline. She had the only violet eyes Bond had ever seen. They were the true deep violet of a pansy and they looked candidly out at the world from beneath straight black brows. Her hair was worn in an untidy urchin-cut. The mouth was a decisive slash of deep vermillion. Bond thought she was superb.'

Honor thought the opportunities presented by the role of Goldfinger's lieutenant and leader of a gang of female air pilots were superb, too. 'What a glorious name!' she enthused at the time. 'Pussy Galore is a bit like Cathy Gale, except that she's not very keen on men. Still, Bond changes all that.'

She also talked about the role of the black-booted Cathy Gale that had made her the rage of television and set a trend for kinky clothes that dominated British fashion for two years.

'I loved doing the *Avengers* series because it got me away from "understanding wife" roles,' she said. 'But you can have enough of slamming an assortment of thugs into walls. I also got tired of counting a dozen bruises every time I crossed my legs. And it was not exactly flattering to have men refusing to shake hands for fear I might toss them over my shoulder!'

Honor was, therefore, pleased that her role as Pussy Galore was 'unbelievable, fantastic, ridiculous, but also great fun.' And she was gratified to be playing someone who wasn't just a cardboard character.

'The role of Pussy Galore had been written to make her an intelligent, thinking woman, and that was the kind of challenge I wanted,' she reflects today. 'I was fascinated with her from the moment I read Ian Fleming's novel.

'Of course, in the book she's a lesbian, although it's very superficially treated. She's supposed to have been raped by an uncle at the age of twelve or something ludicrous – and of course she stops being a lesbian the moment she sleeps with Bond. But they couldn't use that in the film.

'Mind you, I did manage to work in a slight in-joke by calling all my women pilots 'Joe' or 'Charlie' or 'Harry'. There also happened to be a good parallel in that she was antagonistic towards Bond – she was at his level mentally and certainly not in the kitchen sink department.'

She jumped at the chance the picture gave her of learning to fly. 'They offered me a free lesson at Biggin Hill for publicity purposes,' she recalls, 'and I enjoyed it so much that once I had some free time I decided it would be a useful thing to know.'

Although Honor says that after Goldfinger she 'spent the next twenty years running like a stag from the image', she does retain some fond memories from her association with 007. She enjoyed working with Sean Connery who she found good humoured and very single-minded. She has also become a vociferous defender of *all* the pictures against charges of violence.

'They are a joke, a spoof, you can't take them seriously. I certainly don't think they do any harm to children, they see Bond as a super-hero. He's like Action Man. They know he's not real. My own son loves them!'

Now that she is 'no longer a youngster', Honor Blackman finds it a bit ridiculous to be still associated with the images of Cathy Gale and Pussy Galore.

'Mind you, I've got no illusions,' she says, 'the epitaph on my tombstone is going to bear the words, "Remembered as the *Avengers* girl and Pussy Galore in *Goldfinger* – and for other, better roles!" '

Claudine Auger who was Domino in *Thunderball* (1965).

There was yet another change of nationality when the fourth Bond girl was chosen for *Thunderball* in 1965. She was the dark-eyed, Titian-haired, 22-year-old French actress, Claudine Auger.

Claudine was one of 300 girls who were considered for the role of Domino, the plaything of master criminal Largo, who is eventually wooed and won over to the side of law and order by the ever-resourceful 007. In the film, Domino was spared the torture her namesake suffered in the book when Largo discovered that she was helping Bond –

namely to be extensively burned. A fortunate intervention by one of Largo's lackies prevented this fate.

Claudine was making a return visit to England when she came to film *Thunderball* as she had once worked as an au pair girl in Mill Hill. In the interim her voluptuous beauty had won her the title of Miss France and a career in films.

She arrived full of optimism and delighted a press conference with her fractured English. 'I think it will make me famous,' she told the assembled journalists. 'Domino is one of the most interesting of James Bond's girlfriends. She doesn't lie to herself.

'I think I am a little like her. I try to be truthful with myself. I am wilful too . . . And Domino loves love – and I love love, too!'

Today, now past forty and still beautiful, Claudine is married to an English businessman, but occasionally works in television and films. The Bond role had a profound effect upon her life.

'Once you are a Bond girl you are a Bond girl for life,' she says. 'The publicity I got from the film was invaluable, but thereafter I was just offered inferior duplicates of the same part – they were starring roles but bad scripts. I therefore decided I would do good small parts than big bad ones.'

Claudine remains proud of her achievements in the film, however. 'I believe we showed that the Bond women are the women of the nuclear age: they are free and they make love when they want to without worrying about it afterwards.

'The love scene under the water was the first time it had been done in a movie,' she recalls. 'We had this breathing equipment on and then went down to the sandy bottom of the ocean. Then the top of my bikini floated up to the surface. It was very novel.'

Claudine Auger has always loved travel and excitement and hopes to combine this with acting.

'I want to act all my life,' she said recently. 'At seventy-five I want to be a very sexy grandmother . . .'

There were not one but two lovelies for James Bond in *You Only Live Twice* made in 1967 – the top Japanese actresses Akiki Wakabayashi and Mie Hama who brought a touch of Eastern beauty to this hugely spectacular adventure.

Akiki Wakabayashi played Aki, the secretary of Tiger Tanaka, the head of the Japanese Secret Service who joined forces with 007 to locate the headquarters of SPECTRE, cunningly hidden inside a volcano. She brought a mixture of tireless devotion and enchanting gentleness to the part based on years of work in Japanese feature films and television dramas primarily about domestic life. Her love of Bond of course cost Aki her life when she unsuspectingly swallowed poison meant for 007.

The doe-eyed Mie Hama, who played Kissy Suzuki, was at that time widely acclaimed as one of the most beautiful actresses in Japan and pin-up posters of her far outsold those of such famous stars as Marilyn Monroe and Brigitte Bardot. She was perfectly cast as the Ama girl Bond took as a wife in order to help him penetrate the headquarters of SPECTRE.

Neither of these girls have appeared again in Western films after the Bond epic. Said Mie Hama recently, 'It was an exciting experience appearing in that film, for James Bond is very popular in Japan. But I prefer to work in my home country and I have not been tempted to go abroad.

'I don't think either Akiko or I were typical Bond girls – and I should be surprised if anyone like us appeared in the series again!'

Diana Rigg (left), the ill-fated Mrs Bond, in *On Her Majesty's Secret Service* (1969), and (below) the other Mrs Bond, Mie Hama, in *You Only Live Twice* (1967).

The seventh of the Broccoli-Saltzman Bond films, *On Her Majesty's Secret Service*, introduced a new 007 in George Lazenby, with the girl who had succeeded Honor Blackman in *The Avengers*, Diana Rigg.

Diana, of the chestnut hair and almost alarming directness, admitted she was glad of the chance to leave *The Avengers.*

'Emme Peel was destroying me then,' she says. 'She dominated me. I would wake up in the morning and find this Avenger bird in the mirror. It was a sort of looking-glass-war.'

At first, though, she wondered if she might be repeating the mistake by entering the world of James Bond.

'Would I be wasting my talents? I just didn't know. But how many parts are there in movies for women? One needs a vehicle – and I think Bond gives fair motoring.

'I liked the part of Tracy, too. She was extremely rich and devil-may-care and when she met Bond she was no push-over. She was not a victim. She selected Bond on terms of sexual equality – and that was what attracted me.

'Of course,' she adds, 'the part was ill-fated. For Bond is filmland's Bonded warehouse and such a property can't land up with a wife.'

The actual making of *On Her Majesty's Secret Service* attracted headlines almost from the start with stories of an unhappy relationship between the two stars. But Diana, a thoroughgoing professional, is now able to look back at those days with complete detachment.

'It wasn't *that* bad,' she says. 'There were moments of course, but by and large we got on all right. You've got to when you work with someone for eight months. It's a case of get on and shut up.'

She is also equally objective about *why* she thinks she was chosen for the role of Tracy, the daughter of the sinister Draco who became Bond's short-lived bride at the end of *OHMSS*.

'After all those other well-equipped ladies I was a bit of a surprise, wasn't I?' she says with an engaging smile. 'I mean I'm not exactly all teeth and tits am I? I think they wanted me there for weight. George had never acted before so they needed a professional who could feed him his lines.'

Since her foray into Bond, Diana has established her reputation as one of the leading British actresses, and she considers *OHMSS* to have been a step along that path. A not altogether satisfying one, but one that taught her some valuable lessons and did not hamper her development as a serious actress.

'I don't regret it – or my time in *The Avengers*,' she says. 'I can even bear to watch repeats of them all!'

Red-head Jill St John who appeared in Sean Connery's 'return' movie, *Diamonds Are Forever*, has been described as 'one of the few true glamour girls ever produced by Hollywood'. Three times married and with a colourful personality, her beauty nonetheless had still got her marked down by many film-makers as decorative but dumb, though in fact she has an IQ of 162 (genius rating) and was said by Henry Kissinger to be 'among the brightest women I have ever met.'

Jill played Tiffany Case who came to 007's aid to thwart yet another ingenious plot by Blofeld which involved smuggling diamonds to make a highly destructive satellite complete with laser beam. The film varied considerably from Fleming's novel, although Tiffany's first appearance in bra and panties was straight from the printed page.

Interestingly, just prior to the Bond film she had appeared in another spy film, *The Liquidator* (1966) based on John Gardner's novel, where she had played a heavily

The beautiful and super-intelligent Jill St John who played Tiffany Case in *Diamonds Are Forever* (1971).

involved secretary working for British Intelligence.

'Tiffany Case was quite a different girl,' Jill recalls, 'much more lightweight, inclined to get into trouble. Best when she was just looking helpless. But it was still the picture that put my name up in lights!

'It was a fun picture to make, though. I particularly remember filming a love scene with Sean which was shot through a water bed. You could see the fish swimming around all the time.

'Now, I've always been interested in aquaria and it was once my ambition to be a marine biologist,' she goes on. 'So when we were filming I was looking at the fish more than Sean – and as he was whispering words of passion to me I was wondering all the time if they had the right amount of copper sulphate in the water!'

Despite this seeming indifference to 007's charms, Jill says she enjoyed working with Sean Connery, whom she found intelligent and quick-witted.

'So many of the film people I've worked with have been surprised I've got more to talk about than the latest Hollywood gossip, and I think Sean might have been – to begin with. In hindsight, I believe that if only my part in that picture had been given a bit more depth I could have been more than just a bit of decoration on the cake,' Jill says. 'But then, it's all in the past now – though I see I still get written up every so often as "one of the Bond girls". The fate of all of us, I guess!'

Jill's successor, and the girl who first partnered the third James Bond, Roger Moore, also shares some of her views about the problems inherent in being a Bond girl. Although vivacious, Jane Seymour was enthusiastic at the time about her role as Solitaire in *Live And Let Die* (1973), she has since claimed that it *might* have ruined her career.

Jane, the 21-year-old daughter of a well-known Harley Street gynaecologist, seemed perfect casting for the part of Solitaire, according to Ian Fleming's description of his heroine. 'She was one of the most beautiful women Bond had ever seen,' he wrote. 'She had high cheek bones and a wide sensual mouth which held a hint of cruelty . . . an iron will . . . a lack of compromise . . . a face born to command.'

Jane was spotted by the producers in an episode of the TV series *The Onedin Line* and was offered the role 500 other girls had also been after. She herself had never thought of applying for the part of the mysterious seeress whose virginity holds the key to Bond's mission.

'It was an incredible stroke of luck,' Jane said while working on the picture. 'The producers spotted me on *The Onedin Line*, rang my agent, arranged to meet me, and then offered me the part. The only thing I did do when we met was to sweep off this fur cossack hat I was wearing and let my waist-length hair cascade around my shoulders!'

Jane was no newcomer to films. She had appeared in five previous movies as well as learning her craft in the theatre, where she had played a memorable Ophelia. It was felt she could project the mixture of virginal purity and suppressed sensuousness that the part demanded. She herself had a vivid memory of the seduction scene which provided a crucial moment in the picture.

'I was a bit shy then so they shot it in secret about 8.30 one morning in front of a small camera crew,' she recalls. 'You'll remember that Solitaire had mystical voodoo powers and was working with the baddies who were planning to take over the Western World. Bond discovered that the only way for me to loose these powers was for me to loose my virginity.

'He used a pack of tarot cards and each time he turned one over they gave the same message – Lovers. Solitaire believed in the cards and so I had no option but to succumb. What I didn't know was that Bond was cheating with the cards!

'It was not an easy scene to play, though, but Roger was fantastically helpful. In fact I thought he came closer to Ian Fleming's original James Bond. He had the sort of English arrogance that is needed for the part.'

Roger Moore's help went even further. 'He actually saved my life,' says Jane. 'We were doing another scene on a hydraulic lift when suddenly the lift dropped. Roger made a grab for my long hair and stopped me falling twenty feet. All the same I was pretty shaken up and I couldn't do a thing for the rest of the day.'

Jane says she did not read *Live And Let Die* before filming began. 'I was told not to look at the book,' she says. 'They said I'd be better off reading the script. Harry Saltzman actually saw me on the set with a copy of the book and said, "I'll take that." I couldn't find another copy, but I realised it didn't really matter because the only thing they had used was the title!'

Jane also had a taste of the kind of exploitation that can creep up on a Bond girl when she was offered 'a small fortune' to pose nude for Playboy magazine. 'I actually told them they could have "covered-up" photographs of me twice as sexy if I used my hair,' she recalls with a grin.

'I always laugh when people say to me now, "Oh, you must have made a fortune being a Bond girl." When I tell them how much I made in the following year they are staggered. Set me up for life? Far from it!'

What happened was that in the wake of *Live And Let Die*, Jane says she was offered a

Jane Seymour was Solitaire in *Live And Let Die* (1973).

rush of 'girly' parts which she believes could have ruined her career if she had accepted them. Instead, she took on a series of jobs in provincial repertory companies to break the image, and has now established herself on both sides of the Atlantic as a formidable talent.

'The thing is,' she says, 'that inside every James Bond girl there's a Lady Macbeth fighting to get out. But with no chance. I don't think what I did was acting. I just had to scream, run three paces behind the man with the gun, and show a lot of leg. I knew that I could act, that I was worthy of bigger things than Bond, but it took a while before anyone took me seriously as an actress.'

Britt Ekland – Mary Goodnight in *The Man With The Golden Gun* (1974).

Barbara Bach played the Russian spy, Major Anya Amasova, in *The Spy Who Loved Me* (1977).

Britt Ekland, the Swedish beauty who was Roger Moore's second companion, played another of Fleming's most memorable girls, Mary Goodnight, in *The Man With The Golden Gun* made in 1974. She, though, has happier memories of her days of Bondage.

'I actually had a lot of laughs making that picture,' she says. 'A lot of people have asked me whether Roger's terribly English and stuffy – but in fact he's quite the reverse. He's terribly funny and has the best sense of humour of anyone I know.'

Playing secret agent Mary Goodnight who becomes involved in 007's mission to hunt down the merciless Scaramanga, Britt found herself more than once the butt of Roger's jokes.

'I remember we were playing this scene where I was hidden under the blankets of a bed on which Bond was sitting chatting up this gorgeous girl,' she says. 'Suddenly I heard the director shout, "Cut – freeze everyone." I froze – and the next thing all the guys in the studio, about six of them, were on the bed with me! I felt all this bouncing going on, so I pulled the blanket back, and there were all these men crowding in on me. I could tell with one look at Roger's face that he had been in on it!'

Britt, the former wife of Peter Sellers and Rod Stewart, admits that she was very anxious to land the part of Mary Goodnight. 'It was a very lean time for me. From having a lot of money I went down to earning hardly anything at all. Just barely enough to stay in England and keep my daughter in school. But I kept working – and I worked very hard on that Bond film.'

As a result of her experiences on *The Man With The Golden Gun*, Britt says she has come to the conclusion that all the Bond films are 'very peculiar' in certain respects. 'First, because you never take your clothes off. And, secondly, because you never make love and even the kissing is reduced. I mean it goes on up to a point, and then something else has to happen. The producers are obviously very keen to get the right certificate for the films.

'So, however many naked girls you think you see, if you look carefully you'll see that none of them are naked. And however many girls Bond gets into bed with, he only manages to have one kiss then something terrible happens!'

Barbara Bach who played the Russian spy, Major Anya Amasova, in Roger Moore's third Bond film, *The Spy Who Loved Me*, is now married to one of the world's most famous pop stars, Ringo Starr, once of The Beatles.

Russet-haired Barbara, with her wide hazel eyes and high cheekbones, was a former fashion model who graduated to the world of films with all the assurance and ease she had shown when posing for the front covers of some of the leading American magazines.

The role of Anya, a liberated feminine counterpart of 007, was hailed in 1977 as 'the most important part ever to be created for any female Bond protagonist.' What made the part even more challenging was playing alongside the veteran actor Curt Jurgens as Stromberg, and the introduction of perhaps the most memorable of all the Bond villains, Jaws (Richard Kiel).

'I had spent eight years in Italy which gave me valuable training for the part,' Barbara says. 'I was lucky to gain so many personal qualities there because I worked with many more different kinds of actors than I might have done if I'd come directly to Hollywood.'

She is a girl with a cosmopolitan background – Rumanian grandmother, Austrian-born father and Irish mother – and she fitted smoothly into the role of the Russian spy whose emotions get the better of her mission to outwit 007.

'Though there were some scenes in the movie which were shot on exotic locations in places like Sardinia and Egypt, the most exciting thing was working on that huge set at Pinewood with the nuclear submarines. After all the B-pictures I'd made in Italy where you use whatever props are to hand, that set just took my breath away!'

Barbara found Roger Moore highly professional in his approach to acting, though his sense of fun was always ready to erupt when things went wrong on the set.

'He knows how to defuse a situation with a laugh, though sometimes those cigars which he smokes incessantly can be less of a joke,' she smiles.

The role of Major Amasova certainly brought Barbara to international attention – though when she followed this by playing a Yugoslav spy in *Force 10 From Navarone*, she did foresee a problem.

'Imagine making my first two big pictures playing foreigners,' she said in 1978. 'No one knows how much I look forward to playing a role with a straight American accent. I'd even settle for playing a Southern girl!'

If Barbara made a good match for 007, then Lois Chiles who appeared as Holly Goodhead in *Moonraker* in 1979 was actually his equal in almost every respect. As a CIA agent, an astronaut and a scientist she was not surprisingly described by one critic as being 'smarter than a computer in overdrive.'

When Lois, the 30-year-old, green-eyed daughter of a Texan oilman, who had rapidly graduated from modelling into the movies, heard on the film grapevine that the Bond producers were casting for *Moonraker*, she determined to go after a part and fate seemed to play into her hands.

'I was flying home to America after some filming in London when who should I find myself sitting next to than Lewis Gilbert,' says Lois. 'And he was actually on his way to a *Moonraker* conference. I remember thinking to myself, "Wouldn't it be a strange twist of fate if that proved to be my next picture?" '

Which is exactly what it *did* prove to be. Lewis Gilbert himself takes up the other side of the casting.

'In the early days,' he says, 'Bond came into a room, the girl fell, was plundered, and you never saw her again. In the last movie Barbara Bach for the first time held her own. But Lois had even more to do. She is equal to Bond. Her image is very much in keeping

Lois Chiles as Holly Goodhead who got carried away into space in *Moonraker* (1979).

with the evolution of women today.'

And he added, 'We're still pressing for beauty – people expect beautiful women around Bond – but now we must show a lot more of women intellectually. This, of course, presented us with the biggest challenge the series had faced so far: portraying intellectual qualities while presenting Playboy-type visuals.'

Lois has a good measure of both – and proved so in the film. She also has her own views on the Bond girls' sex symbol imagery.

'Being sexy doesn't necessarily mean hanging out of your clothes,' she says. 'That's not my concept of sensuality. Being sexy is a lot of subtleness. So my dresses were cut low – subtle and a bit of a tease. Some people can be very sexy and still keep their clothes on. Look at Sophia Loren!

'I was hired for *Moonraker* for a different kind of sensuality: for being a strong, independent girl,' she says.

Lois believes today that Holly Goodhead was Bond's concession to women's liberation.

'I look back on *Moonraker* with affection,' she says. 'It was fun to make and the people I worked with were fun. In fact, I think that's the way to approach a Bond film – appreciating the opportunity to have fun. It's not something terribly serious.'

There were not many laughs for Lois immediately after *Moonraker*, however.

'I got no more offers after the film,' she says. 'It was as if people felt I'd been given my chance and blown it. I hadn't delivered the goods. I was really disheartened.'

What she did was to live off her earnings from *Moonraker* and go back to acting school. 'Now I'm hopeful again,' she says. 'I'm no longer just someone who sailed into the film business. I'm finally an actress. But it's taken a long time . . .'

The next Bond epic, *For Your Eyes Only*, introduced another French actress, Carole Bouquet, in the part of Melina Havelock, the resolute young girl who set out to avenge her parents killed by a Cuban assassin and found herself knee-deep in 007's mission to recover a top secret piece of submarine equipment.

Carole, another Bond beauty with waist-length dark hair, had actually been earmarked for the role while *Moonraker* was being made. The director of *For Your Eyes Only*, John Glen, explains: 'We'd originally met Carole when she visited the Paris set of *Moonraker*, and we just thought she would be ideal when we came to cast this picture. We couldn't have made a better choice.'

Born in Paris, the 23-year-old actress made a spectacular entry into films while she was still attending the National School of Theatre at the Paris Conservatoire. There she was seen by director Luis Brunel who offered her a starring role in *That Obscure Object of Desire* which he made in 1977. Cubby Broccoli who later saw the movie immediately realised her potential for the 007 saga.

However, both during the making of the picture and since, Carole has very carefully distanced herself from all the Bond ballyhoo.

'I accepted the role because I thought it would be an interesting experience to act in such a popular series,' she says today. 'But I never considered it anything other than an interlude in what I hope will be a long career making serious pictures.'

As if to prove her point, the morning that Carole finished work on *For Your Eyes Only* at Pinewood, she boarded a plane for Prague and there worked for two months with director Werner Schroeter on a film about women in a lunatic asylum. The luxurious hair she had so strikingly worn as Melina Havelock became lank and dirty, the transluscent skin of her face was allowed to go unwashed and she deliberately went without sleep to create bags under her blue eyes. The beautiful Bond girl became quite unrecognisable.

'I did not wish to become involved with all the fuss that surrounds the actresses who appear in the Bond films, because I have heard what it has done to the careers of some of them,' Carole explains further. 'Just let me say that I like to avoid the limelight and get on with my work. I am sure, though, that the Bond films have many years of success ahead of them and I shall not forget my small contribution to the series.'

Carole Bouquet was cast as Melina Havelock in *For Your Eyes Only* (1981).

Maud Adams who was Roger Moore's female companion in *Octopussy* which was filmed in 1983, had actually appeared in a Bond film before in *The Man With The Golden Gun*.

'Mind you, I died rather quickly then,' she says with just a trace of a Swedish accent. 'I was Christopher Lee's lady and I fell for Bond and got a bullet in my chest for my trouble!'

Born in Lulea, Sweden, in 1945, Maud was a model in Paris and New York, before entering the world of television commercials and then into films in 1970. She says that James Bond proved her passport to success.

'Before I appeared in *The Man With The Golden Gun*, I had only played in minor movies,' she says. 'Cubby Broccoli feels that he really discovered me. He had closely followed my career after that and wanted to bring me back. He thought the part of *Octopussy* was perfect for me – though I never believed I had a chance because women don't normally come back in the Bond adventures.'

The fact that Cubby is an admirer may be judged from this quote he made to one journalist in 1979. 'In *The Man With The Golden Gun* she had one of the most beautiful close-ups I have ever seen on the screen,' he said. 'And she is quite an actress. We really threw her in at the deep end. In her very first scene she was sitting in a stadium between Christopher Lee and James Bond. And she was dead – but Bond didn't realise the fact. How's that for openers?'

In *Octopussy*, Maud played a multi-millionairess hotel chain and circus owner who dabbles in smuggling until her partner-in-crime double-crosses her. Then she switches sides to join Bond and revenge herself.

Once called the woman with 'the sexiest cheekbones in Hollywood', auburn-haired Maud was delighted to find that the Bond women were no longer being treated as just sex symbols.

'I think that now all the girls get a chance to show their brains as well as their bodies and that's a big step in the right direction. I also happen to think that *Octopussy* was the best role ever written for a woman in a Bond film.'

Maud remembers her work with Roger Moore as a 'sensational experience'.

'Roger is so much fun,' she says. 'He always keeps everyone in good spirits, joking around, and he's a great person to work with.'

She also thinks highly of the Bond movies as a whole.

'It is good for all of us to have fantasies – and the Bond films are all one big fantasy,' she says. 'I happen to think the films are just as much a fantasy for women as for men. All women would like to be James Bond sensual fantasy creatures. They never have any worries, never have to cook or take the kids to the dentist, or pay the bills.

'And of course all men can identify with being Bond: this very exciting, handsome man who can get any women he wants. I like men to be exciting, unpredictable and provocative like James Bond.'

While Maud Adams was busy filming *Octopussy*, another remarkable development in the Bond saga was taking place. The public were to get a second 007 for their money that same year when it was announced that Sean Connery was returning to the role he had originated in the movie appropriately titled *Never Say Never Again*. Co-starring with him was a stunning 32-year-old Nicaraguan model turned actress named Barbara Carrera.

Barbara was cast as Fatima Blush, the number-one assassin of SPECTRE whose mission was to hunt down and kill Bond. Talking about the role during filming, Barbara said: 'Fatima is not at all good. In fact, she's a very bad lady. But she's exciting.'

The first Bond girl to take the title role, Maud Adams in *Octopussy* (1983).

Barbara Carrera who co-starred in Sean Connery's recent 007 story, *Never Say Never Again* (1983).

Explaining further, she said, 'Fatima finds Bond terribly attractive and she's thrilled that she's the one who has been chosen to give him what she thinks of as the ultimate thrill: death. She sees the act of murder as a sort of ceremony and therefore there is a certain ritual to be gone through beforehand.'

In order to prepare herself for the film, Barbara rented a 13-room villa near Monte Carlo. 'It was the ultimate in luxury,' she recalls. 'It was full of servants and it helped me get in the right mood for my part as the millionairess Fatima. The trouble was that in the beginning the character of Fatima wasn't really defined. So I had to come up with the flamboyant clothes and the exaggerated make-up. I also decided to play her as Kali, the Hindu goddess of death, and mix in with that a little black widow and a little praying mantis. She became anything but your ordinary Bond girl – gutsy, powerful and intelligent: almost 007's female counterpart.'

There were, though, other problems which hung over the production because of the legal battle with EON which was going on behind the scenes. 'The film was made only because Sean Connery agreed to come back to play Bond,' Barbara says, 'but there didn't seem to be one leader saying things must be done this way or that, not even Sean. For instance, we went to Nassau in November to shoot the underwater scenes, but no one told us it was going to be the rainy season!'

Barbara admits she had to nerve herself for the scuba diving scenes in the picture. 'I had a tremendous fear of the deep ocean and never dreamed that I'd be able to go under the water for an hour,' she says. 'But once I saw the beauty underwater my fear disappeared and now I'm addicted to the sport.'

She also did not relish the prospect of allowing a boa constrictor to crawl over her body. 'I loathe the very sight of snakes and knew nothing about the boa constrictor when I accepted the part. But I ended up by kissing it, caressing it and allowing it to slither all over my body and even around my neck underneath the expensive furs!'

But Barbara had no reservations whatsoever about working with Sean Connery. 'He's an incredibly sexy man and all the women I meet around the world – without exception – are in love with him. So it was no hardship playing the seduction scenes. In fact, all the love scenes were very spectacular and erotic and I had to seduce him in the most strange and enticing ways!'

Off the set, Barbara says Sean adopted her like a big brother. 'He is such a warm, loving person and you can really depend on him. Women always say to me that they consider Sean to be the real Bond. He took a very serious, realistic approach to the part, whereas I think Roger Moore has always played Bond much more tongue-in-cheek.'

With the benefit of hindsight, Barbara believes that she made the exotic and sensual Fatima more than just a decorative armpiece for Bond. 'Most of those beautiful, artificial Bond girls have never been given anything to do. They are cardboard cut-outs and they just fade into obscurity. I was determined to make Fatima Blush a Bond girl people would remember.'

The most recent picture, *A View To A Kill*, made in 1985, gave fans not only a blonde Bond bombshell but also another memorable villainess. The stunning blonde was former *Charlie's Angels* TV star, Tanya Roberts, who appeared as Stacey Sutton the geology expert who helps 007 thwart the mad plans of Max Zorin to flood the San Andreas Fault in California. During the mission, the pair found themselves in uneasy alliance with May Day, Zorin's betrayed assistant, who was played by the remarkable singer and actress, Grace Jones.

Tanya Roberts, an ash blonde with pale-blue eyes, was raised in the tough Bronx area of New York and had worked in the theatre and on TV and films before making the Bond picture. On her way to stardom she had also posed for a *Playboy* centrefold which became an instant topic of comment with journalists.

'I was very happy posing for *Playboy*,' the effervescent 29-year-old said firmly while making the picture. 'I was photographed with some large cats and I thought it looked provocative and beautiful. Why not? I've got one of the best bodies in town!'

But in discussing her role as Stacey Sutton, Tanya was quick to stress that she was not just a Bond body. 'She's a very strong, bright and independent girl. She's totally on her own – her father and grandfather are both dead. Stacey is a really good character and plays an important part in moving the story on which was what attracted me to it in the first place.'

Tanya said she had seen all the earlier Bond films, but had never imagined taking part in one until she was contacted by Cubby Broccoli.

'I love the pictures because they're such great escapism,' she says. 'But they are hard work to make and far from glamorous. I mean getting up at four o'clock in the morning and then getting filthy dirty while acting down in a mine is hardly glamorous!'

Tanya said she found Roger Moore 'very consistent and nice, always in a good mood.' And she added, 'You might as well be married to the people you're working with in a film; it *is* a marriage, more or less. You get all kinds of personalities, and it's nice when you get mellow ones like Roger.'

She was not amused, though, when she became the centre of a series of rows which made headlines before *A View To A Kill* opened.

'There's always a lot of rubbish printed about the rivalry between Bond girls,' she says. 'I've given up reading what's printed about me. The worst story was one saying I'd

The two very different female stars of the Bond epic, *A View To A Kill* (1985) – Grace Jones (left) and Tanya Roberts (right).

been rude about Roger. I had a call saying he didn't want me at the première.

'I couldn't believe that anyone would really think I'd actually said those things. I mean, knocking Roger would be like digging your own grave. But fortunately, it was all sorted out in the end. I guess it's the price you pay for being the top-billed Bond girl.'

In fact, Tanya was pretty well matched for headlines by her co-star, Grace Jones, the electrifying Jamaican-born singer and former model, who also talked about her role as May Day during the filming.

'She's sexy and feminine and mysterious and very high society, which is like me. She is also lethal – and that makes for the kind of combination I like.'

Grace added, 'I think I have an image as a rather extraordinary physical creature. I like that, too. You see I work out at least four times a week and I have extensive martial arts training. I was once mugged in New York and resolved there and then it would never happen again. All of that helped me in the role of May Day.'

Grace was also a Bond fan like her co-star. 'I have always loved the movies,' she says, 'especially those with Sean Connery. But I got to know Roger Moore working on the film and he had a difficult role to fill – but the fact he did it just as successfully as Sean says a lot.'

John Glen, the director of *A View To A Kill*, has spoken in equally glowing terms about Grace herself. 'She is probably the most bizarre person I have ever worked with. You cannot miss her, even if she is standing near the back in a scene. She has an incredible physical presence that none of the other Bond girls have had.

'She has amazing strength, too. At one stage she had to lift up a fully grown man – with a little help from special effects – and then throw him. I have to admit we were all a little terrified of her before she arrived because of her reputation for hurting stunt people. But once we explained it isn't necessary to actually *hit* people she was fine!' he added.

Grace herself remembers the movie for the tricks she and Roger Moore pulled on each other. 'He's a great practical joker and I heard stories that he played tricks on all the girls with whom he had love scenes, to try and break the ice.

'I thought I'd get in ahead of him and so I smuggled this piece of electrical apparatus under the sheets of the bed we were using. Actually the batteries were weak so no harm was done – but I guess I could have been the Bond villain to achieve what no other has done. Finishing off 007!' she adds with a broad grin.

The Gadget Master

The tall man with iron-grey hair, direct brown eyes and a poker face, took up the rather old fashioned briefcase from his desk. His big, firm fingers moved over the surface of the case and for a moment it was possible to hear a pin drop in the elegantly furnished drawing room of the Georgian house.

The fingers touched a trigger in the case and a secret compartment slid open. From it, a wicked looking knife sprang into view.

At this, the poker face broke into a smile – an unfamiliar smile, for this is a man not usually given to emotion. Not on the cinema screen at least.

'Ah, it worked,' he heaved a sigh of relief. 'The trouble is, I've been showing this off to people for twenty-five years and sometimes the knife just drops out onto the floor! Like so many of the gadgets I've got, it's getting a bit worn now. Wouldn't do for that to happen to Bond in some tight corner, though, would it?'

Desmond Llewelyn, the man who has been called 'the deadly gadgeteer' and the 'fiendishly inventive armourer' of the James Bond films, smiles disarmingly, and seems a million miles away from Major Boothroyd, or 'Q' as he is more familiarly known, the head of the Secret Service's special weapons unit.

Desmond Llewelyn is a kindly man with a strong sense of humour, and is quite ready to admit that he is not gadget-minded at all. And in real-life in his beautiful home at Bexhill-on-Sea in Sussex, he looks every inch the rural gentleman. The only signs of his involvement in the Bond pictures is his collection of the gadgets that he has used during his years associated with the series: two briefcases, a whole selection of guns and knives, a camera, wrist-watch, pen and such-like. All the most innocent-looking items *until* Desmond lets you into their secrets . . .

After a lifetime in the theatre and latterly on television and in films, fame came late to Desmond Llewelyn – yet playing the ingenious 'Q' has given him enormous satisfaction. Indeed, brief though his appearances have been in the Bond films, only Lois Maxwell, playing Miss Moneypenny, has appeared in more. (He was not in *Dr No* and missed out on *Live And Let Die* because he happened to be in America promoting its predecessor, *Diamonds Are Forever*, at the time shooting took place.)

For many fans of the Bond opus, 'Q' has long been one of the favourite supporting characters, and certainly his appearance with some new gadget in each picture has invariably and immediately heightened the interest of audiences.

'There are so many people interested in the gadgets all over the world,' he says, handling the various superbly made instruments which form his collection, 'and I get lots of letters about them. I take it as a compliment that many people actually believe I've had a hand in inventing the devices that James Bond uses in the films. Also, wherever I go people can't seem to think of me as anything other than "Q"!'

In actual fact Desmond has led an interesting and varied life. And more than one journalist has suggested that he is more Bond-like than most of the imitators of Ian Fleming's hero!

Desmond was born in Newport, Monmouthshire in September 1914, and coming from a family steeped in the traditions of mining, a career in entertainment seemed hardly likely. His grandfather had been a miner, and his father was a colliery general manager. Yet somehow being raised among coal mining folk led him towards acting, as he explains.

'Although the place where I was raised was a mining area of hard working, hard playing people, they were also a people with a great passion for the arts. For the Welsh are fantastic when it comes to making their own entertainment,' he says.

'I remember as a child that so many people sang or took part in local amateur dramatics that you just couldn't help a bit of it rubbing off. Perhaps that's why it has produced so many talented people for the world of entertainment – fine singers and splendid acting stars like Richard Burton and Stanley Baker. They came out of the mining areas of South Wales.'

After being educated at Radley, Desmond spent two years at RADA in London and then served in several provincial repertory companies in Southend, Bexhill and Oxford for three years. In 1939 he was on the verge of breaking into the film business – having made his debut in the Will Hay comedy, *Ask A Policeman*, playing a ghost – when World War II broke out. Naturally enough, he joined the Welsh Fusiliers.

Desmond was trained at Sandhurst, attained the rank of Lieutenant, but scarcely had

Desmond Llewelyn, the deadly gadgeteer 'Q' of the Bond movies, at home with some of his collection of souvenirs.

he become involved in the hostilities in France, than he was taken a prisoner of war during the evacuation of Dunkirk on 27 May 1940. He remained in captivity for five years – although he did try to escape once and was actually captured in a tunnel. As a result of this he was promptly dispatched to a tougher camp, Oflag 9AZ.

There was one good thing about his years in captivity, however, as he also explains. 'We set up little drama groups in the prison camps I was at in Germany and although it wasn't the most comfortable way to develop a career in the theatre, we still managed to put on shows regularly and it was marvellous experience for me.'

After the war, Desmond returned to acting and found regular work on both the London stage and in television. Then in 1950 he struck lucky not once but twice. He won his first major film role playing a Welsh tank driver in a film about the Guards Armoured Division called *They Were Not Divided.* The second piece of luck was the director of the picture, Terence Young, who twelve years later was to give him the role of 'Q'.

'I suppose it was lucky all round,' he reminisces. 'I wasn't in *Dr No*, but the actor who played the part of Major Boothroyd (Peter Burton) wasn't available for the second picture, *From Russia With Love*, so my name was put forward. Now because I'd worked with Terence Young on *They Were Not Divided* he knew my name. I think he liked my work and that's how I landed the part!'

Desmond Llewelyn has made 'Q' an instantly recognisable figure and now knows him inside out.

'He's really just a very conscientious civil servant who has risen to head a department and has a lot of responsibilities,' Desmond explains. 'And Bond happens to be just one of his responsibilities – though a responsibility he sometimes feels takes up too much of his time when he should really be getting on with other things. Outside of his work, he's very much a club man, and I like having the opportunity of wearing different ties in different films – though I have to make sure that they are of the kind of organisations that "Q" would belong to: the Guards, his old university, that sort of thing. I did, though, once wear a fireman's tie after I'd been made an honorary fireman!'

Desmond also sees his role as very much that of a 'straight man' for James Bond to bounce humorous remarks off – and is a fund of stories about his relationships with Sean Connery and Roger Moore both on and off camera.

'During the years we've been making the films, both of them have come out with off-the-cuff remarks which have been left in the films and really got big laughs from the audience. Mind you, I like to think that none of them would have worked if the audience weren't totally convinced that "Q" was a no-nonsense type who is offended by Bond's lack of respect for his inventions.'

This said, Desmond is quick to admit that he thinks some of the gadgets he has had to give 007 were 'ridiculously impractical' and only included for the sake of a laugh. Others, though, have turned out to be real life-savers. At this he turns to his collection and recalls the part each item has played in the respective films of the series . . .

'Most of these gadgets are designed to overcome the enemy,' he says, 'and are consequently lethal – but at the same time terribly simple to operate.'

The briefcase which he demonstrated in his first film, *From Russia With Love*, was a real box of conjuror's tricks and perhaps it is not surprising that this remains the favourite of all his pictures to date.

'It was the first special prop made for Bond, of course, and full of all kinds of hidden gadgets necessary to the spy's trade. The knife which popped out of one side, for instance, and the teargas cartridge which exploded in the face of the Russian played by Robert Shaw. There were also the daggers and the telescopic rifle which Bond used to shoot down the helicopter.'

That rifle was featured on all the publicity posters for the film – and gun enthusiasts might just like to know from 'Q's' own lips that it was an Armalite Survival Gun.

Guns also featured in Desmond's second Bond film, *Goldfinger*, as well as perhaps the most famous of all the secret agent's 'props', the Aston Martin DB-5 complete with its incredible variety of special effects. It is not only for the car that he remembers the 1964 movie, but also because of the effect it had on him as a person and an actor.

'You may have noticed that in *Goldfinger* I'm the one who jumps when a shot is fired,' he says in a moment of confession. 'You see I'm actually gun shy! But it was the film in which I really got to establish my character.'

Goldfinger was directed by Guy Hamilton and again Desmond remembers how the scene in which he was to hand over the Aston Martin to Bond was created.

'I was working at a bench and when Bond came in I got up to greet him. Immediately I did this, though, Guy Hamilton shouted for a cut. "No, no," he said, "You don't do that. You stay right where you are and get on with your work. This man Bond is actually a bloody nuisance to you!" "What do you mean?" I asked Hamilton. "This is the great James Bond surely?"

'Hamilton looked straight at me and explained, "No. He treats you with contempt, don't you see? He destroys every gadget you give him. All your hard work is just tossed away after use. Even when you're describing the car to him he's not really taking any interest." I saw exactly what he meant and that's how "Q" has been played ever since.'

Although Bond showed a seeming disinterest in the car in *Goldfinger*, it proved so popular with the public that it was brought back in *Thunderball* in 1965 – complete with its passenger ejector seat, bullet-proof shield, retractable tire-slashing blades and smoke-screen device. Desmond Llewelyn naturally has a special fondness for the Aston Martin which has remained a crowd-puller wherever it has been displayed.

'Actually,' he says, 'the features on it were not as brand new as you might think. I mean, think of the film *Ben Hur* and you have the knives coming out of the chariot wheels. In Prohibition days, the gangsters used oil slicks to throw off pursuit, and there have been ejector seats in aeroplanes for years. What the designer, John Stears, did was to just put all those things together into one wonderful bag of tricks!'

Among the other 'wonderful tricks' in *Thunderball* were the Bell-Textron Jump Jet suits which had been used by the US Army in commando actions in Vietnam, and the remarkable underwater camera used by Bond.

'When production started on *Thunderball* we needed this special compact camera for taking underwater pictures which "Q" was to give Bond,' Desmond recalls. 'At that time the only cameras in production were great big clumsy things which wouldn't look right. Well, we heard that Nikon were working on different ideas for small underwater cameras and so we got in touch, told them what we wanted, and asked if we could give their prototypes a test. They jumped at the chance to be in a Bond film!

'Now, of course, the cameras like that have been perfected and are on sale generally. But then they were something special – and people were asking, "Who on earth invents such things?"'

The camera, which Bond used to photograph Largo's underwater hideout, was so well used during the filming that although it now enjoys a place of honour in Desmond's collection, it has to be kept stuck together with sticky tape!

Making the 1967 Bond film, *You Only Live Twice*, was memorable for Desmond because it took him to the Far East.

'Making the Bond pictures is not only marvellous for me as an actor, but also because they give me a chance to see the world. By the time *You Only Live Twice* came along, I'd been to France as a soldier, Germany as a POW and Italy as an actor. But the one place I'd always wanted to visit was Japan – and thanks to James Bond I got there.'

Although for many people the enormous hollow volcano in which SPECTRE planned its latest bid for world domination provided the most breath-taking moments of *You Only Live Twice* the scene stealer was probably the little autogyro plane flown by Bond. Again, the man charged with placing this remarkable device in Bond's hands recalls how it came to be a part of the film.

'Apparently Ken Adams heard the man who had invented the plane, Wing Commander Ken Wallis, talking about it on the radio and it immediately struck him how well it would fit into *You Only Live Twice.* So he got onto Wallis and invited him down to Pinewood for a demonstration. Once Ken Adams had decided to use it, there was just the small matter of having "Q" take it apart and pack it into four large suitcases for transportation to Japan!'

The autogyro – nicknamed 'Little Nellie' – was actually designated a WA-116, says Desmond, and had a top speed of 180 miles per hour, a ceiling of 14,000 feet and could land on a surface just twenty-four feet wide!

It was back to the more traditional armaments for the George Lazenby Bond, *On Her Majesty's Secret Service*, before a last fling for 'Q' and Sean Connery on *Diamonds Are Forever*, made in 1971.

Again Desmond rummages among his souvenirs. 'You probably recall the precarious scene where Bond was climbing a sheer face,' he says, 'Well, this is the Piton Gun he employed which is actually used by mountaineers to drive pegs into rock faces.

'Another rather nasty souvenir of the same picture is the Finger Trap which was used to such grisly effect. Mind you, I have to be careful with that one!' he says.

A third item from the picture is one that Desmond really *does* wish works. 'It's a small, square-shaped ring which "Q" used for fiddling the fruit machines in Las Vegas in order to win all the jackpots. One of his most harmless inventions – what a pity I can't get it to work!'

Unfortunately, Desmond was not able to appear in Roger Moore's debut film, *Live and Let Die*, but met the new Bond in *The Man With The Golden Gun*. He has since got to know Roger Moore well – more so than Sean Connery with whom his scenes were usually brief.

'Sean I found a bit distracting because he would often fidget with my gadgets while I was talking,' he says. 'And although Roger has his own habits, too, he is incredibly efficient. He only has to look at the script and he's learned it. He just mops up lines.

'Now for my part I find that difficult. So often the lines are technical and I don't always understand what it's about. I do, though, try to familiarise myself with the workings of the equipment I'm supposed to have created for Bond so that I don't disillusion the public. But the truth is I'm only an actor and not being particularly mechanical I sometimes have a terrible time trying to figure out how they work and then get them to work for me!'

In *The Spy Who Loved Me* (1977) Desmond found himself presenting Bond with the remarkable submersible Lotus sports car equipped with sea-to-air and underwater missiles.

He recalls, 'I thought it was a wonderful idea to have a car that goes underwater. In fact it travelled at fourteen knots but the person in it had to wear a wet suit and oxygen mask.

'Like so many of the other Bond gadgets, I can foresee the day when people will be travelling around under water in cars just like that one. Maybe some of them will even remember the film and think that "Q" was the man behind it all!'

Moonraker in 1979 provided Desmond with the added problem of becoming familiar with space technology when he had to offer gadgets to Bond which he knew were as

Just one of the fabulous machines that 'Q' has handed over to the not-so-loving care of James Bond – the Lotus Esprit which appeared in *The Spy Who Loved Me* with Roger Moore and Barbara Bach in 1977.

impractical as they were funny. *For Your Eyes Only* was certainly more down to earth, but Desmond rather felt the gadgets took second place to the Bond girls.

However, *Octopussy* made in 1983 restored all his old enthusiasm. For a start it provided him with a second briefcase – and one as packed with gadgets as the original in *From Russia With Love*. The two cases now form the centre-pieces of his collection.

Among the items to be found in the case are a Fabergé Egg, a gold fountain pen and a Seiko TV watch.

'The Egg was one of the main things in the film,' he recalls. 'You remember how Bond put a small homing device in it so that he knew where it was. Actually such a thing had already been invented. Not so with the fountain pen, though.

'It was no ordinary pen. It was a solid gold, Mont Blanc pen worth over $1,000! What "Q" did with it was to put a hearing aid in the top and a special mixture of acid which can dissolve steel. Enough to get anyone out of trouble!' he enthuses.

The TV watch was also a precursor of an item that shortly afterwards came onto the market for general sale.

In the latest film, *A View To A Kill*, Desmond was particularly delighted with the highly sophisticated robot surveillance machine called Snooper. 'A real pet that gadget,' he says, 'just imagine what corners it might get into. And the item for detecting hidden listening devices which was disguised as an electric shaver also provided me with another memorable screen moment.

'And what about that small launch camouflaged like a floating iceberg? When I see things like that I wonder what on earth they'll dream up next!'

Desmond is naturally pleased that his gadgets have once again become such a feature of the Bond films after their brief hiatus.

'In the most recent films Richard Maibaum and Michael Wilson have given me back the real character of "Q". He is as disgruntled as ever and criticises Bond all the time. Of course, you have to be careful not to make him *too* disgruntled or it would become boring for the audience. Not to mention a bit monotonous for me as an actor,' he says.

Understandably, Desmond Llewelyn would like 'Q' to feature more extensively in the films, but is aware that by appearing more often during the course of a story he might dilute the eager anticipation with which the audience greets him. In any event, he honestly never expected the character to have lasted as long as he has done – and even now believes he could be dispensed with. 'Really, I'm just there to demonstrate things to Bond. They could just as easily have someone hand a gadget to Bond and get him to reply, "Well, look what 'Q' has sent me this time!" '

Desmond Llewelyn is modest about his own contribution to the Bond saga.

'I have had a very satisfying career,' he says, 'and if I've become typecast as "Q" then I am getting rather old to play too many other parts anyway. I have a nice home and I've been able to raise my family so I have plenty to be grateful for to James Bond.

'I love the filming, and the Bond crowd are really marvellous. They make it all such fun. And, of course, people know my face all over the place. I sometimes get surrounded by people and everyone seems to assume I'm rich. But that's just not true. The Bond films usually amount to only a couple of weeks work in a year – and the rest of the time it's gardening and mowing the lawn!'

Desmond's life on the coast of Sussex is a far cry from the high-speed, dangerous world of 007, and sometimes when he's struggling to mend something in his home or clearing the swimming pool of leaves, he wishes he really *was* 'Q' and could dream up the kind of marvellous gadget that would make such chores easy.

His enthusiasm for the stories remains undiminished, and he has little time for people who try to find special meanings or inferences in the films.

'They are pure entertainment,' he insists. 'Like the old Tom Mix cowboy dramas. Certainly the stories have got more fantastic, they're much bigger than life. I think if they had stuck to the old fashioned things, the films wouldn't have captured the imagination of the young the way they have done. They are pure escapism – the only problem is *what* to do next?'

For the 'Master Gadget Maker' that particular problem does not arise. He merely has to wait and see what incredible pieces of equipment emerge from the imaginations of the writers and the drawing boards of the designers.

Then he will be faced once again with the little matter of making what might seem unbelievable – *believable*. And not just to the ever-casual Mr Bond, but the audience as well.

The Love Of Bond's Lives

The indispensable Miss Moneypenny, whose adoration of James Bond is generally accepted as the longest unrequited love affair on the screen, has been played for twenty-five years by Lois Maxwell, once described as 'the worst girl in Hollywood' and in truth a remarkable lady whose life story is almost as dramatic as a female 007 – let alone a member of the secret service team!

Lois of the auburn locks and enchanting blue-green eyes has appeared in all fourteen Bond films since that memorable introduction in *Dr No* when Bond asked her, 'Moneypenny, what gives?' And she replied with unforgettable insouciance, 'Me – given an ounce of encouragement.'

As M's super-efficient secretary, she has never appeared for long in any of the films, yet her presence in every picture is a unique achievement that has endeared her to fans for a quarter of a century. 'It's only a small part,' she says with beguiling charm, 'but people are affectionate towards it. The Moneypenny scenes have become like a Bond trademark.'

The passing years have treated Lois Maxwell kindly despite the personal and professional demands that life has put upon her, and today – between filming the Bond pictures – she leads an industrious life in her native Canada where she is a partner in a business making crowd control barriers and pursuing her interest in writing with a twice-weekly column in the *Toronto Star* called, inevitably, 'Moneypenny'. The incongruous combination of these two occupations is surely only typical of the woman who has made a cult figure out of a tiny part about which she says she has 'pretty well said the same thing backwards, forwards, sideways and upside down over the last twenty-five years!'

The fact that Lois has made such a success of the part is due in no small measure to having met Ian Fleming and being vastly encouraged both by his verdict on her acting and his fondness for Moneypenny.

'I met him three times,' she recalls, 'and I liked him tremendously. In fact he was rather like my late husband – he had this sardonic smile and attitude. Anyway, he told me that he visualised Moneypenny as a tall, distinguished-looking woman with the most kissable lips in the world. "And you, my dear," he said, "are the epitomy of that woman I visualised." You see, Moneypenny has sexuality. I was very bucked by what he said.'

Lois was christened Lois Hooker, the daughter of school teacher William Hooker and his wife, Ruth, a nurse, on 14 February 1927 in Kitchener, Ontario. The acting bug bit her in childhood, she says, but her mother and father frowned on the idea of her being an actress, and when she got a regular role in CBS's 'Children's Play of the Week' she had to keep her identity secret from them behind the pseudonym 'Robin Wells'.

'I was amazed they never recognised my voice on the radio,' she says today peering over the half-moon spectacles she wears when not on the screen. 'Of course, I could never take home the money I earned, so every week I spent it on presents for the soldiers in the Military Hospital just around the corner from the Toronto studio.'

In 1942, at the age of fifteen, her desire to act made her decide to run away from home and, lying about her age, she enlisted into the Canadian Army who were then looking for talent for their Army Show. She played a 'gag girl' to the two comedians, Wayne and Schuster, as the party toured Canada, then Alaska and the Arctic, before entertaining the crews of minesweepers on the way to England. After this stop-over, the party was due to go on to Italy.

'That's when they discovered my age,' she recalls with a grin. 'They took me off the draft and sent me to see a psychiatrist to ascertain whether I was fit to be fired at! The whole business was complicated by the fact that because of some confusion in the records, Lois Maxwell, 21217, was also posted as a deserter from a battalion of the Canadian Seaforth Highlanders which was then due to sail for Italy! Anyway, they wanted to send me straight back to Canada.'

Lois felt the only solution to her dilemma was to go on the run. So she dyed her uniform and thought she had better find herself a new identity and a new job. So she headed for London and managed to get an audition at RADA with Sir Kenneth Barnes in the hope of obtaining a scholarship.

'After the audition I was dodging coppers and everyone else who was looking for me. Then, just when I had got the news that I had won the Academy's Lady Louis Mountbatten Scholarship, I was walking rather euphorically down the Edgware Road when this voice said, "You're AWOL!"

'Now I was in *terrible* trouble. I was flung into a lorry and taken to Aldershot where they put me in a cell. Eventually I managed to get to a phone and call RADA. "Help!" I said. "I'm in prison." I don't know what they did, but within hours I was out and being discharged from the Army.'

In fact it was Lady Mountbatten who had persuaded the British authorities to free Lois and allow her to stay in the country as her ward and take the course at RADA. Her natural ability helped her to progress quickly at the Academy and – by chance – she had her first brush with another actor who was to share some of the later Bond success with her, for a fellow student at the same time was Roger Moore.

Completing her course, Lois worked in radio, as a photographer's model, and appeared briefly in her first film, *Corridor of Mirrors* made in 1946. Following an appearance on the London stage in Somerset Maugham's play *Our Betters*, she was tested by Warner Brothers and offered work in Hollywood. The two years which followed in the film capital are remembered with distaste.

'They stuck paste behind my ears to keep them flat. They put so much padding on my bosom I nearly toppled over. And they stuck stalks on my eyelashes. Then they stood back, rubbed their hands and said, "Fine, now she looks like a healthy mixture of Barbara Stanwyck and Lauren Bacall!" '

And as for the films she made in Hollywood – *That Hagan Girl* with Shirley Temple

(Left) The unmistakable Miss Moneypenny as immortalised by Lois Maxwell, and (above) Lois Maxwell at home in Toronto today working on her newspaper column, 'Moneypenny'.

and Ronald Reagan (1947), *The Decision of Christopher Blake* (1948), *The Dark Past* (1948), *The Crime Doctor's Diary* (1949) and *Kazan* (1949) – she has this to say:

'Completely forgettable – the whole lot. They always gave me straight roles. I thought with my freckles and long red hair, and knowing how to ride a horse, they would put me in Westerns or comedy. But I was invariably a psychiatric case or dying of unrequited love.'

While learning the art of playing unrequited love might have been good training for her Bond days, it was so frustrating Lois decided to run away again. This time to Italy – ignoring the pleas of Columbia Pictures who had more film ideas for her.

'It was quite a gamble,' she recalls. 'When my boat docked I had just $82 to my name – no home, no work and no knowledge of the language. But things worked out fine – thanks to the fact that *That Hagan Girl* had opened in Rome a few days before I had arrived and the film people knew my name.'

Italy, in fact, proved much more rewarding from a career point of view, and also personally when Lois found herself caught up in the social whirl of Rome society. Her first picture, *Tomorrow Is Too Late* (1950) with Vittorio de Sica, won top prize at the Venice Film festival, and then in *Brief Rapture* she gave what she believes to have been her best acting performance in a story about drug addiction.

Off-screen she went motor car racing, attended parties with Aly Khan, and unsuspectingly had another brush with the world of Bond-to-come when she took up underwater fishing with octopus as her main target.

'I used to go after them with a pressure gun so that I could kill them to eat,' she grins. 'The trouble is one nearly caught *me*. That was nastier than anything in the film *Octopussy*!'

After five years, Lois returned to London and her now well-developed talent earned her work in television and films. She also met someone very special.

'I was catching this plane to Paris one day when I saw this lovely hunk of man who looked like a great white hunter. We sat next to each other on the flight and I read my book upside down all the way. Just before we landed, he introduced himself as Peter Marriott, associate producer with Douglas Fairbanks Jnr. "Oh, my God," I said. "I should have come to see you years ago."'

The couple married in 1957, and Lois now has two children, both grown-up: Melinda, twenty-eight and Christian, twenty-six.

It was, though, a tragedy affecting her husband Peter, when she had given up acting for a time to raise the children, which precipitated her into the world of James Bond and the little niche she has now carved for herself in screen history. The memory of this time still brings a little sadness into her voice.

'It was on my son's second birthday,' she says, quietly. 'Right out of the blue Peter had a double coronary. The doctor's didn't expect him to live and I knew I would have to find work to support us all. So I phoned round some of the people I knew in the film business and pleaded for *anything* they could give me. It was Terence Young who called me back and offered me a part in *Dr No*.

'Actually, I was offered the part of either Moneypenny or the girl Sylvia, played by Eunice Gayson. The thing was I didn't fancy being seen in a pyjama top and I thought there might be a chance of playing Moneypenny again if the film was successful – which would, of course, be good for the family finances.'

Despite the worry of her husband's health, Lois was determined to make something of the part of the super-secretary and her evident infatuation with James Bond. She built up in her mind a background to explain their relationship and the motivation for the wistful smile or few simple words of dialogue she had to speak.

'There was nothing to go on in Ian Fleming's books, you see, so Terence Young, Sean Connery and I had to work something out before we began filming *Dr No*.'

A smile lights up Lois Maxwell's face when she describes the 'relationship' which they determined.

'Actually, Bond and Moneypenny have been secretly in love for years,' she says. 'They met when she was in the typing pool and he was a Ministry of Defence tea-boy. They went off for a weekend together at a discreet hotel and had a splendid time. Since then, though, they have had to keep their distance. Coming together would only cause them to fall hopelessly in love.

Of all the Bond films, Lois says *From Russia With Love* is her favourite, although she also has a soft spot for *On Her Majesty's Secret Service* because of its off-beat ending.

'It has perhaps a little more humanity in it than the others, with Bond's wife being shot and the creation of a situation that everyone in the audience can relate to. And for Moneypenny, of course, it's the end of her dreams. She's just left weeping with her memories.'

Appendix The James Bond Books and Films

1. The Novels

By Ian Fleming:
CASINO ROYALE (1953)
LIVE AND LET DIE (1954)
MOONRAKER (1955)
DIAMONDS ARE FOREVER (1956)
FROM RUSSIA WITH LOVE (1957)
DOCTOR NO (1958)
GOLDFINGER (1959)
FOR YOUR EYES ONLY (1960)
THUNDERBALL (1961)
THE SPY WHO LOVED ME (1962)
ON HER MAJESTY'S SECRET SERVICE (1963)
YOU ONLY LIVE TWICE (1964)
THE MAN WITH THE GOLDEN GUN (1965)
OCTOPUSSY (1966)

By Robert Markham (Kingsley Amis):
COLONEL SUN (1968)

By John Gardner:
LICENCE RENEWED (1981)
FOR SPECIAL SERVICES (1982)
ICEBREAKER (1983)
ROLE OF HONOUR (1984)
NOBODY LIVES FOREVER (1986)

2. The Films

CASINO ROYALE (1954)
Columbia Broadcasting Company for 'Climax!' TV Drama Series.
Produced by Arthur Oldman
Directed by Robert E Brandt
Script by Walter Jordon from the novel by Ian Fleming
Starring: Barry Nelson (James Bond), Peter Lorre (Le Chiffre), Linda Christian (Vesper Lynd), William Lundigan (narrator).

DR NO (1962)
EON Productions
Produced by Harry Saltzman and Albert R Broccoli
Directed by Terence Young
Script by Richard Maibaum, Joanna Harwood and Berkley Mather from the novel by Ian Fleming
Starring: Sean Connery (James Bond), Ursula Andress (Honey Rider), Joseph Wiseman (Dr No), Jack Lord (Felix Leiter), Bernard Lee ('M'), Lois Maxwell (Miss Moneypenny), Peter Burton (Major Boothroyd).

FROM RUSSIA WITH LOVE (1963)
EON Productions
Produced by Harry Saltzman and Albert R Broccoli
Directed by Terence Young
Script by Richard Maibaum and Joanna Harwood from the novel by Ian Fleming
Starring: Sean Connery (James Bond), Daniela Bianchi (Tatiana Romanova), Pedro Armendariz (Kerim Bey), Lotte Lenya (Rosa Klebb), Robert Shaw (Red Grant), Bernard Lee ('M'), Lois Maxwell (Miss Moneypenny), Walter Gotell (Morzeny), Desmond Llewelyn (Boothroyd).

GOLDFINGER (1964)
EON Productions
Produced by Harry Saltzman and Albert R Broccoli
Directed by Guy Hamilton
Script by Richard Maibaum and Paul Dehn from the novel by Ian Fleming
Starring: Sean Connery (James Bond), Honor Blackman (Pussy Galore), Gert Frobe (Goldfinger), Shirley Eaton (Jill Masterton), Tania Mallet (Tilly Masterton), Harold Sakata (Oddjob), Bernard Lee ('M'), Lois Maxwell (Miss Moneypenny), Cec Linder (Felix Leiter), Desmond Llewelyn ('Q').

THUNDERBALL (1965)
United Artists
Produced by Kevin McClory
Directed by Terence Young
Script by Richard Maibaum and John Hopkins based on an original screenplay by Jack Whittingham, Kevin McClory and Ian Fleming
Starring: Sean Connery (James Bond), Claudine Auger (Domino), Adolfo Celi (Largo), Luciana Paluzzi (Fiona), Rik Van Nutter (Felix Leiter), Bernard Lee ('M'), Lois Maxwell (Miss Moneypenny), Guy Doleman (Count Lippe), Desmond Llewelyn ('Q').

YOU ONLY LIVE TWICE (1967)
EON-Danjaq Productions
Produced by Harry Saltzman and Albert R Broccoli
Directed by Lewis Gilbert

Script by Roald Dahl based on the novel by Ian Fleming
Starring: Sean Connery (James Bond), Akiki Wakabayashi (Aki), Tetsuro Tamba (Tiger Tanaka), Mie Hama (Kissy Suzuki), Bernard Lee ('M'), Lois Maxwell (Miss Moneypenny), Desmond Llewelyn ('Q'), Donald Pleasence (Ernst Stavro Blofeld), Charles Gray (Henderson).

CASINO ROYALE (1967)
A Famous Artists Production
Produced by Charles K Feldman and Jerry Bresler
Directed by John Huston, Ken Hughes, Val Guest, Robert Parrish, Joe McGrath, Richard Talmadge and Anthony Squire
Script by Wolf Mankowitz, John Law and Michael Sayers from the novel by Ian Fleming
Starring: David Niven (Sir James Bond), Peter Sellers (Evelyn Tremble), Ursula Andress (Vesper Lynd), Orson Welles (Le Chiffre), Joanna Pettit (Mata Bond), Daliah Lavi (The Detamer), Woody Allen (Jimmy Bond), Deborah Kerr (Agent Mimi), William Holden (Ransome), John Huston ('M'), Barbara Boucher (Miss Moneypenny), Geoffrey Bayldon ('Q'), Terence Cooper (Cooper).

ON HER MAJESTY'S SECRET SERVICE (1969)
EON-Danjaq Productions
Produced by Harry Saltzman and Albert R Broccoli
Directed by Peter Hunt
Script by Richard Maibaum from the novel by Ian Fleming
Starring: George Lazenby (James Bond), Diana Rigg (Tracy), Telly Savalas (Ernst Stavro Blofeld), Ilse Steppat (Irma Bunt), Gabriele Ferzetti (Marc Ange Draco), Bernard Lee ('M'), Lois Maxwell (Miss Moneypenny), Desmond Llewelyn ('Q').

DIAMONDS ARE FOREVER (1971)
EON Productions
Produced by Harry Saltzman and Albert R Broccoli
Directed by Guy Hamilton
Script by Richard Maibaum and Tom Mankiewicz from the novel by Ian Fleming
Starring: Sean Connery (James Bond), Jill St John (Tiffany Case), Charles Gray (Ernst Stavro Blofeld), Lana Wood (Plenty O'Toole), Jimmy Dean (Willard Whyte), Putter Smith (Mr Kidd), Bruce Glover (Mr Wint), Norman Burton (Felix Leiter), Bernard Lee ('M'), Lois Maxwell (Miss Moneypenny), Desmond Llewelyn ('Q').

LIVE AND LET DIE (1973)
EON Productions
Produced by Harry Saltzman and Albert R Broccoli
Directed by Guy Hamilton
Script by Tom Mankiewicz from the novel by Ian Fleming
Starring: Roger Moore (James Bond), Jane Seymour (Solitaire), Yaphet Kotto (Dr Kananga), Clifton James (Sheriff JW Pepper), Julius W Harris (Tee Hee), Geoffrey Holder (Baron Samedi), David Hedison (Felix Leiter), Bernard Lee ('M'), Lois Maxwell (Miss Moneypenny).

THE MAN WITH THE GOLDEN GUN (1974)
EON Productions
Produced by Harry Saltzman and Albert R Broccoli
Directed by Guy Hamilton
Script by Richard Maibaum and Tom Mankiewicz from the novel by Ian Fleming
Starring: Roger Moore (James Bond), Christopher Lee (Scaramanga), Britt Ekland (Mary Goodnight), Maud Adams (Andrea), Herve Villechaize (Nick Nack),

Clifton James (Sheriff JW Pepper), Bernard Lee ('M'), Lois Maxwell (Miss Moneypenny), Desmond Llewelyn ('Q'), Michael Fleming (Communications Officer).

THE SPY WHO LOVED ME (1977)
EON Productions
Produced by Albert R Broccoli
Directed by Lewis Gilbert
Script by Richard Maibaum and Christopher Wood
Starring: Roger Moore (James Bond), Barbara Bach (Major Anya Amasova), Curt Jugens (Stromberg), Richard Kiel (Jaws), Caroline Munro (Naomi), Walter Gotell (General Gogol), Bernard Lee ('M'), Lois Maxwell (Miss Moneypenny), Desmond Llewelyn ('Q').

MOONRAKER (1979)
EON-Les Productions Artistes Associés
Produced by Albert R Broccoli
Directed by Lewis Gilbert
Script by Christopher Wood
Starring: Roger Moore (James Bond), Lois Chiles (Holly Goodhead), Michael Lonsdale (Hugo Drax), Richard Kiel (Jaws), Corinne Clery (Corinne Dufour), Bernard Lee ('M'), Lois Maxwell (Miss Moneypenny), Desmond Llewelyn ('Q'), Walter Gotell (General Gogol).

FOR YOUR EYES ONLY (1981)
EON Productions
Produced by Albert R Broccoli
Directed by John Glen
Script by Richard Maibaum and Michael G Wilson
Starring: Roger Moore (James Bond), Carole Bouquet (Melina Havelock), Topol (Columbo), Julian Glover (Kristatos), Lynn-Holly Johnson (Bibi), Cassandra Harris (Contessa Lisl), Michael Gothard (Emile Locque), Robert Brown ('M'), Lois Maxwell (Miss Moneypenny), Desmond Llewelyn ('Q').

OCTOPUSSY (1983)
EON Productions
Produced by Albert R Broccoli
Directed by John Glen
Script by Richard Maibaum and Michael G Wilson
Starring: Roger Moore (James Bond), Maud Adams (Octopussy), Louis Jourdan (Kamal), Kristina Wayborn (Magda), Kabir Bedi (Gobinda), Steven Berkoff (Orlov), Robert Brown ('M'), Lois Maxwell (Miss Moneypenny), Desmond Llewelyn ('Q'), Walter Gotell (General Gogol), Michaela Clavell (Penelope Smallbone).

NEVER SAY NEVER AGAIN (1983)
Taliafilm Production
Produced by Jack Schwartzman and Kevin McClory
Directed by Irvin Kershner
Script by Lorenzo Semple Jnr based on a story by Ian Fleming
Starring: Sean Connery (James Bond), Klaus Maria Brandauer (Largo), Max Von Sydow (Ernst Stavro Blofeld), Barbara Carrera (Fatima), Kim Basinger (Domino), Bernie Casey (Felix Leiter), Edward Fox ('M'), Pamela Salem (Miss Moneypenny), Alec McCowen (The Armourer), Rowan Atkinson (Consular Official), Pat Roach (Lippe).

A VIEW TO A KILL (1985)
EON Productions
Produced by Albert R Broccoli and Michael G Wilson
Directed by John Glen
Script by Richard Maibaum and Michael G Wilson
Starring: Roger Moore (James Bond), Christopher Walken (Max Zorin), Tanya Roberts (Stacey Sutton), Grace Jones (May Day), Patrick Macnee (Tibbett), Patrick Bauchau (Scarpine), Fiona Fullerton (Pola Ivanova), Robert Brown ('M'), Lois Maxwell (Miss Moneypenny), Desmond Llewelyn ('Q'), Walter Gotell (General Gogol), Mary Stavin (Kimberley Jones).